se!

❧❧❧

DARK TIDE

❧❧❧

DARK TIDE

The Great Boston Molasses Flood of 1919

STEPHEN PULEO

BEACON
150

→→ BEACON PRESS ←←
Boston

Sandro —
My best wishes
and **thanks** for
your support!

Regards
Stephen Puleo

Beacon Press
25 Beacon Street
Boston, Massachusetts 02108-2892
www.beacon.org

Beacon Press books
are published under the auspices of
the Unitarian Universalist Association of Congregations.

07 06 05 04 03 8 7 6 5 4 3 2 1

This book is printed on acid-free paper that meets the uncoated paper
ANSI/NISO specifications for permanence as revised in 1992.

This is a work of nonfiction. All of the characters
and events depicted in this book are real.

Text design by Dean Bornstein

Composition by Wilsted & Taylor Publishing Services

Library of Congress Cataloging-in-Publication Data
Puleo, Stephen.
Dark tide : the great Boston molasses flood of 1919 / [Stephen Puleo]
    p.   cm.
Includes bibliographical references and index.
ISBN 0-8070-5020-2 (hardcover : alk. paper)
1. Boston (Mass.)—History—1865– 2. Floods—Massachusetts—
Boston—History—20th century. 3. Industrial accidents—
Massachusetts—Boston—History—20th century. 4. Molasses
industry—Accidents—Massachusetts—Boston—History—20th
century. 5. Alcohol industry—Accidents—Massachusetts—
Boston—History—20th century. I. Title.
F73.5.P97 2003
363.11'9664118—dc21
2003010433

For Kate

Your eyes smile, my heart dances

Contents

-→-→-←-←-

Author's Note

->-<-

THIS is the first full accounting of the Great Boston Molasses Flood. It was not simply a disaster that occurred on a mild January day in 1919, but rather a saga that spanned a decade, from the construction of the tank in 1915 through the conclusion of a huge civil lawsuit in 1925.

There are no other books on the subject, and little has been written on the flood at all, save for a handful of magazine articles and newspaper retrospectives that have appeared sporadically through the years. A few works of children's fiction allude to the event, but the story lines of these books generally focus on fun and adventure in a fanciful "world of molasses," rather than depicting the event as the tragedy it was.

It is probably not surprising, then, that the disaster—an event that knocked Prohibition and the League of Nations out of the headlines—is little more than a footnote on the pages of America's past. Even in Boston, the flood today remains part of the city's folklore, but not its heritage. A small plaque in the North End marks the site of the flood (placed there by the Bostonian Society in the mid-1990s), and tourist trolleys slow down when approaching the area so the driver can point out the location. One of the converted World War II amphibious vehicles that transport tourists through the downtown streets and into the Charles River, part of Boston's renowned "Duck Tours," is named "Molly Molasses," but most who learn about the city's famous landmarks leave with little actual knowledge about the molasses flood.

Beyond these references, the story of the flood has remained elusive, surfacing occasionally in the folksy myth recounted by cab drivers and citizens alike that on hot summer days, for years after the flood, one could still smell the sweet, sticky aroma of molasses.

There may be several reasons for this indifference.

One is that, in a city defined by so much compelling and pivotal history, from the founding of Plymouth Colony to the Battle of Bunker Hill, from the Abolitionist movement to John F. Kennedy, perhaps it is difficult to make room for an event in which ordinary people were affected most. No prominent people were killed in the molasses flood, and the survivors did not go on to become famous; they were mostly immigrants and city workers who returned to their workaday lives, recovered from injuries, and provided for their families.

Another reason the flood has never attained lofty historical significance may be because of its very essence—molasses. The substance itself gives the entire event an unusual, whimsical quality. Often, the first reaction of the uninformed when they hear the words "molasses flood" is a raised eyebrow, maybe a restrained giggle, followed by the incredulous, "What, you're serious? It's really true?"

But perhaps the biggest reason the flood has not claimed its proper place in Boston's history is because, until this book, the story—if known at all—has been mistakenly viewed as an isolated incident, unconnected with larger trends in American history. *Dark Tide* makes those connections.

I have done presentations about the molasses flood to hundreds of people, and when they hear the *entire* story, wrapped in its full historical context, they are almost always fascinated and anxious to delve more deeply into the topic. Afterward, the inevitable response is: "Why didn't I know about this and where can I learn more?"

Undoubtedly, some of that interest comes from a visceral reaction to the disaster. The molasses flood *was* a tragedy (twenty-one killed, 150 injured), it occurred in a great city, contained a "whodunit" element (why *did* the tank collapse?), spawned in its aftermath a true David vs. Goliath courtroom drama, and created a collection of heroes that saved lives that day and sought justice afterward. These are crucial pieces of any good story, elements that grip the imagination and fuel additional interest.

But the real power of the molasses flood story is what it exemplifies and represents, not just to Boston but to America. Nearly every watershed issue the country was dealing with at the time—immigration, anarchists, World War I, Prohibition, the relationship between labor and Big Business, and between the people and their government—also played a part in the decade-long story of the molasses flood. To understand the flood is to understand America of the early twentieth century.

The flood, therefore, was a microcosm of America, a dramatic event that encapsulated something much bigger, a lens through which to view the major events that shaped a nation.

That is why, when people hear snippets of the molasses flood story, they invariably want to hear more.

That is why, finally, the full story needs to be told.

❧❧❧

DARK TIDE

❧❧❧

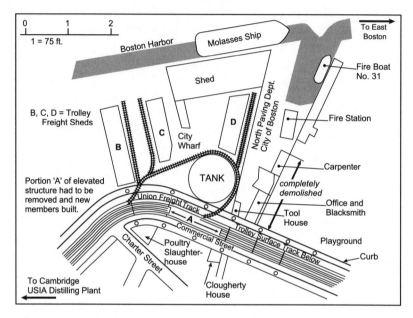

Illustration shows close-up view of molasses tank and waterfront area, including the way molasses ships docked and pumped their cargo through a pipeline into the tank. Configuration of surface-level spur tracks showed how molasses was transported from tank to USIA's distilling plant in East Cambridge. The proximity of the Clougherty house to the tank and the overhead railroad tracks is also shown.

(Map by Sarah Gillis, adapted from map published in Engineering News-Record, *May 15, 1919)*

⚜ PROLOGUE ⚜

ISAAC'S DEMONS

Boston, Late July 1918; 2:30 a.m.

Isaac Gonzales knew what a terrible thing it was to be afraid at night. Night fear had robbed him of sleep and drained him of rational thought. Tossing and turning in the dark, his wife asleep beside him, he was unable to block out the horrible images that flooded his mind and wracked his body with terror. And, once again, his fear drove him from his bed, from his home, and into the night.

Now he was running hard through the darkness of Boston's North End, his heart pounding, sweat rolling between his shoulder blades even in the early morning hours. Summer was strangling the city this last week in July, and the cramped tenements and narrow streets threw off heat long after sunset. Isaac threw off fear—it pulsated from his body in waves—and he felt an odd mixture of shame for his inability to conquer it and satisfaction for his willingness to fight it.

He could feel the buildings pressing in on him, his legs becoming heavier and his breathing more ragged. Sprawling warehouses, cheap wooden storefronts, and dilapidated tenements stood shoulder to shoulder, snuffing out the moonlight from Isaac's path. He saw no other people, but he could hear scattered coughing from the flat rooftops where families had dragged their bedding, escaping the stifling confines of their tiny apartments in search of sleep. He could feel their presence, and he imagined these rooftop guardians watching him, as his rubber-soled boots thumped against the cobblestones.

Isaac ran past Paul Revere's house, into historic North Square, turned left and crossed Hanover Street. Then he stopped and bent over to catch his breath, his throat burning as he gulped the thick, humid air. The smell of oil, salt, and seawater filled his flaring nostrils, carried by a hot, wet wind that blew in from the harbor.

Isaac had run more than two miles across town from his St. Germain Street home in the Back Bay, running to overcome his fear by running *toward* the source of it. The vision had come to him again, not a dream, but what he called his "semi-conscious mind pictures," terrible images that burrowed their way into his brain despite his best efforts to shut them out. This was the fifth time that Isaac had made the cross-town run in the middle of the night, and each time it was the mind pictures that had forced him to the streets. They had become his private demons, taunting him in the blackness of his own bedroom, the images too awful to ignore.

Each time, the pictures flashing through his mind showed the monstrous steel tank near Boston Harbor collapsing, its more than 2 million gallons of molasses smashing into buildings and engulfing hundreds of people. He envisioned a huge molasses wave crashing against brick, splintering wood, and shattering glass. The tank, fifty feet high and ninety feet in diameter, stood in the middle of Boston's busiest business district and at the edge of its most densely populated residential neighborhood, dominating the narrow strip of land between Commercial Street and the inner harbor. As a matter of commerce, Isaac knew that it was an excellent location. Ships from Puerto Rico, Cuba, and the West Indies could conveniently off-load their thousands of gallons of cargo, and the molasses could be transported by railcar to the distilling plant in Cambridge, where it was converted into industrial alcohol. Isaac's employer, the United States Industrial Alcohol Company, owned the tank and the distilling plant, and had agreements with the Boston Elevated Railway and the Bay State Railroad to ensure the swift movement of its molasses.

Each day at work Isaac marveled at the efficiency of the operation, but his admiration for the logistical precision was overwhelmed by the fear that gnawed at him—that the tank would soon collapse. He had felt the tank vibrate and heard it groan each time a new shipment of molasses was pumped into it from one of the big tanker ships. He had watched flecks of steel peeling off the inside walls, falling into his hair and settling onto his jacket like brittle confetti as he climbed deep down into the tank to check the outflow pipes just prior to a molasses delivery. Isaac had seen molasses leaking from the tank in at least a dozen spots, pooling on the ground around the concrete foundation. Small children trespassed on his employer's property to scoop up molasses with their pails or to dip their sticks and slurp the sweet liquid.

He had reported the leaks to his supervisor, Mr. White, and to

White's boss, Mr. Jell, who twice ordered the tank recaulked shortly after its construction. After that, the leaks had continued, but White and Jell ignored Isaac's pleas, accusing him of exaggerating and over-reacting. Isaac had persisted, even traveling to the Cambridge head-quarters to see Jell, a true risk for a lowly manual laborer with no union protection. He had carried rusty shards from the tank's walls into Jell's office to provide hard evidence of the potential danger. "I didn't come here to make these complaints about the tank because I wanted you to consider me efficient, or to try to make myself any big-ger or greater than I really am," Isaac had said to Jell. "I am here from pure necessity." Jell looked at the rusty steel flakes and had replied: "I don't know what you want me to do. The tank still stands."

Jell and White had made it clear that any further complaints could lead to his dismissal, and he needed the job. He worked hard, was ter-ribly overworked in fact, but he was well paid. He called himself a "general man," and his responsibilities ranged from helping to off-load the molasses ships to checking gauges on the tank to filling train cars, trucks, and wagons with molasses for transportation to the dis-tillery. He was good at his work, but it wouldn't matter if he didn't keep his mouth shut.

As he plodded up the hill in front of the Old North Church, Isaac wondered how much more he could take. The visions of the tank's de-struction came to him almost every night and he was frightened all the time now. He believed he had done all he could to prevent a dis-aster. Not only had he alerted his managers, he had even *slept* in the little office next to the tank for several months, believing he could sound a warning if the tank began crumbling. One of those nights he had received a phone call that still made him shudder. A man with a raspy voice had said that the tank would be blown up with dynamite and anyone who worked there would be killed.

The call had terrified Isaac because he believed it was plausible, even likely. The tank and the surrounding property were designated as a federally protected area by the government since most of the mo-lasses stored there was distilled into alcohol to produce munitions for America and her allies for the war in Europe. Isaac did not know much about politics, but he knew enough to deduce that the tank could be a prime target for the antiwar Italian anarchists who had been operating in the North End. After he received the phone call,

Isaac reported the incident to Boston Police and decided that sleeping next to the tank would be a bad idea. He believed that the tank would eventually collapse under the weight of the molasses, but the thought that a bomb could hasten such a calamity was enough to scare him back into his own bed. Still, the visions continued, driving him to the streets in the wee hours to do *something* to prevent a catastrophe that he was convinced would occur soon.

Isaac knew that if anything was to be done, he would have to be the one to do it, however inadequate his actions might be—and at whatever the cost. He had already risked his job, and his marriage was suffering, too. His wife was overwrought by his flailing and frightened cries when the images appeared to him in their bedroom, and equally perplexed by the reasons for his nighttime runs. "What *good* can you do?" she had asked him earlier as he dressed in the dark. "If it is going to collapse, what good can you do?" Isaac didn't respond to her question directly. "I just don't think the tank should be left alone," he said. Then he had kissed her quickly and bolted out the door.

Now, a half-hour after that kiss, he had reached the top of Copp's Hill, the highest point in the North End, and, as the wind swirled around him, he surveyed the scene below. Silence everywhere. Tankers and freighters were moored in the inner harbor. No movement at the blacksmith shop, carpentry building, or stables in the city-operated North End Paving Yard. The elevated railroad trains that traveled over Commercial Street carrying people from South Station to North Station had finished their final trips for the night, as had the freight trains that ran directly beneath the trestle on Commercial Street. The Engine 31 firehouse was dark and peaceful, firefighters asleep inside, its fireboat tied alongside the pier, rocking gently with the swell of the harbor.

And looming over all of them like a silent steel sentinel was the molasses tank. It reminded Isaac of a black mountain, towering above the landscape, its dark outline clearly visible against the starlit sky.

That the tank was still standing was a relief to him, but he needed to take further precautions. He started down the other side of Copp's Hill, crossed Commercial Street, and flashed his access pass to the security guard. Then he entered the property and made his way to the back of the tank to the pump-pit, where the inflow-outflow controls were located. He was alone and he remained motionless for a moment, adjusting to his surroundings. The only sound was the soft lapping of the waves against the retaining wall 150 feet away. The oily smell was stronger now and he caught the pungent whiff of decaying sea animals that had washed up under the nearby pier and dried out among the pilings.

Working quickly, Isaac twisted open a valve and began releasing molasses into the harbor, and along with it, any gasses that had built up inside the tank. After ten minutes, he closed and tightened the valve. He had no idea how many gallons of molasses he had dumped, and practically speaking, knew it would make little difference in the overall capacity of the tank, which held more than 2 million gallons when it was full. Isaac also knew that he would be fired, prosecuted, and most likely sent to jail if Mr. Jell ever found out about these late-night visits. But dumping the molasses helped clear his head and made him feel less helpless.

He slipped out of the pump-pit, bid goodnight to the guard, and walked quickly off the property. He turned once and looked up at the tank. Had it groaned, or was that a foghorn from a tugboat in the harbor? The early-morning summer wind blew warm off the ocean, but Isaac shivered as he crossed Commercial Street and began the long run home.

For another night at least, he had banished the demons.

PART I

A Monster in Our Midst

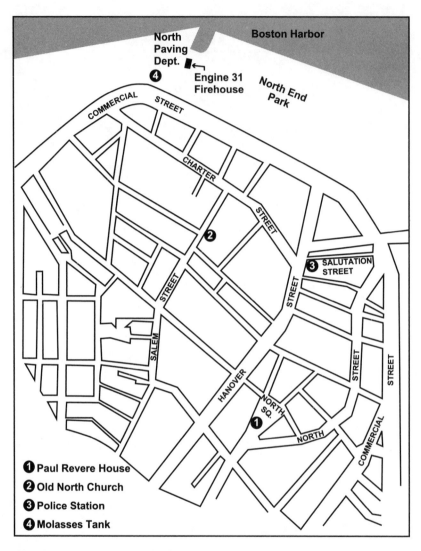

Map shows Boston's North End and proximity of the molasses tank, paving yard, and fire-house to Paul Revere's House, the Old North Church, and the Salutation Street police station, which was firebombed by anarchists in December 1916. This was part of a pattern of violent anarchist activity in Boston that USIA argued was responsible for the destruction of the molasses tank. *(Map by Sarah Gillis, based on Boston Redevelopment Authority maps)*

ONE

DEADLINE ON THE WATERFRONT

Boston, Late December 1915

An icy wind roared across Boston's inner harbor, scraping salt pebbles from the ocean-spray spilling over the seawall and flinging them into Arthur P. Jell's face. Jell tasted the salty grit between his teeth and felt the sting against his cheeks. Shivering, he cursed the wind as it sliced through his topcoat and into his chest, and flexed his aching fingers inside his thin cloth gloves. December could be Boston's cruelest month down at the water, if only because it was so unpredictable. Bostonians *expected* the shocking cold that swept in from the Atlantic every January and February. December, though, was a seasonal tease, red-raw as a fresh wound some years, others as soft and muted as an early-morning drizzle with no indication of the deep winter to come.

This year, to Jell's annoyance, winter was not being cheated her first month, and the cold settled into his bones and his consciousness early. Every place he turned reminded him of the horrendous December weather: piles of grimy snow that workers had dumped against the freight sheds, puffs of frozen breath encircling the heads of crew members as they exhaled, relentless wind shrieking off the harbor. Winter had squeezed the color and depth from the world in front of him, leaving a series of flat, pale grays—water, sky, clouds, ships, the Bunker Hill monument across the bay in Charlestown, the seagulls that squealed overhead, dipping and gliding on the wind currents—all blending to form a bleak two-dimensional background painting.

In the foreground, the massive shell of the coal-gray tank stood out in stark contrast, the only thing that seemed real to Jell, something majestic being born from something ordinary.

✼ ✼ ✼

The weather was only a little less foul than Jell's mood as he watched crews of workmen scurrying up ladders and across shaky scaffolding.

They were as anxious as he was to erect the tank. *His* tank. That's how he felt about the gigantic steel structure that stood before him, so close to completion, but as yet unfinished, a promise unfulfilled. It was an embarrassment *because* it was still incomplete, more than a year after his bosses had put him in charge of the project with the clear and sober instructions that he should give it his highest priority. It was a race against the calendar to get it finished before the molasses steamer from Cuba docked at Boston Harbor in just three days. On the afternoon of New Year's Eve, the ship would arrive, its crew ready to pump into the tank seven hundred thousand gallons of the viscous liquid that Jell's company would later distill into industrial alcohol.

Delays had plagued the project from the start, but Jell still had time to salvage his reputation and his career with his employer, the Purity Distilling Company, and, more importantly, its parent company, U.S. Industrial Alcohol (USIA), if he could meet the December 31 deadline. After months of frustrating negotiations to lease the Commercial Street waterfront location, Jell was scrambling to speed construction along. He had ordered the Hammond Iron Works, the manufacturers and assemblers of the tank, to employ extra crews to finish the job—thirty men now toiled day and night on the tank. He had even approved the installation and expense of additional electric lighting so those crews could work around the clock. "It may be that objections will be raised to our running riveting machines at night, but until we are prevented from doing so, we wish to work both a day and a night shift," he wrote in a letter to Hammond officials.

Now, Jell watched as workers bent the last of the giant steel plates into place and bolted them together with thousands of rivets. The full height of the tank would be achieved by fastening together seven vertical layers of rounded steel plates, each overlapping the layer below and held in place by a horizontal row of rivets. Vertical rows of rivets sealed the seams of each of the eighteen steel plates that formed the tank's cylindrical shape. The tank would be the largest in the region by far, standing fifty feet tall, ninety feet in diameter, 240 feet in circumference, with the capacity to hold more than 2 million gallons of molasses.

USIA/Purity Distilling needed the huge tank to store the molasses after it was off-loaded from steamers that transported their shipments from Cuba, Puerto Rico, and the West Indies. Crews could then load molasses from the tank onto railcars that would transfer the sugary substance as needed to the company's manufacturing plant in nearby East Cambridge. There, a small portion of molasses would be distilled into grain alcohol for rum, but most of it, more than 80 percent, would be distilled into industrial alcohol that would be used as a major ingredient in the production of munitions, especially dynamite, smokeless powder, and other high explosives.

USIA and its subsidiaries, including Purity, would sell the alcohol to major weapons manufacturers in the United States, as well as to the British, French, and Canadian governments, to produce munitions for the war against Germany that had broken out in Europe in August 1914. Since then, the demand for industrial alcohol to feed the munitions manufacturing process was greater than Jell had ever seen. Now, despite President Woodrow Wilson's promises of neutrality, many citizens believed that the United States would become involved. If that happened, the U.S. War Department would become USIA's largest customer and would order the company to ratchet up production even more.

Even without America's involvement in the war, the demand for industrial alcohol by friendly European governments was straining current manufacturing capabilities. USIA, one of the nation's largest industrial alcohol producers, was always in need of a readily available supply of molasses to produce alcohol more quickly and manage inventory more efficiently. Up until now, without a Boston tank of its own to store huge quantities of molasses temporarily, the company was forced to purchase smaller amounts of molasses as needed from a third-party broker with a tank in South Boston. This drove up costs, ate into profit margins, and left USIA at the mercy of another supplier at a time of burgeoning demand for industrial alcohol.

For USIA's Boston operation to operate at peak efficiency, the Commercial Street molasses tank was the answer. Its enormous storage capacity along with its ideal location, sandwiched between ship traffic in the busy inner harbor and Boston's major freight rail lines that ran along Commercial Street in Boston's North End, made it a critical component in USIA's growth plans.

As treasurer of the Purity Distilling subsidiary, Jell knew those corporate plans all too well, and realized that the company would lose out on profits if the tank was not finished by the time the molasses steamer arrived in Boston. The ship, owned by another subsidiary of USIA, the Cuba Distilling Company, would be delivering about half of her 1.3 million gallons of cargo to USIA distilleries in New York and the remaining molasses to Boston. If the Boston tank were not ready to accept the remaining molasses, the ship would have to find another USIA location to accept the delivery or even dump the product at sea. Either way, this would cost the company time and money.

Already the delay in finishing the tank was costing USIA dearly and causing Jell personal embarrassment. He had hoped the tank would be completed long before this, but negotiations had been difficult with the Boston Elevated Railway Company, whose waterfront land USIA was leasing for the tank site. He had begun discussions with Boston Elevated in January, but they stalled in the spring and early summer, and were not concluded until late September. It then took one month for the Hugh Nawn Construction Company to build the concrete foundation upon which the massive steel tank would sit. Fabricated steel plates for the tank didn't arrive in Boston until the first week in December.

Even with a perfect December, Jell had recognized that the construction schedule would be tight—and December had been far from perfect.

✥ ✥ ✥

First, death had visited the tank construction site. On the morning of December 8, Thomas DeFratus of Charlestown, a thirty-five-year-old laborer, toppled from a staging plank and plunged forty feet inside the tank to his death. Jell still remembered the doomed man's scream and the anxious shouts of the other men. He felt sorry for DeFratus and his friends, many of whom were crying as they pulled their comrade's broken body from inside the tank shell and awaited the medical examiner. But Jell was most distraught because the incident cost him a precious half-day of work by the time the body was finally removed to the North District Mortuary. Worse, for several days afterward, he watched the careful movements of the other men, their white-knuckled grips on the rungs as they climbed ladders, the methodical step-by-step high-wire walk across scaffolding, their boots sliding tentatively along planks searching for a toehold, their fingers brushing the side of the tank for balance. They were frightened men working in slow motion. Jell recognized that their fear had to run its course, and he was relieved three days later when the work pace had finally returned to normal.

His relief, though, was short-lived. On December 13 and 14, a vicious storm with gale-force winds pounded Boston. The newspapers called it a "superstorm," the worst in a dozen years. Two massive fronts collided in upstate New York and dumped more than twenty inches of snow west of Boston as well as a torrential rain and a driving sleet within the city. Trains were delayed and streets were rendered impassable due to the flooding. Heavy wind knocked down electric power lines, chimneys, trees, and signs that hung outside of storefronts. The popular roller coaster at Nantasket Beach, south of Boston, was toppled by the wind, falling across the street, snapping wires and crashing against utility poles.

The superstorm with the fifty-mile-an-hour gale meant a two-day construction delay at the Commercial Street molasses tank. And even on the third day, crews spent most of the morning clearing debris from the site and pumping water that had collected in the well of the tank. Jell took some solace that the wind had not damaged the tank's shell, which then stood about thirty feet high.

Workers made good progress between December 15 and Christmas Day—another lost workday for Jell—and then, as if to taunt him, a December 26 sleet storm forced him to stop work for another day. In a bizarre case of déjà vu, winds in this storm were so severe that they destroyed the Boston area's other landmark roller coaster, this one on Revere Beach, north of the city.

Jell saw the weather as just one more obstacle jeopardizing the tank's completion and one more factor conspiring to humiliate him.

✣ ✣ ✣

The stinging wind continued to howl off the harbor, rattling the tank's steel superstructure. Jell wriggled his toes, now numb inside his leather shoes. He clenched and unclenched his fingers to get his blood moving. Across the entire wharf area Jell saw men working; stevedores, longshoremen, and teamsters. They were big men with rough hands and strong backs, guiding horse-drawn wagons loaded with beer barrels, driving hogs from the railroad sheds to the steamers moored along the pier, or unloading heavy wooden crates from the cargo holds of those ships. He even saw a blacksmith pounding out shoes in front of the city-owned stables. Jell was not comfortable among such men or around such work, preferring the certainty of numbers and the warmth of his office to the randomness and discomfort that surrounded him on the wharf. These men earned their livings with the threat of injury, miserable weather, and erratic ship traffic always lurking. A longshoreman who wrenched his back or a stevedore who dropped a beer barrel and shattered his foot could be out of work for months with no means to support himself or his family. A teamster delivering tomatoes to the dock might see his product rot if a ship were delayed for days by a storm.

He also was uncomfortable in this neighborhood. To him, it was sooty, noisy, and crowded, filled with poor Italian immigrants speaking a strange language and practicing even stranger customs, and Irish city workers whose brashness made him uneasy. He longed for the project to be finished so he could return to his Cambridge office.

He recognized, though, that this was the *perfect* location for the molasses tank, a little more than two hundred feet from the ships, easy access to the tank for railroad cars along the spur track, and a fast one-mile rail trip to the East Cambridge distillery where the molasses would be distilled into alcohol. He had negotiated hard for this location and would bear standing in the cold now to watch the site take shape.

Behind him, Jell heard the clatter and screech of the elevated passenger train from South Station as it rumbled above Commercial Street, straining to negotiate the hard left bend in the track toward North Station. Jell did not turn, but imagined the sparks that flew when the train's steel wheels bit into the searing cold rails. His eyes were drawn to the crews working on his tank and he watched the men wield hammers and bolt rivets, wondering how they could work in this kind of cold. Their problem, but his too. Speed was his overriding concern right now.

✤ ✤ ✤

Arthur P. Jell had spent his entire working career in clerical, administrative, and financial positions, beginning at age fourteen when he had become an office boy with distillers Hiram Walker & Sons. In 1909, at the age of thirty, he moved to Boston to become secretary of the Purity Distilling Company. After two years as secretary, Jell was promoted to treasurer, the position he held when he was given responsibility for the molasses tank project in late 1914.

USIA president Frederic M. Harrison and vice president Nelson B. Mayer had been dangling a parent-company vice-presidency in front of him, the next logical step in Jell's career. Such a promotion would include relocation to headquarters in New York City. When Harrison ordered him to begin work on the Boston tank project, there was more than a veiled implication that his success on this project would expedite his promotion and failure would doom his future with the company.

Jell had first contacted Hammond Iron Works in late 1914 to draw up plans for the Commercial Street tank and Hammond furnished completed blueprints in early April 1915, along with a price tag of $30,000 for the manufacture and erection of the tank. Since then, Jell had been involved in frustrating negotiations with Boston Elevated to agree on leasing terms for the site. "It looks as though the matter will be settled within a very few days," Jell wrote to Hammond on April 9, 1915, a prediction that had proved laughable.

The leasing discussions with Boston Elevated ground to a halt over money and the details of the complicated arrangement. Boston Elevated had to assign USIA rights to build the large tank and an accompanying pump room, moor vessels alongside the wharf to unload molasses, install a 220-foot underground pipe to carry molasses from the ships to the tank, store the molasses, build a small auxiliary tank that acted as a molasses feeder between the large tank and the railroad cars, and build a "spur track" that would enable railroad cars to travel back and forth between the tank site and the main Commercial Street tracks.

Both sides also had to agree to language governing charges for gas, water, and electricity onto the property, as well as liability for any damages that occurred during USIA's regular commerce. All of this took time, much more time than Jell or his company had estimated. "We regret very much that we are still unable to give you any definite shipping date for the 90-foot tank," Jell wrote to Hammond on May 6, 1915. "We are far more anxious than you are to commence work on this, and we can assure you the delay has been unavoidable."

The pressure on Jell to finish the tank project increased the very next day, May 7, when the British luxury liner *Lusitania* was sunk by a German submarine in the North Atlantic. America was outraged when the press reported that nearly 1,200 people had been killed, including 128 Americans, and sentiment began building for the United States to enter the war against Germany. Even the normally temperate *New York Times* editorialized on May 8, 1915: "From the Department of State, there must go to the Imperial Government at Berlin a demand that the Germans shall no longer make war like savages drunk with blood." If America entered the war, the War Department's demand for munitions, and therefore for industrial alcohol produced from molasses, would grow exponentially.

Even now, the demand for industrial alcohol from the big munitions companies—du Pont, Hercules Powder, Aetna Explosives—was hard to keep up with as they worked to feed the British and French war machines. The French and Canadian governments also placed large orders directly, and alcohol shortages were becoming commonplace. The production of munitions, quite simply, was America's number one growth industry.

For USIA to get its fair share of this booming trade, Arthur P. Jell needed to finish the molasses tank on the Boston waterfront no later than the final day of 1915.

❖ ❖ ❖

On September 24, 1915, after months of haggling, Jell had signed a twenty-year lease with Boston Elevated to rent the seventeen-thousand-square-foot waterfront parcel at 539 Commercial Street, sandwiched between the North End residential neighborhood and the inner harbor, for an annual fee of $5,000. The lease was to commence on November 1. "We are extremely anxious to have the work proceed as rapidly as possible and are quite willing to pay any additional expenses there may be in pushing the work forward so that the tank can be completed promptly," Jell wrote to Hammond on October 1, 1915. Then on October 19: "We confirm the understanding whereby you are to furnish sufficient men to complete the tank by December 15th and we agree to pay ... any additional expenses which may be necessary in order to hurry the work as much as possible."

The Hugh Nawn Construction Company began work on the three-foot thick concrete foundation during the first week of November, and Hammond Iron Works shipped the steel plates to Boston around

Before the flood, the molasses tank towered over adjacent structures and the elevated railroad tracks. (*The Bostonian Society/Old State House*)

the first of December. When Hammond suggested that it might lose some time applying for proper permits from the Boston Building Department, Jell wrote back promptly: "You apparently did not understand that we had arranged so that it would not be necessary for your foreman to take out a permit in Boston, as the contractors who are building the foundation will allow us to erect the tank under their permit." The building department considered the tank a "receptacle" and not a "building," so the permit for the foundation was all that the city required.

With his deadline approaching like a locomotive, Jell made an executive decision in late December. The contract with Hammond called for the fifty-foot-high tank to be tested for leaks upon its completion by filling it with water. Jell knew that the amount of water he would need to fill the tank would be so vast that he would have to tap into the municipal water supply, an expense he refused to authorize. Jell also knew it would have taken many days, perhaps weeks, to fill the tank. It was time he did not have. Instead, Jell ordered crews to run only six inches of water into the tank, enough to raise the water level above the first angle joint at the base of the structure. When no leaks occurred, Jell pronounced the tank sturdy, sound, and ready to use.

On December 29, 1915, two days before the Cuba Distilling Company molasses steamer arrived with seven hundred thousand gallons of molasses to off-load, Hammond Iron Works posted a letter to Jell along with a final invoice for the tank. ". . . In order to include it in this year's business, and even if the tank is not, technically speaking, completely finished by December 31, we trust it will be satisfactory that our invoice is rendered under this date."

Two mornings later, the huge tanker arrived in Boston and disgorged her molasses cargo smoothly, filling the tank to a level of about thirteen feet.

Nearly a year of frustration had ended. Arthur Jell had met his impossible deadline and USIA was in business on the Boston waterfront.

❖ ❖ ❖

From the first day of the tank's completion, USIA paid the Boston Police Department for a policeman to be on a "fixed post" at the tank. Jell and USIA were taking no chances. Anarchists, who were militant radicals who opposed the war, hated government, and loathed capitalism—especially those large American corporations that fed the war effort—were making their presence known across the country with incendiary speeches, audacious threats, and violent activities.

During November and December of 1915, there were suspicious explosions and fires at strategic manufacturing plants across the country. Fire destroyed the Bethlehem Steel Works in Pennsylvania, which was producing guns for the Allies. An explosion rocked the du Pont Powder Mill in Wilmington, Delaware, killing thirty men and injuring five. A man was arrested in Pittsburgh after threatening both to blow up the Westinghouse Electric and Manufacturing Company plant and assassinate President Woodrow Wilson. Guards were doubled at principal government buildings in Washington, D.C., including the State, War, and Navy departments after numerous bomb threats and a bomb explosion destroyed a room in the Capitol in the summer of 1915. Throughout 1914 and 1915, a rash of bombings shocked New York City. In one brazen attempt, a bomb was placed in the courtroom beneath the seat of magistrate John L. Campbell, who had convicted and sentenced an anarchist for inciting a riot. The judge was about to ascend to the bench when the bomb was discovered and disarmed.

At the start of 1916, Jell and other Bostonians saw the danger creep closer to home. On New Year's morning, a Massachusetts State House night watchman making his rounds discovered a wicker suitcase tied to the doorknob of the sergeant-at-arms' office. Suspicious, he called state police to investigate. They discovered a pipe inside the suitcase filled with several sticks of dynamite—a faulty fuse had prevented the bomb from exploding. On the morning of January 2, an explosion rocked the New England Manufacturing Company in the Boston suburb of Woburn. Rumors quickly circulated that the company had received a letter two weeks before threatening to blow up or set fire to the plant unless it stopped producing goods and shipping them overseas to the warring nations in Europe.

Beyond these incidents, Boston Police had issued warnings that Boston's North End was fast becoming the headquarters for some of the leading Italian anarchists in America, who preached the violent overthrow of the U.S. government and the capitalist economic system.

Jell feared that because the USIA Cambridge factory converted molasses into industrial alcohol for munitions, the Commercial Street molasses tank could be an inviting target for anarchists or others who opposed the war in Europe. After the prolonged delay in securing a location for the tank, the company had lost precious time and significant revenue. USIA's bottom line would be strained severely if the North End tank were damaged in any way—or, worse, destroyed.

Arthur Jell considered twenty-four-hour police protection a worthwhile investment.

Boston, February 1916

His first day on the job, Isaac Gonzales watched and listened intently as his new boss, William White, led him around the tank property and explained the logistical operations involved in getting molasses from the waterfront to USIA's manufacturing plant in East Cambridge. He learned how the ten-inch-wide discharge hose from the molasses tankers was to be bolted to the permanent pipeline on the wharf using two flanges with a gasket in between. He learned how to control the flow of molasses into the 220-foot main intake pipe that traveled from the wharf to the tank to prevent clogging. He learned how to climb down into the tank when it was being filled to be sure the intake pipe opening remained clear. And he also learned to discharge molasses from the big tank to the auxiliary tank and then into the railcars when orders came in, so the trains could transport the thick liquid to the Cambridge distilling plant.

Isaac felt at home around ships, the sea, and molasses. Born in Puerto Rico, he spent four years as a seaman and often traveled back and forth between his home island and Cuba to load molasses for the trip north. He settled in the United States after he was discharged from his ship in Baltimore, making his way to Washington, D.C., where he worked as a messenger for a lawyer specializing in international law, and later, for the U.S. attorney general's office as an engine repairman at a D.C. office building. In 1910 he moved to Boston, where he worked at a series of laborer's jobs before joining Purity/USIA. Like many others during the recession of 1913 and 1914, Isaac had been down on his luck. He was living at the Boston YMCA when staff members told him about this job, and he was determined to succeed.

It was freezing when Isaac arrived at the Commercial Street dock early in the morning, and the deep cold continued into the mid-afternoon. The wind off the harbor slashed at his face and tossed cold, gray seawater onto the wharf. Isaac wore a heavy wool coat, a knit hat pulled low over his ears, thick gloves, and heavy work boots. White asked him to attach the hose into place, which forced him to remove the gloves to get a grip on the flanges, the gasket, and the nuts and bolts. Isaac made a note to wear thinner gloves the next day, cold or not.

Looking up at the tank, Isaac saw that thick molasses was seeping from between many seams, congealing around the rivet lines and spreading slowly downward and outward. It did not flow rapidly down the sides of the tank because of the cold—molasses never really froze, but Isaac knew it developed the consistency of heavy pudding in frigid temperatures. More troubling than the seeping, though, were the noises that came from inside the tank. He heard low rumbles over the wind, like distant rolls of thunder.

Isaac knew the sound that molasses made as it was fermenting, "boiling" as he called it, a phenomenon that became even more pronounced with dramatic temperature changes. But this sound seemed different to Isaac. Maybe it was the way the wind snapped and whistled as it bounced off the tank's walls. Maybe it was something else. But the rumbling noises in the tank made the hairs on the back of his neck tingle. It was as though the giant steel container was alive and he was hearing the low growl of an angry animal.

✦✦✦

President Woodrow Wilson, speaking on February 1, 1916, from the rear platform of a train at whistlestops throughout Iowa, addressed thousands of Midwesterners who braved subzero temperatures, waved American flags, and listened intently to his plan to keep the United States out of the European war. He insisted that the best way to accomplish this was for the people and Congress to support his national defense preparedness program, which involved increased munitions production for the purpose of shipping arms to friendly nations overseas. A well-supplied England and France would lessen the need for U.S. intervention.

Munitions production was good for the U.S. economy, too. In fact, it had been the astounding growth of this sector throughout 1915 that had rescued America from economic recessions in 1913 and 1914.

Wilson's biggest challenge was convincing Iowans and the country that munitions manufacturers were not influencing his policy decisions. Wilson told a crowd of fifteen thousand people in Davenport: "It seems to be supposed that a small body of men, who have a chance to make money out of the manufacture of munitions, have something to do with the policy of the government of the United States. I have yet to discover any such influence." The government, Wilson said, would control the supply and prices of munitions, "and prevent any undue profit to anybody."

Wilson, in part, was responding to a so-called "monster petition," signed by more than a million people, that had been delivered to the Senate and called for an embargo on arms and ammunition production and exports from the United States to warring nations. The petition consisted of a thousand rolls of paper—each tied in red, white, and blue ribbon—that reportedly would stretch more than fifteen miles if the unrolled sheets were laid end to end.

The petitioners were misguided, Wilson said. Defense preparedness at home and assistance to friendly nations abroad were the most effective ways for the United States to exert its influence to end the war. "Do you want the situation to be such that all the president can do is to write messages and utter words of protest?" he asked the crowd. "If these breaches of international law should touch the very honor of the United States, do you wish to do something about it? America can not be an ostrich with its head in the sand."

For Arthur Jell and U.S. Industrial Alcohol, the president's message was important and welcomed. It meant, most likely, that munitions production, already booming, would continue to increase. Even with government oversight of production, pricing, and profits, this was good news indeed.

✿✿✿

Later in February, Jell formally acknowledged Hammond Iron Works' efforts to complete the tank on time, writing, in part: "We take this opportunity of expressing our appreciation of the manner in which you rushed this work, as by completing the tank at the time you did, we saved a considerable amount of storage charges. We feel that considerable credit is due to your foreman and the men under him for the assistance they rendered in hurrying the work forward ..."

↣ TWO ↢

NEIGHBORHOOD WEEPING

Boston, Wednesday, March 15, 1916; 4:30 a.m.

Martin Clougherty locked the heavy wooden front door of the Pen and Pencil Club in Dock Square and started home in the early morning chill. Another good night, especially for a Tuesday. The club was a waterfront gathering spot for Boston newspaper reporters, and Martin made sure that in addition to an ample supply of liquor, his establishment had the appropriate accoutrements to satisfy his clientele: a billiard room, a recreation room, and a library with overstuffed chairs so the conversation and debate flowed as freely as the whiskey. Martin took good care of his customers, and with their regular patronage of the Pen and Pencil, they were taking good care of him.

For the past three years, he had owned the club with two other partners, but finally in January, Martin had scraped together enough money to buy the Pen and Pencil outright. A risk worth taking; since the beginning of the war in Europe in 1914, the club had been hopping every night. Newspapermen loved nothing more than to enjoy a few drinks and smokes when there was important news to discuss and debate. Each night, amid the clink of glasses and the swirl of haze from thick cigars, Martin listened to the city's top reporters argue about German aggression, the future of Europe, and the role the United States should play in the European war. The heartier the conversation, the more his customers ate and drank, and, particularly since the sinking of the *Lusitania* last year, Martin could not imagine livelier banter taking place anywhere else in the city. His patrons imbibed and swapped barbs until he closed the bar at 2 A.M., which meant that Martin could not begin cleaning and sweeping in earnest until closer to 3 A.M., when the last of them vacated the Pen and Pencil Club.

Walking home now along Atlantic Avenue, he heard the clip-clop sound of a single-horse wagon echoing a short distance away, most likely delivering fresh fruit or vegetables to the pushcart peddlers in Haymarket, the city's busiest produce district. It was still dark, but when he glanced out at Boston Harbor he could discern the faintest hint of pink brushed low across the eastern sky. In a few hours, sunlight would sparkle off the gray-green water, but he loved this time of the day best, just before dawn. He loved the stillness of the city's waterfront, the odd incongruity of his day ending while most of the city's working men were just beginning theirs, the immense satisfaction he felt from another successful night at the club.

Martin knew the Pen and Pencil Club represented an enormous opportunity, a *liberating* opportunity, for him and his family. At the age of thirty-six, he lived with and supported his widowed mother, Bridget, his sister Teresa, and his feeble-minded brother, Stephen, plus two boarders, in a three-story wooden house at 534 Commercial Street, on the corner of Copp's Hill Terrace. The family had lived there for nine years, and while it had served them well after Martin's father passed away, it was time to look elsewhere for a more suitable home. The boxy house was neat, clean, and modernized with a new plumbing and gas system that he had installed himself, but it sat directly across the street from what had become Boston's busiest and noisiest center of commerce—the Commercial Street wharf and the North End Paving Yard.

All day long, stevedores shouted as they unloaded ships, and horse-drawn wagons and motorized trucks clattered onto the wharf to deliver goods that would be shipped across the world. Sometimes the cargo would be live animals, pigs or chickens, and squealing would fill the air, punctuated with the screeching of seagulls overhead. From the paving yard came the sounds of the stonecutters splitting rock to be used in the construction of subway platforms and sidewalks across the city, and the clanging of the blacksmith's hammer at the adjacent city stables, ensuring that the city-owned horses were properly shod. Adjacent to the Clougherty house was a poultry slaughterhouse, which the Italians in the neighborhood would visit early to select fresh chickens for their evening meal. The incessant clucking and squawking from inside, muffled by the wooden walls of the building, reminded Martin of the steady din of debate that took place inside his club.

The worst of the noise, though, came from the trains. Locomotives hauled boxcars and tank cars along Commercial Street in front of the

Clougherty house, groaning as they turned onto the spur track that led to the wharf. Directly above Commercial Street, the Boston Elevated Railroad passenger trains traveled between North Station and South Station, every seven minutes all day long. Martin considered it a minor miracle that he was able to get any sleep at all during the day. When he lay his head on his pillow, he was no more than thirty feet from the trains and eighty feet from the interminable wharf racket that began before 7 A.M. and continued for the next twelve hours, every working day.

The noise was only part of the problem. Martin hated the smell and the dirt and the darkness, too. The coppery stench of blood from the slaughterhouse mixed with the pungent odor of manure from the horse stables could make his eyes water if the wind was blowing right. And Martin hated to watch his sixty-three-year-old mother hang wet laundry out to dry on the front porch, only to see her white linens coated with a thin layer of soot a few moments later, as fine black dust from the street and the trains clung leech-like to the damp fabric. Each day when he climbed into bed, he crawled between sheets gritty with Commercial Street dirt.

But the darkness was the worst. His mother woke at 5 A.M. each morning to prepare breakfast and begin her household chores, but she never got a real chance to see the sun rise over the harbor. For years, the overhead train trestle blocked most of the light, and now, within the last few months, the five-story steel monstrosity that contained millions of gallons of molasses snuffed out the rest of the morning sun. Prior to the tank's completion two months ago, Martin could look out the kitchen window and glimpse patches of ocean between the support girders of the overhead train trestle. Now, when he looked out that same window, he had a full frontal view of the gray molasses tank.

All of this made Martin ready to move his mother and siblings somewhere else. It had been their home for nine years, but the pace of activity at the Commercial Street wharf had made living conditions close to intolerable. Besides, the neighborhood had changed so much that it didn't even *feel* like home anymore. Most of the Irish were gone. The few that were left huddled in small pockets near Battery Street and Salutation Street along the waterfront, or near Thacher and Endicott streets on the northern side of the neighborhood facing Charlestown. The Italians had virtually taken over the North End, and while Martin had never encountered any problems with them, he had to admit their bizarre customs and strange language were unsettling. His mother, who had emigrated from Ireland and whose brogue was as heavy today as it was when she arrived forty years ago, had told him many times that living among the Italians made her feel as though *she* were the foreigner.

Martin thought he would like to move to Quincy or Revere, somewhere close enough to give him easy access to the city, the club, and his friends, but far enough removed to enjoy occasional peace and quiet. He had seen advertisements for homes costing between $2,000 and $3,000 that were large and comfortable enough for his family. He had been working hard to save while paying all of the Clougherty household bills. A powerfully built and athletic man, he had once been a club boxer, and now was a boxing referee. He worked bouts between Irish fighters or Irish and Italian fighters (the Italians usually changed their names to Irish names to attract the predominately Irish crowd that patronized boxing matches), and the income he received had supplemented the money he and his partners had made at the Pen and Pencil Club. Now that he owned the club, he believed he could accelerate his timetable for moving out of the neighborhood—perhaps within three years.

It was nearly 5 A.M. when Martin approached his house. He had made the mile-and-a-half walk at a brisk but unhurried pace, savoring the early morning silence. He paused on the top step. Wharf deliveries had not yet begun. Boat traffic was still. No trains moved. The horses were asleep in the city stables. *This* was how quiet it would be all the time once he moved out of the city. He inhaled deeply; the strange combination of horse dung and seawater and molasses hung on the damp air, an oddly pleasant mixture at this hour. The early-morning stillness made everything better. He nudged the door open and stepped inside, hoping sleep would come before the Commercial Street waterfront awakened and interrupted his dreams.

Boston, Later That Morning

Thirty-four-year-old Boston firefighter George Layhe stepped off the ferryboat from East Boston and onto the Commercial Street dock.

The ferry had fought the late winter Atlantic chop all the way across the inner harbor, and the morning papers had forecast cold rain or snow, but today neither turbulent water nor inclement weather could dampen his spirits. Today was his fifth anniversary as a member of the Boston Fire Department, and his knowledge of marine engineering and boats made him one of the most valuable members of his company. His latest pay raise had brought him up to $1,400 per year, and save for a three-day suspension for fighting with a hoseman one night in 1913, his record was unblemished, and he had the full respect of his superiors and colleagues. His deputy chief, Edward Shallow, would say later that Layhe was a "strong, able fellow, in good condition, who attended to his duties strictly, all the time."

For his part, Layhe loved the camaraderie he shared with his buddies in the department, men like William Connor and Paddy Driscoll. There were always spirited discussions or a game of billiards or cards during the noon hour. George had been assigned to Engine 31, the fireboat headquarters, since he began working for the department on March 15, 1911, and he considered these men his brothers. He was proud to be part of their family. He was especially close to Connor, who was George's age and had started his service on the same day. Today, after the shift was over, they would celebrate their anniversaries by dropping in to one of the dockside taverns for a beer.

A handsome man with soft, intelligent eyes and an angular face, Layhe had other reasons to be grateful today. He and his wife, Elizabeth, owned their home on Saratoga Street in East Boston, and with the addition of their infant daughter, Helen, who arrived just two months ago, they now had three beautiful children. The boys, Francis, eleven, and George, eight, were growing fast, and the tight-knit Irish community in East Boston seemed the ideal place for them to make friends and remain safe. It reminded him of the neighborhood in which he had grown up in Fort Plain, New York, where his parents, Daniel and Elizabeth, had settled after emigrating from Ireland.

The difference, of course, was that George Layhe was a widely respected man *outside* of his neighborhood and he had the opportunity to work at something he loved. His father, like so many Irish immigrants arriving in America in the aftermath of the Great Famine, had been the victim of intense discrimination and had little opportunity to do anything but to perform unskilled labor as he struggled to support his family. George had discussed this topic often with Bill Connor. The worst of the treatment against the Irish was mostly over now, but it had taken place not so long ago. Their good friend, John Barry, a stonecutter for the city who was twenty years older than Connor and Layhe, recalled firsthand how he had been denied work, insulted, and spat upon because of his heritage.

But times had changed rapidly. Now, Boston had elected two Irish mayors in the last six years, John F. "Honey Fitz" Fitzgerald in 1910 and James Michael Curley in 1914, the latter of whom proclaimed himself the "mayor of the people" and enjoyed widespread support within the fire department. Curley had tweaked the Yankee Brahmins immediately after taking office when he proposed that the city sell the famous Public Garden for $10 million. Half the money would go into the general fund and the other half, Curley suggested, would be used to purchase new public gardens in various neighborhoods of the city where they would be more accessible to the public.

George thought the idea made sense and hoped that Curley's idea would become a reality—East Boston could use a public garden. But it quickly became clear that Curley's proposal was a mischievous attempt to draw the battle lines between the old "downtown" blue-bloods and the new Irish leadership that focused more on the ethnic neighborhoods. He sharpened those lines to a point shortly thereafter when he boasted publicly: "The day of the Puritan has passed, the Anglo-Saxon is a joke, a new and better America is here. (The Brahmins) must learn that the New England of the Puritans and the Boston of rum, codfish, and slaves are as dead as Julius Caesar."

George and the other firefighters felt as though someone at City Hall was fighting for them and looking out for their welfare. This was reinforced when Curley, with a flourish, ordered long-handled mops for all the scrubwomen at City Hall and announced that the only time a woman would go down on her knees in his administration would be when "she was praying to Almighty God." The firefighters had cheered, and the Curley legend was born. An Irishman was mayor of Boston, George Layhe was a respected firefighter and a new father, and just about all was good with the world.

As George walked along the pier to the firehouse, he took in the early morning scene around him and marveled at the increase in activity since he began work five years ago. Commercial Street now was one of the main arteries in Boston. It linked North and South stations and supplied the piers and wharves on the north side of the city. From these wharves departed practically all of the coastal shipping out of Boston, as well as the passenger ferries to Charlestown and East Boston, the latter of which Layhe took to and from work each day. From the big freight sheds on the dock everything from leather goods to livestock to beer would be loaded on ships and transported to destinations along the East Coast or to Europe. It was barely 7:30 A.M., and already George saw teamsters, stevedores, railroad messengers, freight handlers, and delivery boys beginning their day in the crowded, noisy wharf area. Adjacent to the firehouse, at the North End Paving Yard, he exchanged quick greetings with John Barry, the stonecutter for the City of Boston Street Department. Barry worked in one of several contiguous wooden buildings that included an office, a blacksmith shop, a stable with more than twenty horses, a wagon house, and a carpenter shop.

Dominating this scene, since the beginning of the year, was the giant molasses tank. The tank towered over everything in the area, including the wharf itself, the tenements across Commercial Street, even the elevated tracks that ran above the busy thoroughfare. It sat just three feet from Commercial Street and fifty feet from the firehouse, which gave George a clear view of the tank every workday. It was painted a depressing charcoal gray color, but depending on how the sun slanted over the harbor, there were hours and moments when the huge receptacle gleamed and seemed to be almost inspiring in its size and power.

It would be hard for anything to ruin George Layhe's day today, but he became a little queasy when he stared up at the tank and witnessed a sight that had become all too familiar in the two months that it had been standing.

Thick lines of molasses oozed down its walls and painted rust brown stains across its charcoal gray steel face.

Boston, That Same Day, 8 p.m.

Giuseppe Iantosca trudged into the kitchen of his home at 115 Charter Street in Boston's North End, dirt caked around the knees of his heavy work pants and etched into the lines that ran from the corners of his eyes. He would be forty-one years old in three months, but he felt much older after working for ten hours laying and repairing track for the Boston & Maine Railroad. Lifting and maneuvering the heavy steel rails and swinging a pick and sledgehammer most of the day left his shoulder muscles aching and sharp pain shooting across his lower back. After his shift today, Giuseppe took the train back from Cambridge, then had to stop at the market to pick up some vegetables for dinner. The B&M paid Giuseppe forty cents an hour, and the $4 he earned for today's long labor seemed especially meager. Worse, the railroad had already announced it would be cutting back the shifts to eight hours, meaning Giuseppe's pay would drop to $3.20 per day, less than $20 a week even when he worked six days. Giuseppe barely spoke English, but he could add and subtract, and he knew that the new pay schedule would bring him and his family less than $1,000 per year. He and his wife, Maria, had six children—the youngest, Josephine, born just two days before—meaning the dollars he earned would be stretched further than ever. Meat and fresh milk, virtually nonexistent during the week, would now be a rarity even at Sunday dinner, and Maria's pasta dishes and lentil soup would be the family's food staples. His children would forgo new shoes this year; each of them knew how to jam wads of newspaper into the holes in the soles.

Maria sat at the kitchen table now, the infant unmoving in her arms. The child was so still that he was alarmed at first.

"Josie?" he said, unsure.

"Asleep," Maria smiled and nodded to the child. Giuseppe stepped over to them, reached down, stroked his wife's cheek, and then the baby's, with palms rough as sandpaper, hewn from years of pick-and-shovel labor. Maria's face was pale and drawn; she was exhausted from the rigors of childbirth on Monday. She had delivered Josephine with the help of Carmela Distasio, who lived upstairs, but since then Carmela had been able to provide Maria with only limited help. Carmela had four children of her own that needed care. The two Iantosca boys, Pasquale, seven—whom they called Pasqualeno or "Little Pasquale"—and Vincenzo, five, often played together with Maria Distasio, eight, and her six-year-old brother, Antonio.

Giuseppe bent, pain clawing his back, and kissed his wife softly so the baby would not awaken.

"The other children?"

"Asleep," she answered. "Pasqualeno had a busy day." She thrust her chin toward the ceiling to refer to the upstairs apartment. "With Maria." Giuseppe stood silent, waiting for more of the story. "Look over there," his wife said, nodding to the kitchen counter.

Giuseppe saw three large cans standing uncovered on the dingy countertop. He shuffled over and peered inside. All three were filled with thick, brown molasses.

"They went over to the tank after school," Maria Iantosca said. "Pasqualeno, and Maria and Antonio. They bring the cans. The molasses leaks from that tank all day long and they go there and scoop it up. We can use it. Otherwise it goes to waste."

"Can the kids get in trouble?" Giuseppe asked. "Can they get hurt?"

"If the railroad men see them they just chase the kids away, so there's no trouble," Maria said. "I don't see how they can get hurt."

"No, I guess not," Giuseppe said. He dipped his finger in one of the cans, tasted the molasses, turned to his wife and smiled.

In her mother's arms, Josephine stirred, scrunched her face, yawned, and continued to sleep.

Giuseppe was ready to do the same.

✤ ✤ ✤

The North End in which Martin Clougherty, George Layhe, and Giuseppe Iantosca lived and worked was one of America's oldest, most historic, colorful, and crowded neighborhoods.

In the early years of the country, the North End had been Boston's most fashionable address, home to colonial governor Thomas Hutchinson and the city's most famous midnight-rider, Paul Revere. It was a springboard for the settlement of Boston in Puritan and colonial years, it was the nexus of activity during the American Revolution, and later it became a center of shipping and commerce in a growing city.

By the mid-1800s, however, the economic condition of the North End had deteriorated, as successive waves of German and then Irish poor had settled there. The Irish potato famine of the mid-1840s provided the impetus for this flood of poor immigrants, and by 1850, the North End had become Boston's first slum neighborhood. John F. Fitzgerald, "Honey Fitz," a future mayor of Boston and grandfather of a president of the United States, was born in 1863 in a small wooden North End tenement, the son of a grocery store owner. (John's daughter, Rose, who would one day become the mother of President John F. Kennedy, was born twenty-seven years later on Garden Court Street in the North End.) In 1880, there were about twenty-six thousand people in the neighborhood, and the Irish still made up the vast majority of the population—about sixteen thousand. The combined Jewish, Portuguese, and Italian populations numbered only about four thousand.

Those numbers changed dramatically over the next forty years. More than 4 million Italians came to America between 1880 and 1920, 80 percent of them from southern Italy and Sicily, a great influx that altered the ethnic makeup of American cities in general, and the North End population in particular.

Like the Iantoscas, who hailed from the town of Montefalcione in the province of Avellino, most Italians settled in urban neighborhoods in tight-knit enclaves with others from their particular region, or *paese*, in Italy. These became not so much *Italian* neighborhoods as a collection of individual enclaves of immigrants from Sicily, Abruzzi, Calabria, Avellino, and Genoa. Giuseppe Iantosca and Vincenzo Distasio were *paesani*, as were their families. They lived in the same building, kept an eye on each other's children, socialized together, and often shared meals. Like Giuseppe, Vincenzo worked to support his family as a laborer, the most common occupation among Southern Italians, who had high rates of illiteracy and were largely unskilled.

As Irish and Jews assimilated and earned more money, both ethnic groups moved out of the North End to better areas of the city, although small enclaves remained in the neighborhood well into the 1930s. The Cloughertys were among the few Irish families that still lived in the North End by the First World War. Most other Irish had moved to South Boston, across the Charles River to Charlestown, or to East Boston, where George Layhe settled after he moved to Boston from New York. The Italian population in the North End continued to soar—by 1910, after a decade of unprecedented immigration, the neighborhood's population approached thirty thousand people, of whom more than twenty-eight thousand were Italians.

The North End became the center of Italian life in the Boston area. The narrow streets pulsed with vitality, as hacks, pushcarts, delivery trucks, and people competed for right of way. Jerre Mangione and Ben Morreale, authors of *La Storia: Five Centuries of the Italian-American Experience,* described the general Italian neighborhood in America: "Above the streets, the fire escapes of tenements were festooned with lines of drying laundry, while housewives exchanged news and gossip with any neighbor within shouting distance. The roofs became the remembered fields of Italy where residents could visit one another on summer Sundays while the young played in the tar-filled air."

But the colorful culture of the neighborhood belied the mostly miserable housing conditions endured by thousands who lived in the congested sections. Tenements were cold and dark. City investigators found the buildings adjoined so closely together that sufficient air and light could not enter inside rooms, except for those on the top floors. Crowding in the North End had become horrific. The inhabitable portion of the neighborhood is only about a half-mile square—only about eighty acres. In 1910, the neighborhood rivaled Calcutta, India, in population density, according to historian William DeMarco.

Arthur P. Jell's decision to build one of America's largest molasses tanks in one of its most congested neighborhoods was not due solely to the North End's prime geographic location. Yes, the tank's proximity to the inner harbor and to railroad routes *were* major factors. But other waterfront locations in the city had rail access, including the nearby Irish strongholds of South Boston and Charlestown, and there is no evidence that USIA discussed or even considered these areas to build an aboveground receptacle capable of holding more than 2 million gallons of molasses.

Instead, Jell and USIA saw an opportunity to travel down the road of least resistance with their selection of the Commercial Street site.

Two overriding realities no doubt played a part in their thought process and ultimate decision—social attitudes toward Italians and a lack of political participation among Italian immigrants to control events in their own North End neighborhood.

One of the lesser known and most unseemly aspects of the Great Immigration period is that Italians, especially those from southern Italy, and including those who settled in Boston and the North End like Giuseppe Iantosca and Vincenzo Distasio, were among the most vilified immigrant groups ever to arrive on America's shores.

The scope and breadth of discrimination against Italian immigrants was remarkable, ranging from physical mob violence in the early years to less overt, yet extremely damaging anti-Italian pronouncements and writings from politicians and journalists. Italian immigrants were lynched more frequently in America than any other group except African-Americans.

The worst single day of lynchings in American history took place in New Orleans in 1891, when eleven Sicilian immigrants, nine of whom had been acquitted and two of whom were awaiting trial, were killed by a mob in retribution for the murder of nationally prominent police chief David Hennessy. The killing of the Italians produced enormously serious repercussions, leading to the near-impeachment of President Benjamin Harrison and bringing the United States to the brink of war with Italy. It also began a period of more than thirty years—bracketed by the trial, conviction, and execution of Nicola Sacco and Bartolomeo Vanzetti—of systemic discrimination against Italian immigrants and Italian-Americans.

Leading "respectable" voices often led the way. Shortly after the New Orleans incident, Henry Cabot Lodge said: "Southern Italians are apt to be ignorant, lazy, destitute, and superstitious. In addition, a considerable percentage of those from cities are criminal." In 1902, the five-volume *History of the American People,* written by Woodrow Wilson, who would later become president, gave his bias against southern Italians the status of a scholar's judgment. These immigrants, he wrote, came from the "lowest class of Italy . . . They have neither the skill, nor energy, nor initiative, nor quick intelligence. The Chinese were more to be desired."

At the heart of the discrimination against southern Italians and Sicilians, considered inferior to their countrymen from the north, was the widespread view that immigrants from southern Italy belonged to a different race entirely. This perception was prevalent for many reasons: their darker complexions, their tendency not to speak English, and their tendency to be illiterate in their own language. Discrimination against southern Italians during this time was as much racism as xenophobia. The Bureau of Immigration reinforced these entrenched biases, classifying Italian immigrants as two different "races"—northern and southern. One official U.S. immigration report stated: "While industrious, Southern Italians ... and Sicilians are less steady and less inclined to stick to a job, day in and day out, than other races." There were other reasons for discrimination against southern Italians, the ethnic group who made up about 80 percent of the North End's population by 1915. Most were not citizens, and many traveled seasonally between Italy and the United States, a migratory pattern that earned them the disparaging label "birds of passage" from other Americans, many of whom perceived Italian immigrants as uncommitted to the United States.

The net result of this discrimination angered, frustrated, and discouraged Italians, especially during the first decade of the twentieth century, causing some to return to Italy and others to insulate themselves more tightly within their own ethnic enclave. Italians focused on working hard, supporting their families, creating a support network of *paesani,* opening small businesses, and avoiding conflict whenever they could. They dedicated themselves to their immediate and extended families, and in most cases, *la famiglia* was the sole social unit to which they belonged and, together with *paesani,* the only people they felt they could trust. Italian immigrants created thriving neighborhoods, in Boston and other urban areas, but most were neither community activists nor particularly civic-minded. Quite simply, Italians paid little attention to what was happening outside of their immediate families and circle of friends.

The exception to this rule, of course, were the anarchists, whose violent preachings and activities contributed to the negative perceptions of Italians. Years of poverty and government oppression in Italy fueled the passions of Italian anarchists, shaped their revolutionary philosophy, and drove them to be among the most radical of all ethnic anarchists. Italian anarchists, more fervently than any other group, believed that capitalism and government were responsible for the plight of the working class and the poor, for the "poverty and squalor in the midst of plenty," in the words of Nicola Sacco years before his arrest. Historian Paul Avrich pointed out that Italian anarchists like Sacco were sure that, "in the end, truth, justice, and freedom would triumph over falsehood, tyranny, and oppression. To accomplish this, however, would require a social revolution, for only the complete overthrow of the existing order, the abolition of property and the destruction of the state, could bring the final emancipation of the workers."

While the overwhelming majority of Italian immigrants were apolitical, the radical anarchists and their followers frightened Americans and made them even more suspicious of the entire ethnic group.

✣✣✣

The discrimination Italian immigrants faced in America fueled their disdain for politics, their suspicion and distrust of government, and their aversion to civic activism. This, coupled with their very high illiteracy rates and inability to speak English, had a profoundly negative effect on the assimilation of southern Italians into American life. Most importantly, these factors discouraged Italians from swearing allegiance to their new country by acquiring citizenship, a necessity if they ever were to vote and wield political power. By 1910, only about 25 percent of Italians in Boston had been naturalized.

"The Italians without doubt take the least interest in politics of any nationality," historian Frederick A. Bushee wrote in 1903. "They are at the foot of the list by every mode of calculation. Migration of single men (back to Italy) helps to break up organized political work among the Italians, but the chief reason is that Italians themselves have developed little interest in politics." Immigrant leader Gino Speranza wrote in 1904: "As a nationality, Italians have not forced political recognition. Though numerically strong, there is no such 'Italian vote' as to interest politicians. They have no representative press outside of their neighborhoods and well-organized movements among them for their own good are rare." Little had changed in Italian enclaves by 1915.

Italians continued to marry, have children, buy property, start businesses, and create bustling commercial and residential communities, including the North End. But because most were not citizens and could not vote, they had little recourse when external forces reached into their neighborhoods and threatened their quality of life. And because of the persistent bigotry that labeled southern Italians as an inferior people, few allies were willing to stand and fight with them.

All of this was good news for U.S. Industrial Alcohol.

The plight of North End Italians emboldened USIA to construct its mammoth molasses tank in Boston's most congested neighborhood. The company *expected* and received virtually no opposition—the poor, vilified, mostly illiterate, and politically toothless Italian immigrants who lived and worked in the shadow of the tank day and night had neither the inclination nor the political power to offer organized resistance.

A few Boston-Irish city workers who labored adjacent to the tank *did* comment on its size during construction, but offered no real protest. They left the North End at night, and their homes and families were far removed from any danger. These men worked on the waterfront, but work and home were two decidedly different places. Boston city workers were grateful for both their jobs and the fact that the molasses tank did not stand in the middle of *their* neighborhood.

So it was understandable that when the tank started to leak shortly after its completion—save for the warnings of Isaac Gonzales—the North End once again remained silent.

By 1916, the munitions companies were on a roll and, by extension, so were the companies that supplied them. Big Munitions and Big Steel, the sinews of war, had rescued America from the widespread business recessions that shook the country during the first two years of the Wilson Administration. When war broke out in Europe in August 1914, the outlook for economic recovery in America was gloomy. Factories were working at 60 percent capacity, estimates of the unemployed reached close to a million, and hundreds of thousands of unemployed were near starvation level.

Hard times continued into 1915, but the rapid growth of the munitions trade revitalized the U.S. economy. The value of explosives exported from the United States increased from $2.8 million in March of 1915 to $33 million in November. But 1916 was truly a watershed year for the war industries and the companies that supplied them. In August of that year, the value of explosives exported from the United States reached $75 million, compared with only $14 million the previous August. Some estimates put the total value of munitions exports—explosives, firearms, ammunition, and related equipment—at an astounding $1.3 billion for the calendar year 1916.

U.S. Industrial Alcohol rode the coattails of the munitions companies to its own meteoric growth. From 1915 to 1916, its net profit more than doubled; from 1914 to 1916, USIA's net profit increased nearly *ninefold.* In 1914, USIA stock returned investors just under 2 percent; by 1916, it generated a return of more than 36 percent. Twice in 1916, USIA filled its Commercial Street tank to nearly 2 million gallons, just barely less than capacity, in its efforts to keep up with the industrial alcohol production necessary in the manufacture of high explosives —and this was *before* America entered the war.

Munitions factories began operating three shifts, unemployment was dropping, and financiers like Rockefeller and J.P. Morgan were loaning money for expansion and capital investment. President Wilson firmly believed that the United States should assist the Allied governments to the greatest extent possible within the bounds of American neutrality, a bonus for Big Business, which initially viewed Wilson's inauguration and liberal policies with apprehension.

"America was already well advanced on the road to war, and she was not to be checked by the weak barriers of neutral obligations," historian Charles Tansill wrote in 1938.

Nor was her munitions industry to be checked.

Italian immigrants in the North End *had* remained silent when the USIA molasses tank was built, and afterward, once it started to leak. Realistically, though, even if they had the political strength to speak as one, by the middle of 1916, their voices likely would have been drowned out by the roar of the munitions industry juggernaut.

Boston, Early June 1916

Patrick Kenneally, a boilermaker by trade, sat on a rigging chair suspended twenty feet above the ground, wiping away dark molasses that leaked from the tank's seams. The chair hung suspended from ropes that were fastened to the top of the tank, and guidelines dropped to the ground to allow Kenneally's partner to move the rigging apparatus around the tank once he signaled down that he had finished working on one section of the steel wall.

Kenneally worked with a soft rag, a light caulking tool, and a hand hammer. After wiping away the molasses, he would use his tools to flatten the steel on each side of the leaky seam to push it closer together, and then press the steel to seal the leaks.

This was his third day at the Commercial Street tank. They had begun their work on ladders, caulked as high as they could, and then staged the rigging chair to reach the spots that were further up the tank. Kenneally was unaccustomed to working so far above the ground. When he caulked boilers to make them watertight, his work was most often done in a shop. He knew from his decade of experience as a boilermaker that it wasn't unusual for a newly constructed tank to weep. Although you did what you could to ensure that a new tank was watertight from the beginning, you never really knew whether it would leak until you filled it with water and watched.

What struck him about this tank was that some of the leaks, especially on the harbor side, started high where the walls met the conical-shaped steel cover and seeped molasses all the way to the bottom. They created a series of brackish, fifty-foot streams that meandered to the ground and pooled around the base of the tank.

This didn't seem right. This tank was doing a lot more than weeping, Patrick Kenneally thought.

It was crying—long, thick tears of brown molasses.

USIA Facility, Brooklyn, New York, June 24, 1916

Millard Fillmore Cook, Jr. assumed the unsigned letter was a hoax. He never actually expected to find a bomb.

Since 1912, when he had become supervisor of USIA's Brooklyn facility, Cook had operated the large plant expertly, supervising molasses shipments into the five tanks on the site and managing a hundred men in the industrial alcohol distillery on the same property. The tanks were nowhere near as large as the company's new Boston tank; Cook was responsible for two 630,000-gallon tanks, two 180,000-gallon tanks, and one tank that held approximately 140,000 gallons of molasses. Cook also was under pressure to meet production quotas for the plant's big customers, the du Pont Powder Company and the Hercules Powder Company. USIA considered Cook one of its best plant managers. This supervisor, whose parents had named him after the thirteenth president of the United States, never seemed to get rattled, even when the plant added a third shift to accommodate the demand for industrial alcohol production after war began in Europe in 1914.

Now, though, Millard Fillmore Cook *was* rattled. The package the policeman had given him was about five inches wide and eight inches long, wrapped in thick paper, and carefully tied and knotted with cord. From the end of the package extended a three-inch-long fuse that had, thankfully, malfunctioned and fizzled out before it burned down to the three sticks of dynamite wrapped inside. Police had discovered the bomb under one of the tanks, exactly where the letter had instructed them to look. USIA's Brooklyn tanks rested on a cribwork of wood, which in turn was supported by concrete columns. This left a gap of about eighteen inches between the tank and the concrete, and it was there that police found the bomb.

USIA had operated the Brooklyn plant since 1902, but Cook knew it had never been as busy as it was now, nor was its work ever as controversial, especially in the minds of the anarchists and radicals who were becoming more daring, not just in Boston, but in New York and around the country. Police had found the bomb under the tank that was closest to Greenpoint Avenue, the main street that led to a bridge connecting the Greenpoint section of Brooklyn with a small settlement across Newtown Creek in Long Island City. Cook knew the Long Island City enclave was thickly populated with foreigners. The warning letter he received was written in broken English. You didn't need to be a detective to know that the letter most likely had been penned by some radical from the other side of the creek.

The only positive aspect to all of this was that the letter *had* been mailed and the bomb discovered before any damage had been done. Next time, USIA might not be so fortunate. Corporate officials in New York City ordered Cook to question all of his employees and double the guard in Brooklyn to prevent further unauthorized access.

They did not have to tell him twice.

Boston, Monday, December 18, 1916

What shocked William White most was the extent of the destruction. A dynamite bomb explosion had ripped a gaping hole clean through the three-foot-thick brick wall of the North End's Salutation Street Police Station, shattered every window on one side of the building, blew out the window sashes, and split the window casings. White had heard from people on the street that the bomb had been placed in a jail cell in the basement of the station, directly under rooms in which three policemen were sleeping early yesterday morning, a Sunday. They were fortunate to have escaped injury when the direction of the explosion blew outward against the station's lower wall rather than upward toward the basement ceiling and the first-floor sleeping area. Police officers had told him that inside the station, floors and walls had cracked, furniture had splintered, and ceiling plaster covered everything.

But the damage stretched far beyond the station house. The bomb had smashed every pane of glass in the tenements across Salutation Street—from Commercial Street to Hanover Street—as well as those in several homes on Battery Street, Commercial Street, and North Street. It had exploded just a few short blocks from the molasses tank. White was USIA's supervisor of the waterfront structure, and he had walked up here today to see for himself what these North End rabble-rousers were capable of, and what additional precautions he needed to take to protect the tank. He was not naïve; he knew the tank was the neighborhood's most inviting target for antiwar radicals and anarchists operating in the North End who seethed about USIA's close relationship with the munitions companies.

Now, kicking rubble and glass out of his way as he walked along the debris-strewn street near the police station, he knew that these law-breakers needed to be dealt with harshly. It was a stroke of fortune that the explosion had taken place so early on a Sunday morning; the streets surrounding the station were deserted and no passersby had been in the blast's direct path. Still, police officers inside the station and innocent civilians living in the nearby tenements could have been injured or killed by this cowardly act. The state chemist on the scene, a man named Walter Wedger, told police that *eighteen to twenty sticks of dynamite* had been used to fashion this bomb, and that the explosion could be heard and felt across the harbor in East Boston. "This is without any question the biggest explosion of this character which has ever happened in Boston," Wedger said.

White knew that anarchists had been active in the North End during the last few months, knew also of the bomb that had been found at USIA's Brooklyn plant in June and that yesterday's explosion had been much too close for comfort. White also theorized that the police station bomb was planted in reprisal against Boston Police for the arrests of several anarchists after a violent antimilitary preparedness riot in North Square in early December. The newspapers called it the "liveliest riot" the neighborhood had ever seen. More than twenty-five shots were fired by police and protestors, though no one was hit by gunfire. Ten demonstrators were arrested, including Alphonsus Fargotti, who was charged with assault with intent to kill for slashing a police officer with a fifteen-inch knife blade. The Friday before the explosion at the police station, a judge bound Fargotti's case over for action by a Suffolk County grand jury, a decision Saturday's newspapers reported. White believed that Fargotti's allies made a bold and violent statement in response, striking at law enforcement's heart—a station house where police worked and slept.

What White did not know was that Fargotti was a militant anarchist, and that dozens of his allies, who were disciples of Italian anarchist leader Luigi Galleani, had taken part in the early December North Square demonstration. The event had been organized by the International Workers of the World (IWW), also known as the "Wobblies," who had engaged in protests across America, sweeping eastward from the Rocky Mountain states, demanding economic justice for the country's lowest paid workers. Their efforts began in 1905 with miners in Idaho, Wyoming, and Colorado, and then grew to include unskilled, semiskilled, and migratory workers of all stripes, many of them blacks, women, and immigrants. Wobblies led strikes in mines, in lumber camps, and at textile mills. One of their goals was to organize workers into one giant union that would one day topple capitalism, a mission that suited anarchists just fine.

The Wobblies found particularly sympathetic ears among poor wage-earners who worked at dangerous jobs and unskilled urban immigrants who struggled to make ends meet, even amidst a robust war economy, and returned from work each day to substandard living conditions. The Wobblies and the anarchists both believed that the war was producing exorbitant profits for business at the expense of downtrodden workers. Though their agendas were not precisely the same—Wobblies favored a Socialist form of government while anarchists believed in *no* government—their staunch anticapitalist stands made them practical ideological bedfellows. It was no surprise that they often joined hands in protest movements around the country.

The early December North End riot began with an IWW meeting

held in North Square, in front of the Italian immigrant Church of the Sacred Heart. Police officers had seen the rally beginning and warned IWW leaders not to speak and to refrain from distributing radical literature. One of the officers cautioned some of the audience to move along and not block the sidewalk, and the riot began. Fargotti slashed at patrolman William Cogan with a butcher's knife, slicing the officer's overcoat and severing a tendon in Cogan's right hand. Close by, a few people in the crowd started shooting. One police officer wrested a .32 caliber automatic from a demonstrator. The sound of the riot was heard blocks away. Additional officers from the Salutation Street and Hanover Street stations arrived quickly, dispersed the crowd, and made arrests. Police found a fully loaded pistol in Fargotti's pocket after they arrested him.

The North Square riot and the Salutation Street Police Station bombing proved to White that the IWW and the anarchists had grown bolder. They preached passionately against government, Big Business, and the war in Europe, and the USIA tank on Commercial Street was an instrument—and a symbol—for all three. "Continue the good war," Galleani had written, "the war that knows neither fear nor scruples, neither pity nor truce ... When we talk about property, State, masters, government, laws, courts, and police, we say only that *we don't want any of them.*"

William White's assistant at the Commercial Street tank, Isaac Gonzales, had been suggesting for months now that USIA erect a chain-link fence around the tank property. The idea was for the tank itself to be fully surrounded by fencing and for two large swinging gates to be installed on the Commercial Street side to allow railcar access to the pumping area. The gates would be padlocked at the close of business, effectively sealing the property. White had resisted Gonzales's suggestion, believing a fence was costly and unnecessary. Police officers guarded the tank property day and night and, up to now, their presence had provided a strong deterrent against trespassers.

But this police station bombing, a few blocks from the molasses tank and just a week before Christmas, had changed things. Authority meant nothing to these people, White thought, nor did the spirit of the season. If they were capable of sneaking a bomb into a police station and exploding the device during the holiest season of the year, they were capable of most anything.

Now White believed Gonzales was right about the fence. He would talk to Mr. Jell in the morning about authorizing the expense. USIA had signed contracts with the country's largest munitions producers, and the company could face financial disaster if its Commercial Street operation were sabotaged.

A fence around the molasses tank would be one added level of precaution. These days, you couldn't be too careful.

THREE

ALONG THE GULF STREAM

At Sea, Late January 1917

Captain Frank Van Gelder maneuvered *Miliero* expertly, hugging the coastline and riding the Gulf Stream as he headed north toward Boston and New York, carrying a full cargo of molasses. The steamer was the pride of U.S. Industrial Alcohol's Cuba Distilling Company, the island shipping subsidiary responsible for negotiating with and purchasing molasses from the sugar cane plantation owners in Puerto Rico, Cuba and the West Indies, and transporting the thick brown liquid north to USIA's distilling facilities in Baltimore, New York, and Boston.

Van Gelder had worked for USIA as a master of oceangoing steamers since 1910, and *Miliero* was the finest ship he had ever commanded. Launched from the Fore River Shipyard in Quincy, Massachusetts, just six months earlier, the newest steamer in the Cuba Distilling/USIA fleet was also the largest. It weighed 5,500 tons, measured nearly four hundred feet from bow to stern, and was capable of carrying more than 1.5 million gallons of molasses. Her hold was divided into sixteen separate steel compartments, each large enough to store between 100,000 and 120,000 gallons. Pumps aboard ship were used to transfer the molasses from the *Miliero's* compartments through a ten-inch-wide discharge hose that linked to permanent pipelines connected to USIA's different molasses tanks in the Northeast.

Van Gelder loved piloting ships, loved the sea, had captained oceangoing vessels for more than thirty years and never tired of it. He had been a master of sailing vessels up to 1893 before becoming a master of steam-powered ships. Steam power was easier to handle, and ships made more accurate time when they were not forced to rely on the randomness of the wind. Steam was better for commerce and improved the profits for the ship owners; a sailing ship caught in a dead calm halfway up the East Coast for a day or more could put a serous strain on a company's financial resources. Not to mention the

fact that a becalmed sailing ship would make a more inviting target for the Germans, who were threatening loudly to resume their
U-boat submarine campaign against U.S. shipping, which they had
suspended in 1916 amidst American protests.

But for all of steam's advantages, Van Gelder missed sailing, the *art*
of sailing more than anything else; figuring the gusts and the swells,
positioning his crew on the sails to take advantage of a sudden shift in
wind direction, the feeling of being an underdog in the battle of man
against weather. The steel-hulled steamers were larger, faster, sturdier,
sleeker, and more reliable, but decidedly less challenging to him.

Still, Cuba Distilling paid him well and had increased his salary
since the war had begun in Europe. Under pressure to produce industrial alcohol at an unprecedented rate to meet the demands from
the munitions companies, USIA had delivered clear policy messages
to Van Gelder and the other Cuba Distilling captains: make sure the
steamer storage tanks were filled with molasses when they left the islands; journey northward with the utmost speed; and carry out unloading procedures day and night at the storage tanks in Baltimore,
New York, and Boston. Depending on the temperature of the molasses and the air temperature at the port cities, it could take several
days to discharge hundreds of thousands of gallons of molasses. USIA
ordered its captains to do anything they could to expedite the process, though Van Gelder was familiar enough about the peculiarities
of molasses to know that the viscosity of the substance itself usually
determined the pace of the transfer from the ship's holds to the tank.

Actually, Van Gelder welcomed the opportunity to get in and out
of Boston as quickly as possible. This was his third visit to the North
End waterfront since the company had built the new 2.3 million-
gallon tank. The previous two times, he had witnessed a sight that
made him queasy in a way that thirty years at sea had never done, a
sight that actually forced him to avert his eyes and carry on grimly with
the mundane tasks of connecting the discharge hose to the dockside
pipes and pumping molasses from the *Miliero's* hull compartments.

It was a strange and chilling sight he and his crew members saw,
though they never spoke about it, either during the pumping process
or even as they pulled away from the dock and pointed the *Miliero* seaward. It was one thing for a tank to leak a bit; he had seen it dozens of
times when he made deliveries up and down the East Coast.

But the steel tank in Boston, which went into operation only about one year ago, leaked more molasses through its riveted seams than any other he had seen.

✦✦✦

Frank Van Gelder transported molasses along the East Coast following the same route that captains before him had traveled since the early 1600s. For three centuries, the molasses trade had been a vital part of the American and the New England economy, as important as fishing or textiles, and a critical component in the country's political and social development.

This dark-brown viscous liquid, a by-product in the processing of sugar cane, played a major role in some of the biggest events in American history: in the colonial discontent that led directly to the Revolution; in the introduction of slavery to the New World and, thus, the Civil War; in the growth of rum and liquor distilleries throughout the United States, and the resulting Prohibition movement; and in ensuring the superiority of Allied firepower that would eventually lead to victory in the First World War. It all started in Boston and New England.

✦✦✦

"Our orders are that you embrace the first fair wind and make the best of your way to the coast of Africa, and there invest your cargo in slaves." According to historian James Pope-Hennessy, these were instructions issued to a ship's master, not in the Deep South, but in Salem, Massachusetts. It was from Salem, as well as from Boston, Newport, and Bristol, Rhode Island, Portsmouth, New Hampshire, and New London, Connecticut, that the slaving ships set sail for the coast of West Africa, their holds laden with barrels of rum. Once they arrived, they traded the rum to African coast merchants in exchange for black slaves, whom they sold, in turn, in the West Indies for local products—most notably, molasses. These ships then transported molasses to New England to be used as a cheap sugar substitute, and to distill into rum. The cycle then began all over again. The "Triangle Trade" was born and became the backbone of New England's economy and prosperity before the American Revolution.

The first American-built vessel to carry slaves was the *Desire*, sailing out of Salem, Massachusetts, in 1638, and the trade continued to enrich New England merchants for nearly two centuries. One historian said it was probably "not an exaggeration to say that the slave trade was the lubricating oil that kept the machinery of the colonial New England economy moving smoothly." Another added: "Indeed, one of the grievances of white Southerners in the nineteenth century—probably even a covert grievance still today—was that the Yankees who had become so vociferously humanitarian over the evils of slavery were the direct descendants of the chief American traders in slaves."

Up and down the West Coast of Africa, New England traders purchased slaves with rum made from molasses. Early records show that African men fetched 115 gallons of rum each and African women ninety-five gallons apiece. Most New England ships took their slaves to sell in the West Indies, many of whom were later sent to the colonies in America. Boston was by far the most important slaving port in the first half of the eighteenth century, and many of her leading merchants sent vessels to Guinea, on the African coast. New England merchants plunged into the rum trade with such enthusiasm that they often created a glut of rum on the Guinea Coast. This, in turn, created an overabundance of slaves in the West Indies, men and women shipped from Africa to the islands, as part of the "middle passage" of the slave trade.

To alleviate the excess, many slaves were imported into the Southern colonies to support the plantation system that had begun to spread throughout the region. By the early 1700s, the average Southern plantation covered more than seven hundred acres, and many of the Virginia and South Carolina plantations were much larger. Thus, the New England-Africa-West Indies triangle slave trade formed the genesis of the "peculiar institution" in the Southern colonies and states, a way of life which would tear the country apart and plunge it into Civil War a century and a half later.

Molasses was at the center of it all.

Beyond its role in the commercial distillation of rum, certainly its most important contribution to the colonial economy, molasses was a staple among families. A cheap sugar substitute, molasses is a by-product extracted during the sugar refining process. Sugar cane is crushed to remove the juice, which is then boiled to extract sugar. The remaining syrup, after the sugar has been crystallized, becomes known as "first molasses," the sweetest variety. The leftover syrup from the second boiling is called second molasses—less sweet and cheaper—and the syrup remaining after the third extraction of sugar from sugar cane is known as "blackstrap molasses," a dark, bitter-sweet, unpleasant-tasting liquid that was used in the production of industrial alcohol by USIA and other companies.

Colonists not only used molasses to produce their own beer and rum, they considered it a vital part of their diet. New Englanders made baked beans, brown bread, and pumpkin pie with it. The German communities in Pennsylvania used molasses in shoofly pie and pandowdy, a baked apple-and-spice dish. In colonial Carolina, molasses went by the name of "long sugar" and was said to "serve all the purposes of sugar, both in eating and drinking." Historian John J. McCusker, in his comprehensive 1989 study of the molasses trade and rum production in the thirteen American colonies, points out that in the town of Colchester, Connecticut, at least one Thanksgiving celebration had to be delayed until additional molasses could be procured. During Christmas, molasses was the key ingredient in the traditional gingerbread. In the mid-1700s, each colonist was consuming about three quarts of molasses per year.

Molasses played an even greater role in the distilling industry. In 1750, there were twenty-five distilleries in Boston and about ten others in coastal towns around Massachusetts. By 1770, the number had grown to fifty-one across the colony, thirty-six of which were in Boston. Massachusetts produced more than 2 million gallons of rum, or more than 40 percent of the total distilled in North America. Another two dozen distilleries operated in Rhode Island and Connecticut, and all of them distilled molasses to produce rum. In 1770, New England imported fifteen times the amount of molasses that the colonies of Massachusetts and New Hampshire had imported a half-century earlier, mostly to support the burgeoning rum business. New England also exported thousands of gallons of molasses to other colonies and to Canada during this period, and cash from molasses trading helped the colonists repay their debt to England.

Molasses—whether for eating, for export in exchange for cash, or for use in rum production—had become an indispensable part of the Massachusetts and New England economy by the eve of the American Revolution.

Which is why, when Parliament renewed and enforced the Molasses Act of 1733 as the Sugar Act of 1764, colonists viewed it as a threat to their livelihoods and their lifestyles, and protested vehemently. The act imposed new or higher duties on sugar, textiles, molasses, and other goods from non-British territories and mandated that colonists could ship these goods only to English ports. This was the first law Parliament enacted specifically designed to raise revenue from the colonies, part of a broader effort to help reduce England's national debt after the Seven Years' War.

But angry colonists dubbed it "taxation without representation" —the first widespread use of the phrase—because their elected representatives sat in colonial legislatures and not in Parliament. Colonists began corresponding with each other and agreements were made in a number of cities not to import British goods. This set the stage for the stauncher, bolder resistance that followed over the next several years when Parliament imposed the Stamp Act and Tea Act. The colonists simmered, revolution was brewing, and the trade in molasses contributed decisively to both.

Years after the American Revolution, former President John Adams wrote to a friend: "I know not why we should blush to confess that molasses was an essential ingredient in American Independence. Many great events have proceeded from much smaller causes."

A sharp drop in sugar prices following the Revolutionary War meant that molasses was used less as a sweetener, but it continued to provide the raw material for the Massachusetts rum and distilling businesses. Industrial alcohol became a significant part of the economy by the late 1800s. It was used in cleaning products, solvents, dyes, and lacquers, and companies like U.S. Industrial Alcohol relied on molasses to produce these products for a country whose economy was expanding and becoming more industrialized. The production of industrial alcohol from molasses continued steadily into the early 1900s, and then spiked dramatically just before and during the First World War, when munitions production soared.

By the time U.S. Industrial Alcohol built the tank on the Boston waterfront in 1915, by the time Frank Van Gelder, Isaac Gonzales, and George Layhe noticed its disquieting amount of leakage, molasses had developed deep and integral roots in the New England and Massachusetts economies, based on nearly three centuries of nautical and economic tradition.

Molasses was as much a part of the fabric of Boston's history and personality as the Old North Church, the Common, and the fishing boats that departed the wharves for deeper Atlantic waters in the early morning darkness.

Boston, February 1917

Twelve days after Frank Van Gelder brought the *Miliero* into port and connected its discharge hoses to the molasses tank's two-hundred-foot intake pipe, his crew pumped the last of the seven-hundred-thousand-gallon cargo from the ship's hold.

The temperature had plummeted to 10 degrees below zero on the morning they arrived and had not warmed up much during their entire stay. The men were anxious to be on their way. They still had a stop to make in New York before turning southward toward the islands again. Pumping molasses was difficult with the air temperature so cold; under these conditions, it didn't flow so much as crawl through the ship's ten-inch-wide discharge hose and through the permanent pipeline that ran from the ship's hose to the molasses tank. Van Gelder's fingers stung like they had been cut with shards of glass and his feet were blocks of ice. His men had been shivering for a week, but there was no rushing the molasses. Van Gelder had seen it behave like it had a mind of its own. "Molasses is queer," he had been known to say. "Sometimes you would get a molasses that was heavy. You would think you would have trouble with it, and it would pump all right. Other times you would have thin molasses and sometimes it wouldn't pump good. You can't explain the reason."

This trip, the molasses had been finicky, almost reluctant, as though it did not want to leave the relatively warm confines of the ship's hold only to be deposited into the cold tank. When molasses left the islands, its temperature generally hovered between 75 and 80 degrees Fahrenheit; by the time it reached Boston, it usually had only dropped to between 65 and 70 degrees. Even this trip, when the temperatures were as cold as Van Gelder could ever remember, the molasses temperature hadn't dropped below 52 degrees. The reason:

Van Gelder and other captains followed the warm Gulf Stream north-ward. The molasses held its temperature for most of the trip—its thick consistency enabled it to hold its temperature better than water or oil anyway—and did not begin to cool until about twenty-four hours from port. That's when the big molasses steamers veered to-ward shore. The frigid temperature had cooled this shipment more quickly than usual, and now the pumps strained and squealed as they forced the molasses toward the enormous storage tank that towered over the wharf.

While Van Gelder and his crew pumped molasses and smoked, stamping their feet and thrusting their hands into their armpits against the bone-chilling cold, USIA's Isaac Gonzales bent over the connection adjacent to the tank to make sure the inflow hose was tight. He had been outside for the last twelve days, too, checking that the pumps worked properly, that no air was being sucked through any loose connections and into the inflow pipes, and that the small heater pump through which the main connector pipe ran operated effec-tively to warm the thick molasses flowing inside.

Even with the heater pump, this shipment of molasses seemed to have the consistency of wet sand. As Isaac straddled the pipe and gripped the flange to examine the bolts, he could almost hear the molasses shifting and slurping inside the pipe, could *feel* it wriggling inside, like a long thick worm inching toward its home.

Behind him he heard something else, an unnatural wail that sent a chill through him that had nothing to do with the weather. He tried to shut his ears to the groan and the long roll of rumbling that came from inside the molasses tank. But it was no use. When the sound happened again, Isaac's chill became an icy pang in his chest, like the flat of a knife-blade pressing against his heart.

Washington, D.C., April 2, 1917, Evening

President Woodrow Wilson strode into an antechamber in the Capi-tol building, shaking raindrops from his coat and wiping his glasses. He had driven through a drizzle from the White House, appropriate weather to mark tonight's events. This morning he had called for both houses of Congress to assemble and hear his request for a dec-laration of war against Germany. Thinking he was alone, Wilson walked to a mirror. Concealed from view, a magazine editor later described the president: "Chin shaking, face flushed, he placed his left elbow on the mantel and gazed steadily at himself until he composed his features." Then Wilson left the anteroom and entered the swinging doors of the House chamber.

He could not believe that events had reached this point. Wilson and America had been walking a neutrality tightrope since the outbreak of the European war, and as late as January 22, Wilson had delivered his "peace without victory" speech to the Senate. The war must be ended on terms that would establish, "not a balance of power, but a community of power, not organized rivalries but a common peace." The only way to achieve that end was through "a peace without victory . . . victory would mean peace forced upon the loser" and would therefore "rest only as upon quicksand. Only a peace between equals can last."

Interventionists sharply criticized Wilson for a view that they considered at best naïve, and at worst a sign of America's weakness. "Peace without victory is the natural ideal of the man who is too proud to fight," said former President Theodore Roosevelt. He called Wilson a spiritual descendant of the Tories of 1776 and the Copperheads of 1864, who had also demanded peace without victory. Massachusetts senator Henry Cabot Lodge rejected peace without victory, declaring that lasting peace "rests upon justice and righteousness."

Wilson's position was irrevocably undermined by the Germans when, on the afternoon of January 31, 1917, Count Johann von Bernstorff, German ambassador to the United States, delivered an official correspondence that as of midnight, America's merchant ships would be sunk on sight by German submarines. The opening of unrestricted submarine warfare against Allied and neutral shipping caused President Wilson to break diplomatic relations.

The downward spiral toward war had begun.

America's entry into the European hostilities was hastened further when British intelligence intercepted a telegram from German foreign minister Arthur Zimmerman to the German minister in Mexico. The message disclosed a plan for Germany to enter into an alliance with Mexico if the United States entered the European war. If Germany and her allies were successful, Mexico's reward would be the return of its "lost territories" of New Mexico, Texas, and Arizona. When newspaper headlines revealed the existence of the "Zimmerman Telegram" and proclaimed Germany's treachery across the country on March 1, explosive anti-German propaganda had begun in the United States, and public opinion surged toward war.

Wilson knew that the neutrality tightrope had snapped. Four days later, March 5, 1917, at his second inaugural address, he told the crowd: "We are provincials no longer. The tragic events of the thirty months of vital turmoil through which we have just passed have made us citizens of the world. There can be no turning back. Our own fortunes as a nation are involved whether we would have it so or not."

Later in March, to Wilson's horror, several unarmed American merchant ships were sunk in the Atlantic by German submarines, and many crew members drowned. Hysteria gripped the country, and Wilson, desperate to avoid war but astute enough to realize that events had overtaken him, was forced to act.

Now, standing before a packed House chamber, all of his vigorous peace efforts for naught, Wilson spoke against German outrages, including the sinking of medical ships and of those vessels carrying relief supplies to Belgium. This was "warfare against mankind," he said. The United States could not "choose the path of submission and suffer the most sacred rights of our nation and our people to be ignored or violated." And then, bringing the House to its feet shouting and applauding, Wilson declared: "America is privileged to spend her blood and her might for the principles that gave her birth and happiness and the peace which she has treasured. God helping her, she can do no other. The world must be made safe for democracy ... We desire no conquest, no dominion. We seek no indemnities for ourselves, no material compensation for the sacrifices we shall freely make. We are but one of the champions of the rights of mankind."

Later that night, according to authors Meirion and Susie Harries, Wilson wept openly while reliving the speech with his private secretary. "Think what it was they were applauding," he said of Congress. "My message today was a message of death for our young men. How strange it seems to applaud that."

Two days later, the Senate voted 82-6 to declare war; the House concurred two days after that, 373-50. Wilson signed the war resolution on April 6, 1917, at 1:18 P.M. The United States was joining the fight against Germany, the war to end all wars, the war that would—

in President Wilson's words—make the world safe for democracy. To be successful, she needed her industrial plants to produce goods and manufacture weapons and war materiel at extraordinary and unprecedented levels.

Like businesses across America, U.S. Industrial Alcohol stood ready to help.

⋆ FOUR ⋆

WAR AND ANARCHY

Boston, April 1917

President Wilson's request for a declaration of war against Germany fueled a patriotic fervor in Boston during the first week of April that sent thousands to the streets to cheer at huge rallies, or to gather on downtown corners to sing the National Anthem, eyes skyward, watching as enormous American flags were unfurled from the upper floors of the city's tallest and most prominent buildings, snapping in the wind as they billowed down the face of each structure. Boston had begun showing its support for Wilson's decision *before* his speech on April 2 when nearly two hundred thousand people thronged the Boston Common at noon in a gathering remarkable not only for its size but for the fact that it was virtually unorganized. Mayor Curley had issued a simple proclamation a few days earlier asking Bostonians to join together on the Common for a flag-raising. On this day, anticipating the magnitude of President Wilson's speech later in the evening, people arrived from every section of the city, streaming onto the historic forty-five-acre grassy parcel from all sides, as Boston shut down during the noon hour.

"It was unorganized, nothing was prepared," one newspaper account read. "And yet more men, women and children came to see the American flag raised ... than ever came before to the Boston Common for any single event ... from banks, from stores, from halls of City and State Government, they came." Two-and-a-half centuries earlier, Bostonians had gathered on this "common land" to exercise their horses, graze their cattle, and drill their militia companies. Now they gathered to express their full-throated support of America's entry into a European war.

Throughout the week, similar smaller rallies continued at locations around the city, as flags were raised over dozens of Boston buildings to the accompaniment of music and speeches. At a Faneuil Hall rally, Mayor Curley told fruit peddlers and meat packers that, "it isn't

56

necessary to talk patriotism to men who work within sight of the greatest beacon light of liberty this old world has ever known, Faneuil Hall." He reminded the men that "the president of the United States has not asked for a declaration of war on the German people, but on the German government," a sentiment that elicited a roar from the crowd. At another North Station ceremony, Mayor Curley praised President Wilson and predicted to a cheering crowd of about a thousand people that American blood would not have to be shed to end the war, but that the German people would rise up and overthrow their government.

Curley's prediction notwithstanding, Boston shifted into a war mind-set rapidly during the first week of April. The *Boston Globe* reminded its readers that April was "a war month" for America, noting that the American Revolution, the Mexican War, the Civil War, and the Spanish-American War had all begun in April, implying that Wilson's call for America's entry into the current European conflict was wrapped in a cloak of historical appropriateness and destiny. In response to President Wilson's call for a standing military 2 million strong within two years, young men flocked to recruitment centers across the city. Lines at the Tremont Street Army and Navy recruitment centers blocked the stairways to the third-floor offices and stretched out the door, and men streamed into the Marine recruiting station in nearby Scollay Square.

At the nearby Charlestown Navy Yard, more than 1,500 men applied for enlistment within three days of Wilson's speech to Congress. "The naval officers are much pleased with the type of young men they are getting, young, growing boys, active and alert," one newspaper reported. "However, there is an urgent need also for the slightly older, more solidly built men, and particularly for skilled men, plumbers, blacksmiths, electricians." Each day, papers listed the "non-slackers" for the day, praising those who had enlisted.

Along with the rush to enlist came a sharp increase in the number of people applying for marriage licenses, in Boston and across the country, as couples scrambled to marry before bridegrooms-to-be shipped overseas. In Chicago, more than eight thousand applications for marriage licenses were received at City Hall within ten days of Wilson's speech, and in Boston, applications doubled over the previous year. Many ministers around the country spread the word that they would not marry "slackers"—men either had to have enlisted or had a good reason for not doing so.

Aside from enlistments, the first week of active war preparation was a flurry of activity in Boston. The Navy closed Boston Harbor at dark, allowing no vessel in or out. Navy divers laid mines and stretched wire netting across the floor of the harbor to thwart German U-boats. Armed patrols were established along Long Wharf, Rowe's Wharf, and Commercial Street Wharf, the latter within a few feet of the molasses tank. German merchant ships docked in harbors across the country were seized and their crews detained, including seven large ships in Boston. Nearly two hundred German crew members were shipped to Deer Island in Boston Harbor, technically as prisoners of war, though their cells—described as "large and excellent quarters"—remained unlocked, and they were allowed free movement around the island.

Meanwhile, Boston's district attorney was warning the city against potentially violent anarchist activity, claiming that Boston was in "grave danger from disturbances by anarchistic bands who are holding nightly meetings, planning what they can do to tear down the structure of Government while the country's eyes are fixed on danger from without." Joseph Pelletier urged that additional guards be stationed in every bank and that manufacturing companies increase precautions. "A few hand grenades, effectively used, would put Boston in darkness for six months," he warned. Pelletier advocated a "thorough survey" of Boston, "that we may get the names and addresses of all who are not citizens. Then we must learn what these people are doing. We must know their purpose in being in the city."

During the next several days, between April 8 and April 10, Pelletier's warnings appeared prophetic as a series of activities in other cities, but not Boston, were blamed on anarchists. The Capitol Police presence was increased in Washington, D.C., after the Secret Service relayed a tip that anarchists were planning to dynamite the Capitol building, a report that proved to be false. In Pittsburgh, authorities blamed anarchists for an arson fire that destroyed a portion of the Aetna Chemical Company, one of the country's largest munitions manufacturers and a major customer of U.S. Industrial Alcohol.

And in the most tragic event, 116 workers, many of them teenage girls, perished in a massive explosion at the Eddystone Ammunition

Corporation in Chester, Pennsylvania. The explosion occurred in the pellet room of the shrapnel building, where the girls worked polishing shells. Officials believed that "foreigners" working in the factory planted the bomb, taking their own lives in the explosion. "It is very difficult to have five thousand people working in a munitions factory and not have some foreigners employed," lamented the factory manager.

Though no violent anarchist activity occurred in Boston during this time, the city, now very much on wartime alert, remained vigilant.

Cambridge, Mass., Two Weeks Later

Arthur P. Jell had taken seriously both the explosion in Pennsylvania and the Pelletier warning. Within days of each, he had hired his own guards and had them sworn in as special police, replacing the single Boston police officer who had guarded the tank on a fixed post. While the possibility of sabotage was an unpleasant thought to consider, he also had been heartened by additional news from Washington. The Council of National Defense had created a General Munitions Board to oversee munitions and equipment production for the Army and Navy, coordinate military purchases, and assist the munitions companies in acquiring raw materials for their manufacturing facilities. The General Munitions Board had enormous power, virtually Cabinet-level influence, and could also direct certain manufacturing facilities to switch from domestic to defense production if necessary.

Jell knew that this decision elevated the status of the industrial alcohol distilling business, ensured that red tape could be cut quickly if it jeopardized production or distribution activities, and virtually guaranteed USIA's double-digit growth for as long as the war continued. He also believed that America's entry into the war was a good chance for him to show the New York home office that the Boston tank and the Cambridge distilling plant could handle soaring production quotas.

But this morning, sitting in his tidy Cambridge office just ten days after he had hired his own guards for the Commercial Street site, Arthur Jell's enthusiasm was waning and his irritation was increasing. The problem was Gonzales and his paranoia. USIA's general man at the Commercial Street molasses tank stood to jeopardize Jell's and the company's success in the coming months if he could not be controlled.

First, there was his unauthorized visit a few days ago, complaining sanctimoniously about molasses leaking from the mammoth storage tank. Gonzales said the tank leaked from every seam every day, that workers on the dock had questioned him about it, and that the Italian neighborhood children gathered around the base of the tank each noon hour to collect molasses in their small pails. "The children also dip sticks into the pools of molasses and slurp it into their mouths; it even drips onto their clothes," Gonzales had said. "I spread sand around the base of the tank to keep the molasses from flowing too far, but with my other duties, I can't keep up with it."

Gonzales then had thrust rusty steel flakes that he had collected from inside the tank into Jell's hands, brushing the last bits from his own palms and into Jell's as though they burned his skin. "These fall like snow into my hair and onto my clothes each time I go inside the tank," he had said with a plea in his voice.

Jell told Gonzales there was nothing to worry about, that the tank was strong and sturdy, that some leaking was normal, especially after the large molasses shipment that the *Miliero* had delivered to the tank in February. He had ordered Gonzales to do a better job of running the trespassing children off of the property so they wouldn't come back. He had not spoken angrily, though he *was* angry that Gonzales had traveled to Cambridge, had tracked cakes of mud from his work boots onto Jell's office carpet, and had lectured Jell on the construction of molasses tanks, as though Gonzales were some sort of engineering expert rather than a manual laborer whose job it was to take direction from his supervisor each day.

The visit had been intrusive enough, but then Gonzales had revealed that he had been sleeping at the tank for several months, bedding down in the pump-pit shack. "I'm afraid the tank is not safe, and if it should start to fall, I can sound a warning," he said to Jell. Shocked by his employee's admission, Jell had told him to go home at the end of his work shift. He reminded Gonzales that the tank had been caulked completely last year. "The tank still stands—the tank will stand," Jell had said.

Yesterday, Gonzales was at it again. In the late afternoon he had called Boston Police in a panic reporting that he had received a phone call from a man with a raspy voice threatening to blow up the tank. "Is this the supervisor of the molasses tank on Commercial Street?" Gonzales said the man asked. When Gonzales said he was merely a worker, the caller became angry and said: "You're a damn liar and we're going to dynamite the tank." Much to Jell's chagrin and that of tank supervisor William White, Gonzales had called police, who came to the wharf to investigate. White told Gonzales that calling the police had been a foolish thing to do, and Gonzales had the audacity to reply, "I don't care whether it is foolish or not; the police captain sees fit to give help." Two officers had even stayed on the site throughout the night. Jell knew anarchists were a threat, but he didn't trust Gonzales and didn't believe there actually had been any call.

Jell had stressed to White this morning that he must do a better job of controlling Gonzales. Firing him would be impractical at this time. Too many young men were enlisting and Jell had no time to train a new man now that alcohol production was on the upswing. But Jell thought Gonzales's behavior was bizarre—*sleeping* at the tank, for God's sake!—and that he needed to be watched closely for the sake of the business. It did not serve USIA's purposes to have Gonzales complaining about leaks to anyone who would listen, nor did it help to draw further public attention to the tank through the presence of more police. When word got out that Boston Police responded to a phone caller who was threatening to blow up the tank with dynamite, and word spread quickly along the waterfront, it could give anarchists destructive ideas. Jell had enough pressure worrying about *real* dangers from violent men who hated that America was at war and hated even more those businesses that would become successful by feeding the war machine. He did not have the time or energy to worry about phantom phone callers.

The USIA operation was humming along smoothly. Jell had made his position clear to both Gonzales and White. He did not need anyone gumming up the works.

June–October 1917

With America at war, it was no surprise that socialists, the IWW, and anarchists became prime targets of the government's antiradical crusade. Fears of radicalism, heightened by the recent Bolshevik revolution in Russia, fanned a "Red Scare" in America and a spirit of reaction that would mount as the war progressed, historian Paul Avrich noted. The U.S. government viewed radical agitation of every kind as obstruction of the war effort, and therefore anti-American, and increased its surveillance of anarchists and other militants. "Their uncompromising opposition to the war brought down on them the full panoply of government repression," Avrich wrote. "Throughout the country, anarchist offices were raided, equipment was smashed, and publications were suppressed." Law enforcement efforts reached a peak on June 15, 1917, when three of the leading anarchist leaders in America were arrested.

In New York, federal agents broke into the offices of the radical publication *Mother Earth*, and charged Emma Goldman and Alexander Berkman with conspiracy to interfere with the draft. Longtime comrades and reportedly lovers, Goldman and Berkman were well known among anarchists and law enforcement officials. They had both emigrated from Russia in the 1880s, became involved with radical Jewish labor groups, and, following the Chicago Haymarket riots in 1886, both became active anarchists. Berkman and Goldman had conspired to assassinate Henry Clay Frick, chairman of Carnegie Steel, after the violent Homestead labor strike of 1892. Berkman, who actually shot and stabbed Frick, was convicted of attempted murder and served fourteen years in prison. He and Goldman founded and edited *Mother Earth* after his release, and in the intervening years, preached against capitalism, Big Business, worker oppression, and militarism. When the United States entered the war in April, they ardently opposed a forced draft. After their arrest on June 15, 1917, they were convicted and sentenced to two years in prison.

The other prominent anarchist arrested on the same day was Luigi Galleani in Massachusetts. The Justice Department considered him "the leading anarchist in the United States," and described his radical newspaper, *Cronaca Sovversiva (Subversive Chronicle)*, as "the most rabid, seditious and anarchistic sheet ever published in this country." On June 15, following an editorial critical of draft registration, federal agents raided *Cronaca's* offices in Lynn, Massachusetts, and arrested Galleani at his home in Wrentham, Massachusetts, where he lived with his wife and five children. He was charged with conspiracy to obstruct the draft, entered a plea of guilty, and was ordered to pay a fine of $300.

Galleani's arrest led to police actions against other Italian anarchists, in Boston and elsewhere. Some were arrested and threatened with deportation for starting a defense fund for Galleani and his colleagues. Others found themselves tossed in jail for insulting the American flag or failing to register for the draft. Still others, including Boston's Sacco and Vanzetti, fled to Mexico, where for several months during 1917, they conspired to retaliate against what they saw as repression in the United States through the use of bombings and other violence. A Justice Department agent later speculated that this group had gone to Mexico to receive instruction in the use of explosives.

By the fall of 1917, most of these comrades had returned to the United States. For the next three years they would live an underground existence and employ bombs as their primary weapon against government authority.

They would, as the title of a previously published Galleani collection of articles suggested, go *Faccia a faccia col nemico*—"face to face with the enemy."

France, January 1918

With a flourish, Major Hugh Walker Ogden finished penning the letter to his friend, Horace Lippincott, secretary of the General Alumni Association of the University of Pennsylvania. Ogden had signed with his familiar "HWO," rather than the "H.W. Ogden" or "Hugh W. Ogden" that he reserved for more formal correspondence. His note to Lippincott served as a cover letter to the Penn Alumni Society's request for information about the war records of its graduates now serving in the military. Half a world away, sitting in war-torn France, Ogden had dutifully filled in every line of the form, and then written his personal note, complete with his usual bold penmanship and succinct, yet passionate, observations: "This is veritably the greatest thing on Earth and I would not exchange my present duty for any in the Army. These are wonderful days we are living in and over here is where all history is heading to its greatest climax."

Perhaps more than anything else he had written in a long and distinguished legal and military career, Hugh W. Ogden believed these words with all his heart. Boston would send more than forty thousand of her sons overseas to fight this war that had begun with the assassination of a member of the Austro-Hungarian royal family, and had rippled across Europe, spreading death and destruction over the continent. Of all of those men, none believed more than Hugh Ogden in the rule of law and the strength of military—right and might—to achieve a just end. If history's greatest climax meant the defeat of a Germany run amok with expansionist aggression and brutality, then Ogden would truly welcome victory as "the greatest thing on earth."

Broad-shouldered, with a mustache, high forehead, and dark, wide-set eyes ablaze with a fighter's intensity, Ogden was Boston's most prominent citizen-soldier and one of the city's best-known attorneys. A graduate of UPenn and an 1896 graduate of Harvard Law School, where he served as editor-in-chief of the *Harvard Law Review*, Ogden had enjoyed a career as a partner in the firm of Whipple, Sears & Ogden for nearly two decades, specializing in equity and corporate law, before America entered the war and Ogden answered his call.

For if his profession was law, his love was soldiering. Indeed, the latter was in his genes. He was the grandson of Isaac Ogden, a general in the New York Militia, and a descendant of John Ogden, who served with a colonial regiment after emigrating from England and settling in what later became Elizabeth, New Jersey. The son of Episcopalian minister Charles T. Ogden, Hugh Ogden was born in Bath, Maine, on December 7, 1871, six years after the end of the Civil War. He became interested in the military at a young age, and in 1897, shortly after his graduation from Harvard Law, he enlisted in the First Corps of Cadets, Massachusetts Volunteer Militia, as a private in Company A. The Commonwealth of Massachusetts dispatched the First Corps as part of the coast defenses during the Spanish-American War, but the unit was never mustered into active service. By 1900, Ogden had become a first-class marksman, and on June 2 of that year, he married Lisbeth M. Davis of Riverton, New Jersey. The couple had four children.

While practicing law with Whipple, Sears & Ogden, he became a second lieutenant in the 1st Troop, Massachusetts Provisional Cavalry, which was later absorbed by the Massachusetts National Guard.

His fascination with things military would seem to be incongruous with not only his legal career, but with many of his other pursuits, including his interest in religion, and in particular, the Episcopal Church. Ogden served as clerk of the corporation of the Emmanuel Church in Boston and as a member of the vestry of Christ Church (the Old North Church) in the North End. He was described as one of the "outstanding Episcopal laymen" of Boston and an authority on canon law. One of his great delights was collecting rare books on church history. He was wealthy enough to do so, both in his own right, and through the $300,000 estate that he and his wife inherited when his father-in-law, John C.S. Davis, died in 1913.

It was this meshing of legal, religious, and military training that shaped Hugh Ogden's character and beliefs, teaching him about fairness, preparedness, and a devotion to duty. When the *Lusitania* was sunk in 1915, Ogden assumed that America would become involved in war, and he learned to speak French in preparation for shipping out overseas. Though the United States remained neutral for nearly two more years, Ogden was ready when the call came. He enlisted and was commissioned a major in August 1917, at age forty-five, began active duty in New York in September, and was shipped overseas shortly thereafter. "He arranged his business and personal affairs and packed up his effects within the brief space of 48 hours," according to the *Boston Globe*. "His departure was very quiet, and little was said about the adventure upon which he was embarking. But he went nevertheless, to engage in an undertaking of very great importance to his country and its cause, and to fill a position of the highest dignity and service in that enterprise."

His background and training had prepared Ogden for his current position, which was judge advocate of the celebrated 42nd Infantry "Rainbow" Division, responsible for virtually all legal issues and matters of punishment within the division. "His position demands a special endowment of the judicial temperament," one writer noted in a profile after Ogden's division had been shipped to the front. "Moreover, it is in practice a post of some little isolation, for the officer who is to be fair and unprejudiced cannot afford to be on intimate terms with his fellow officers or to have close friends among them—he must remain more than usually aloof, and he can have no favorites."

The formation of the Rainbow Division had been the vision of a stern and feisty colonel named Douglas MacArthur. Amid the rush by America to mobilize, individual states had competed with each other for the honor to be the first to send their National Guard units to fight overseas. To minimize the negative implications of this competition, the Army decided to create a division composed of hand-picked National Guard units from twenty-six states and the District of Columbia. Thus, the 42nd was born, "a division that stretches like a Rainbow from one end of America to the other," in the words of MacArthur—and the nickname had stuck. The 42nd had arrived in France in November 1917, and was scheduled to enter front-line fighting in March 1918.

Ogden's service with the Rainbow Division would continue through the end of the war, through the division's 175 consecutive days of virtually face-to-face combat with the enemy, through its courageous participation in the Luneville, Baccarat, Champagne-Marne, Aisne-Marne, Chateau-Thierry, Saint-Mihiel, and the Meuse-Argonne offensives. He would be promoted to lieutenant colonel in September 1918, and would be cited for "high ability and talents and valuable services" while with the division. When the war ended in November of that year, he would serve with the American Army of Occupation in Germany as a legal adviser. In 1919, he would be asked by the Army to serve on a committee investigating court martial procedures and articles of war.

After the war, Hugh W. Ogden would receive the Distinguished Service Medal of the United States, and years later, the decoration of the Officer of the Legion of Honor of the French government, honors he certainly could not have predicted in early 1918 when the outcome of the Great War was still in doubt.

Nor could he have predicted today—sitting at his desk in France and sealing the letter to his dear friend, Lippincott—that shortly after his return to Boston, he would preside over one of the country's most celebrated civil lawsuits, stemming from one of the most unusual disasters in United States history.

Massachusetts, February 1918

As war raged in Europe's muddy trenches, tensions smoldered at home between U.S. government authorities and anarchists. On

February 22, a team of federal agents and local police again raided the office of the anarchist newspaper, *Cronaca Sovversiva*, in Lynn, Massachusetts. They seized thousands of documents, including a photograph of Bartolomeo Vanzetti with Luigi Galleani, and a mailing list of about three thousand names, including those of Sacco and Vanzetti.

Based on these raids, the Department of Labor's Bureau of Immigration issued about a hundred arrest warrants for Galleanists considered "liable for deportation." Nearly half of these lived in New England, mainly in the Boston area. Many of them were among the most active in the anarchist movement, and either wrote for *Cronaca* or raised money for the cause. Anthony Caminetti, the commissioner general of immigration in Washington, D.C., ordered Boston immigration commissioner H.J. Skeffington to take aliens into custody and to hold hearings aimed "to establish their anarchist views and activities." Immigration officials and local police carried out the arrests throughout the region. Luigi Galleani himself was arrested in May, but released after he was questioned extensively. He would remain free for nine more months.

On July 18, 1918, authorities finally outlawed *Cronaca Sovversina*, on the grounds that it was subversive, undermined the American war effort, and in the words of the Justice Department, was "the most dangerous newspaper published in this country."

Anarchists in the North End simmered at the decision.

Spring and Summer 1918

Nearly 5 million men served in the United States Armed Forces during the First World War, about five in one hundred citizens, but it was not until the major German offensive in March 1918 that America made its supreme contribution to the Allied effort, transporting 1.5 million soldiers to France within a six-month period. Of the more than 2 million men who reached France, 1.4 million of them saw active service on the front line.

The munitions industry kept pace. They supplied American forces with the ammunition, high explosives, and smokeless powder that the troops needed to fight and win on foreign soil, and provided employment in the United States for those whose efforts supplied the soldiers overseas. Between April 1917 and November 1918, more than 632 million pounds of smokeless powder was produced in the United States, equal to the combined production of England and France. As for high explosives—TNT, ammonium nitrate, picric acid and others—U.S. production was more than 40 percent larger than England's and nearly double that of France for all of 1918. One expert pointed out that the remarkable success of America's munitions production effort was best illustrated by the fact that "the artillery ammunition program was never held up for lack of either the powder which hurls the bullet or shell from the gun, or the high explosive which makes the shell effective when it reaches its destination." As they had since 1915, the companies that produced munitions continued to reap unprecedented profits during 1917 and 1918.

Their suppliers did, too. USIA manufactured the industrial alcohol that was used in the production of fulminate of mercury, acetone, and cordite—critical components of high explosives and smokeless powders. The company continued to distill enormous quantities of molasses to produce the alcohol at its Cambridge plant. The Commercial Street molasses tank on the Boston waterfront reached the 2 million-gallon level *seven* times during 1918, beginning in March and continuing through December.

As a result, Isaac Gonzales worked harder during the spring and summer of 1918 than he ever had, but his exhaustion had less to do with the manual labor he performed at the tank during the day than it did with the stress and physical exertion he subjected himself to at night. For even as the big molasses steamers arrived from Cuba and the islands to unload their millions of gallons of cargo, the Commercial Street tank still leaked, and Isaac was despondent.

When July rolled around and the heat had baked into Boston's streets and buildings, Isaac had begun his cross-city runs in the wee hours of the morning to check on the condition of the tank and make sure that it was still standing. At 2 A.M., at 2:30 A.M.—he never left the house later than 3 A.M., lest he linger too long at the tank and be spied returning home by puzzled neighbors who arose at first light. On the night of each of these runs, he had left his wife, concerned about him but also contemptuous, lying frustrated in the darkness of their tiny bedroom. Isaac knew of her feelings, but he couldn't help himself. He had to check the tank.

During the day, the grueling work pace kept him from obsessing about the tank's collapse. Helping to unload the molasses steamers, climbing into the tank to clear the outflow pipe, bolting the tank's hose assembly to the flange atop the railroad cars—these tasks were enough to keep his mind and body occupied.

The torrid heat wave was also a distraction. The last week in July was the hottest on record in Boston, with temperatures climbing to the high 90s. Four people had died in the heat wave and several others were treated for heat exhaustion. Another death occurred the first week in August. Although some industrial plants had mechanical cooling systems for specific processes during this period, it would be several years before Willis Haviland Carrier, the "father of air conditioning," would improve his product to the point where it could cool large buildings. Thus, Boston workers removed their ties and left their sweltering offices in droves by midday and headed to Revere Beach on the North Shore and Nantasket Beach on the South Shore. Firefighters flushed the streets by opening hydrants during the day, and Boston mayor Andrew Peters (who defeated Curley in December 1917) ordered that the "lightless nights" policy that had been implemented citywide to conserve energy during the war would not apply to Boston's parks.

During these uncomfortable nights, most people in the city's crowded neighborhoods abandoned attempts to sleep indoors, and in places like the North End, carried bedding to the tenement rooftops or fire escapes to find relief. Isaac had heard their nocturnal noises as he ran through the North End streets—a cough here, a sneeze there—and had been gripped by an irrational fear that they would try to stop him if they had awakened. Yet no one had ever called out to him.

The intense heat and work pace helped distract Isaac's thoughts about the condition of the molasses tank, but never for very long. When he took a water break, or paused to wipe the sweat from his eyes with the back of his sticky hand, the tank filled his field of vision, and the molasses leaking from its seams looked like a series of brown waterfalls.

Isaac was not alone in noticing the leaks. Many days he had chased the little Italian children who lived across the street off the property —Maria, her brother Tony, and their friend, the one they called

Pasqualeno—though usually not before they had filled their pails with molasses. The firefighters talked about it in the early morning when they gathered outside the firehouse and prepared to launch their boat to patrol the harbor, their anxious voices carrying across the wharf on the warm, dawn air, before the roar of the elevated railroad trains and the clatter of horse-drawn wagons began in earnest. A stableman for the City of Boston Paving Department asked Isaac what was going on inside the tank. "Sounds like the molasses is bubbling or boiling, or doing something," he had said. Another worker told Isaac that he liked to lean up against the tank to feel the vibration against his back. "It's a regular vibration, as though the tank is bulging in and out."

In some ways, Isaac felt heartened by these comments; they proved that other people saw what he saw, that he wasn't overreacting or, worse, losing his mind. In other ways, the remarks frightened him and heightened his fear and uncertainty. If the leaks were clear enough for others to see, why didn't his company do something? What if the tank collapsed? What if someone bombed it? Wasn't the tank more vulnerable to dynamite if it was structurally weak to begin with? Why did Mr. Jell and Mr. White ignore his warnings? White, as superintendent, was at the tank site every day. He saw the children with their pails, heard the firefighters and the city workers talking. He knew the leaks were excessive, yet he remained silent and ordered Isaac to do the same.

Fine. Isaac would remain silent, but he had told White about his late-night crosstown runs, relished the telling, in fact. He had wanted White to know how strongly he felt, all but *dared* White to stop him. The tank superintendent had merely grunted and turned away. The question now was: What would White do about it? If he had meant to fire Isaac, he would have done so on the spot. That had not happened. Throughout July, Isaac waited to see if his pleas about the tank would be heeded or ignored; he waited to see if his bosses would take action.

In early August, Isaac got his answer. One morning, on orders from Mr. Jell, a crew arrived and spent the next two days painting the tank, covering its steel-gray shell with a rust-brown color. Isaac and everyone else on the waterfront noticed right away that it became more difficult to see the thick molasses streaming down the sides of the tank.

The sticky liquid now blended, chameleon-like, with the fresh coat of paint, indiscernible from the tank's wall, dropping toward the ground invisibly and silently, like a thief in the night.

❖❖❖

Isaac had seen enough. He had warned his superiors about the tank's condition, and they had responded with a paint job. They thought they could *hide* the danger. On September 1, 1918, insulted and distraught, his heart heavy, his nerves raw, worried about his own sanity and in despair over the future of his marriage, Isaac quit his job with United States Industrial Alcohol and enlisted in the United States Army. He was assigned to the 13th Battalion, 50th Company and sent to Columbus, Ohio, for training. Isaac did not know it, but the war would be over before he could be transferred overseas and he would spend his full seven months of service in Columbus.

He also didn't know—though perhaps his nocturnal premonitions had continued even as he sought sleep in his bunk—that when he returned to Boston in March 1919, the Commercial Street wharf area would be changed forever.

Boston, November 1918

Early on the morning of November 11, 1918, before Boston firefighter George Layhe boarded the ferry in East Boston to take him across the harbor to the Engine 31 station; before Giuseppe Iantosca left his Charter Street home to begin another grueling day with a pick and shovel; before Bridget Clougherty had finished cleaning the breakfast dishes in her Commercial Street house, while her son, Martin, slept upstairs—before all of this—Boston newspapers were already proclaiming with jubilant headlines that the armistice had been signed. The war in Europe was over.

"Whole World in Delirium of Joy," shouted the *Boston Globe* on its front page, and its editorial effused, "it is victory, victory at last. The old day is over, its long, dreadful night of war is past. A new day dawns." Church bells and fire bells rang out across the city and in the suburbs. Historian Francis Russell describes the day this way: "The downtown air quivered from the shrillness of the tugboat whistles and the foghorn in the harbor. For Boston, as for all the other thronged and delirious cities, that morning was the beginning of the new, the bright promise of a future that combined the ineradicable American belief in progress with the memory of a prewar golden past that never existed but was now to be recaptured." The day was climaxed by an impromptu victory parade featuring an effigy of the Kaiser carried on a stretcher by Haymarket Square workers and led by Mayor Peters.

The next day was designated "Victory Day" in Massachusetts by Governor Samuel Walker McCall, one of his last acts before he left the corner office to Calvin Coolidge, the Massachusetts lieutenant governor who won the state's top executive office in elections that were held a little more than a week before the armistice. More than a million spectators clogged Boston's downtown streets for the Victory Day parade, "the largest out-pouring of humanity that ever watched a parade in this city," the *Boston Globe* reported.

The armistice had occurred at the right time for Bostonians, who needed a reason to celebrate after they, and much of the world, had endured a dreadful 1918 autumn battling an influenza epidemic that first showed up in early September. In a little more than two months, it had wreaked havoc of biblical proportions. When it was over, more than five hundred thousand Americans would lie dead, and estimates ranged from 20 million to 100 million worldwide. More than 25 percent of the U.S. population became ill, and an estimated eighteen thousand servicemen died of the virus; the government estimated that it would pay the beneficiaries of soldiers and sailors a total of $170 million in insurance premiums.

In Boston, the horror started in late August when sailors aboard a training ship at Commonwealth Pier had come down with the flu, and by early September, thousands of soldiers at Fort Devens had contracted the disease. The army camp became a scene out of hell. One doctor wrote in a letter: "Camp Devens has about 50,000 men, or did before this epidemic broke loose. The flu has developed so rapidly that the camp is demoralized and all ordinary work is held up till it has passed ... One can stand to see one, two, or twenty men die, but to see these poor devils dropping like flies gets on your nerves. We have been averaging about 100 deaths a day, and still keeping it up."

By October the flu was rampaging through Boston with the alarming death rates hitting the North End particularly hard. Congested tenements, a lack of fresh air, and cold buildings all added to the spread of the flu.

Across the city, theaters, clubs, and other social gathering spots were shut down. Boston schools were ordered closed when the death toll in Boston climbed to more than two hundred victims. One prominent Boston historian noted that, with the death toll rising so fast and gravediggers becoming scarce, circus tents were used to cover stacks of unburied coffins in local cemeteries. By the first of November, the epidemic began to subside, although doctors attributed a small recurrence later in the month to the number of people who crowded onto the city's subway trains.

By the time of the armistice on November 11, Bostonians were ready to express their joy after two months of misery. The Victory Day parade was as much a celebration of the waning influenza plague as it was the end of the war.

❖❖❖

In the offices of U.S. Industrial Alcohol, Arthur P. Jell viewed both the influenza epidemic and the armistice from a different perspective. Many of his Cambridge employees had become sick from the flu, a few had died, and his production schedule had been totally disrupted. But he had a bigger challenge. Since the late summer, munitions demand had been dropping. Now that the war had ended, USIA had to find additional sources of revenue to tide it over until the country could fully make the transition to a peacetime economy, and the demand for nonmilitary industrial alcohol grew again.

Company executives, with full support from Jell, decided that they could retool the Cambridge plant's manufacturing processes to produce grain alcohol for the rum and liquor industries. USIA had produced some grain alcohol early in its existence, prior to its shift to industrial alcohol, and Jell was sure they could do so successfully again.

But even this strategy represented a timing challenge, one that had to be managed carefully for the company to benefit. After years of momentum, it now appeared certain that a Prohibition amendment would be ratified shortly by three-quarters of the states and that an 18th amendment would be added to the U.S. Constitution, banning the sale and consumption of alcoholic beverages.

The influence of the Anti-Saloon League, a temperance organization that began operations in 1893, had grown stronger in the second decade of the twentieth century. In December 1913, a parade of more than four thousand Leaguers marched down Pennsylvania Avenue in Washington, D.C., singing temperance songs. League speakers, some twenty thousand strong, spoke at gatherings across the country. Letters and telegrams "rolled into Congress by the tens of thousands, burying members like an avalanche," according to Wayne Wheeler, lobbyist for the league. The league viewed Prohibition as a way to reduce crime, poverty rates, and taxes created by prisons and poorhouses, as well as improve health and hygiene, the economy, and the quality of life in America.

The World War had accelerated the cause. The frenzy of feeling against the Germans and support for American boys in uniform gave the league a tool to use against the saloons, since most of the brewers were of German extraction. "Kaiserism abroad and booze at home must go," Wayne Wheeler said. The League also argued that resources used for the production of alcoholic beverages were being diverted from the war efforts.

Jell knew that Prohibition would hurt the alcohol distillers while encouraging black market production. Nonetheless, if the 18th amendment were ratified, the law called for Prohibition to actually take effect after a one-year grace period, beginning in early 1920. That gave USIA a narrow window of opportunity. If it could distill enough grain alcohol in the first quarter of 1919, there would be ample time to ship it to brewers, and for them to distribute liquor to saloons and stores, before Prohibition slammed the window closed. In mid-November 1918, Jell had ordered another huge shipment of molasses from Cuba—it was due to arrive in mid-January of 1919. He would spend the time between now and then closing the books on 1918 and preparing a round-the-clock production schedule in anticipation of the January molasses shipment.

He would also have the big molasses tank on the Commercial Street wharf caulked one more time. White, his superintendent on the site, said molasses continued to leak steadily from many of the seams. Caulking would be a good idea before any new molasses was pumped into the tank. Jell had hired a caulking crew that would begin work in early December.

All in all, he was glad 1918 was winding to a close. It had been a good year for USIA, but business had begun to slow in the late summer. The end of the war had injected uncertainty into a business that had grown swiftly in the past three years. The influenza plague had been frightening, and he was not sure it had completely ended. Anarchists had the city on edge. That pesky Gonzales had created disturbances with his strange warnings and even stranger behavior; the odd man's resignation from USIA was about the best thing that happened in 1918.

It had been three years since Jell had shepherded the Commercial Street molasses tank to completion, and throughout the war, he had managed the East Cambridge distilling plant flawlessly, meeting USIA's daunting production quotas and helping the company achieve record profits. Assuming the molasses steamer arrived on time in mid-January, the new year also promised to get off to a strong start. Jell believed 1919 would be the year his loyalty and hard work would pay off in his long-awaited vice presidency and his transfer to USIA's New York headquarters.

Yes, 1919 was *his* year. Arthur P. Jell could feel it.

⌁ FIVE ⌁

HEAVY LOAD

Boston, December 20, 1918

John Urquhart, a boilermaker for Walter W. Fields & Sons in Cambridge, knew ten days ago when he first started caulking the Commercial Street molasses tank that he would have a difficult job ahead of him. Molasses leaked from several different seams, squeezing through the rivets and sliding down the steel walls like lazy brown rivers, plopping onto the pavement below and spreading slowly into thick pools. When Urquhart first washed the molasses off, pinheads of the dark liquid reappeared instantly on the lap seams, like blood refilling a cut.

Urquhart had been busier than ever during the last few months, and the influenza epidemic had disrupted his schedule by depleting his best crews. Many of his finest workers had become ill or had died, and Urquhart had been forced to hire men who were less skilled and less reliable. There had been complaints from some of his customers, so he had decided to undertake his most important jobs alone. This had given him peace of mind, but had set him back on some of his key projects. The Commercial Street molasses tank was one of these. It probably should have been caulked earlier, but he was not able to begin the job until December 10, and, because he worked alone, it had taken him twice as long. For ten straight days, as raw wind whipped off the inner harbor, stinging his eyes and burning his face, he washed the stubborn molasses off with hot water, caulked the seams with his tools, then washed the pinheads again and recaulked.

Working alone on this job, perched on a rigging chair high above the ground, John Urquhart had had plenty of time to think. It had only been a month since the whole city and the entire country were celebrating the end of the war, and already, things were starting to change for the worse. Like the molasses oozing stealthily across the pavement below him, Urquhart believed that the pain and fear caused by the flu epidemic was spreading into other areas, too.

Many men were out of work, and Urquhart knew that two factors were responsible for it. First, war industries—mainly steel plants and munitions companies—were retooling their factories or shutting down abruptly. Urquhart had read that these industries employed 9 million workers, and he wondered where they would all go. Second, soldiers and sailors were already starting to return home; 4 million men would return to America, forty thousand to Boston alone. Would there be jobs for them? Would they expect factories to hire them out of gratitude for their service and fire other men? How could the factories hire anyone if they were closing down?

And then there were the labor unions. Urquhart knew many union men, and knew also that the big organizers, like tough-talking Samuel Gompers of the American Federation of Labor, were already threatening strikes if wages or work hours were cut.

Everyone was concerned about prices, too. The Boston Elevated had just raised its fares from seven to eight cents; Urquhart remembered that it was only five cents two years ago. The price of coal was going up, and so was the cost of clothing and food.

It seemed to Urquhart that last month's victory celebrations may have hidden many problems that were lurking just below the surface. Now those problems were squeezing their way out, just like the molasses inside this tank, and he didn't think there was any equivalent of caulking that could push them back in. Some workers on the Commercial Street wharf had whispered that U.S. Industrial Alcohol should scrap this tank and build a new one that didn't leak. Urquhart thought the same about the economy; that the country would now have to scrap its reliance on war production and replace it with something new to accommodate all the working men without jobs. Otherwise there could be trouble.

He remembered the recession before the war. Men who worked with their hands had suffered the most, their families cold in the wintertime and hungry all year long. Today, the unions were stronger, workers resented the profits the big corporations were making, and soldiers and sailors returning from Europe would surely feel that their country owed them a living. Urquhart did not think that these people would tolerate hunger or cold or unemployment meekly or quietly. It made him feel a little queasy that President Wilson was in France to discuss peace in Europe even while tension and unrest were growing at home.

Urquhart knew that all of these issues were out of his control and would be decided by smarter men. What he *could* control was his handiwork on the molasses tank, and finally today, just a few days before Christmas, he had finished caulking. The tank was ready for the big molasses ship that was scheduled to arrive in mid-January and pump hundreds of thousands of gallons of molasses from its hold compartments. John Urquhart had been a boilermaker for fourteen years and was proud of his talent and his attention to detail. When a man paid him for a job, he did that job well, and the molasses tank was no different.

Urquhart climbed down from his rigging chair and looked up at the massive tank. He squinted against a pale-gray sky and let his eyes scan each seam, slowly, taking care not to confuse molasses with the rust-brown paint that covered the tank's walls. He nodded his head with a sense of satisfaction. It had seemed like an overwhelming task, an impossible task, when he began, but that just proved that if you stayed with something day after day, you would eventually accomplish your goal.

Urquhart had definitely accomplished his goal this time. After ten days of nonstop caulking, the leaks had stopped. The real test of Urquhart's skill would come when the new molasses was pumped into the tank's well—but he was sure the lap joints would hold.

Cambridge, Massachusetts, January 10, 1919

Arthur P. Jell squirmed in his chair after the upsetting telephone conversation with the Boston Police. The new year was not beginning the way he had hoped. He had thought that the end of the war would bring about an end to violent anarchist activity in Boston, but apparently that was not the case. A Boston police officer had discovered a number of placards tacked onto Commercial Street buildings threatening violence, and the police department was contacting North End business owners to alert them. The officer told Jell that the placard apparently was in response to Congressional action two months ago that toughened the existing Immigration Act by making it easier to deport anarchists. That triggered the issuance of a deportation warrant for Luigi Galleani, leader of the Italian anarchists in Boston, and eight of his closest associates. They were regarded by the Bureau of Immigration as being "among the most dangerous aliens yet found within this country." The police officer told Jell that legal maneuvering had delayed Galleani's deportation and he had remained free.

The notices were entitled "GO-HEAD" and condemned the "senile fossils ruling the United States" for passing a deportation law affecting all foreign radicals. Jell had written down the exact text as the officer read the message: "Do not think that only foreigners are anarchists. We are a great number right here at home. Deportation will not stop the storm from reaching these shores. The storm is within and very soon will leap and crush and annihilate you in blood and fire. You have shown no pity to us! We will do likewise. We will dynamite you."

The notice bore the signature, "The American Anarchists," but police said the circular was the unmistakable work of Galleani's followers; their mentor was the prime target of the new deportation law. Witnesses told police that they saw an old man and a boy distributing the notices. Police assured Jell that they tore down the signs quickly.

Jell took this threat seriously. Although the war had ended, the Commercial Street molasses tank still represented a symbol of war and Big Business to the anarchists; the newspapers were full of stories about the enormous profits realized by the munitions industry and the companies that supported it during the past four years. The bomb that had been discovered at USIA's Brooklyn plant in 1916, undoubtedly planted by foreign anarchists living nearby, was still fresh in Jell's mind, as was the telephone threat that Gonzales had reported last year. Jell had been skeptical at the time, had doubted that any call had taken place, and believed the whole incident was a figment of Gonzales's twisted imagination. But what if that wasn't the case? What if Gonzales was telling the truth, as the discovery of these most recent anarchist posters indicated? Jell was awaiting the arrival of a molasses steamer from the Caribbean in just a few days. Any disruption at the tank could prove disastrous to his plan to outrun Prohibition by producing alcohol as rapidly as possible at the East Cambridge distillery.

All of these were good arguments to rehire the private security guards at the tank that Jell had dispensed with after the armistice.

Still, Jell had to balance the anarchists' threats against the cost of hiring full-time private security guards. The molasses distilling business had taken a downturn since munitions demand had plummeted late in the summer of 1918. Until production ramped up again and USIA realized revenue from the sale of alcohol to liquor distributors, Jell had to hold the line on costs. And his superintendent, William White, worked at the tank site for most of the business day and could watch for suspicious characters lurking about the area.

No, Jell decided he would not rehire a full-time private security force. Now that the police were aware of this latest threat—they had made *him* aware of it, after all—he was sure they could provide adequate security on the waterfront. The warning from the police department about the anarchist placards was unnerving, but it wasn't enough to panic him into boosting his expenses.

"The tank will be safe," Jell said aloud, sitting alone in his office. "The ship arrives next week. We'll be ready to go."

France, January 10, 1919

The day dawned bittersweet for Hugh Ogden. As of the first of the year, he had been relieved from further duty with his beloved 42nd Division, and assigned permanently to the Office of Civil Affairs at the headquarters of the 3rd Army of Occupation. Today was the day he would leave France and the brave men of the 42nd, and travel to Coblenz, Germany to advise officials on procedures as the Germans attempted to set up a civilian government. He had just finished writing to his friend, Lippincott, at the University of Pennsylvania, about his reassignment, suggesting "it might be of interest to some of my friends among the alumni." Ogden looked forward to his new assignment and was thankful that the war had ended. But he would miss France and miss the Rainbow Division, *his* division, a band of men that he felt epitomized the definition of courage under fire.

France had been the scene of much bloodshed and horror during this terrible war, but for Ogden, it had also been the place where the troops of the 42nd had fought with valor and honor, not because they liked to fight or wanted to die, but because they sought peace. Ogden believed that some men were willing to sacrifice their own lives in war so that many more could live, and the Rainbow Division was made up of such men. He believed those men exemplified the importance of a strong standing army. Military strength not only could win a war, but could prevent future wars. "There are those who visualize the horrors of war and probably believe that the way to abolish war in general is to abolish the army," he would write years later, after his return to Boston. "Inadequacy or lack of military strength has never yet prevented a nation from going to war. It never will. We must profit by the lessons of the Great War by insisting upon an adequate degree of military and naval preparedness."

Hugh Ogden had learned a great deal about men in this war. He learned that a man would scream when shrapnel tore his flesh—and scream louder when swarming trench rats did the same, as he lay wounded and helpless, his buddies unable to get to him before the hungry rodents ripped him apart. The rats, millions of them, many as big as cats, had feasted on food scraps and dead bodies in hundreds of miles of trenches across France and Belgium. Toward the end of the war, they had become emboldened enough to also attack those wounded men who were too weak to fend them off.

Ogden also learned that even the strongest man would sit down on the battlefield and weep, or try to gouge his own eyes out, or simply go mad with terror when the incessant pounding of artillery fire first shattered his eardrums and then his sanity. The shell-shock cases were the worst to see, strong men breaking down, shaking with terror, babbling incoherently, facing torment for months or years or forever.

He had learned about heroes, too, good men who had put themselves in harm's way to save their comrades. The Rainbow's poet, Joyce Kilmer, was one of these. Sergeant Kilmer was leading a few other soldiers into a wooded area in search of enemy machine guns, when he was killed on July 30, 1918, his dream of writing a major book about the war dying with him. His men buried him at the edge of a little copse known as the Wood of the Burned Bridge in France, a peaceful spot fit for a soldier-poet.

Ogden knew of other brave men. One had hurled himself onto a live grenade that had been thrown into a trench among five soldiers; he was killed, but the other men survived. Another had single-handedly charged an enemy machine gun nest to clear the way for his unit's advance; he took out the nest but shortly thereafter he bled to death, his upper leg cut to ribbons by the merciless rapid fire. Two more men had risked running across an open, muddy field carrying a stretcher, under blistering enemy fire, to rescue a wounded buddy. Though further hampered on their return by the weight of the wounded man and the thick mud sucking at their boots the whole way across the field, they managed to somehow avoid the gunfire and reach the safety of the trench.

Gen. John J. "Blackjack" Pershing and Col. Douglas MacArthur were the renowned members of the Rainbow Division, but Ogden knew that it was the everyday infantrymen, the Doughboys, who were the heart and soul of the 42nd.

Ogden did not often become friendly with these soldiers—his position as judge advocate would not allow it—but he admired their bravery and grit and mettle in the face of death, pain, suffering, disease, and cold. War had provided Ogden with an opportunity to observe men laboring under extraordinary hardships, something he had never seen before. As one of Boston's most prominent corporate attorneys, the battles he fought had been confined to boardrooms and courtrooms and the exclusive Harvard Club—rarefied circles and dignified places where men of refinement and good breeding talked in hushed tones and negotiated reasonable compromises, then retired to side rooms to drink brandy from snifters and smoke expensive cigars. At the very worst, a bad decision could cost these men money, but never their lives. He once considered the stakes to be high in these corporate dealings, until he had traveled to the killing fields of France and watched the Rainbow Division in action.

Then he had learned what high stakes were all about.

This lesson had helped Hugh Ogden reach a decision. He expected to be in Germany for a few months, and then would return to Washington, D.C., to review Army court martial procedures. He was likely to be discharged in the summer of 1919. After that, he would return to Boston, but not to his old law firm. He needed a change, a new start where he could apply the lessons he had learned from the 42nd, of sacrifice, of helping others, of committing to a cause greater than oneself.

The only way to do that was to establish his own law practice. He would work alone and make his own decisions. He would still specialize in corporate work, but when an individual came to him, a man who was not wealthy but needed legal help nonetheless, perhaps even a former member of the Rainbow regiment, Hugh Ogden could take the case without concerning himself with the firm's reputation or standing in the Boston power structure. There would be a monetary price to pay, at least initially, but money was not an important factor at this point in his career.

What was important was for him to make a small difference when he returned stateside, to dedicate his civilian life to accomplishments that symbolically exemplified the *major* difference the men of the 42nd had made in the trenches and on the battlefields of Europe. "They will not sleep in Flanders Fields unless we pick up the torch they bore so high and carry on in the great cause for which they had died," he would declare in a speech several years later. "We have to make safe the cause of liberty by living for it—perhaps, indeed, a harder task than theirs who died for it. They did not give their lives so the great might have further privilege to oppress the small, so that the rich might abuse the poor, and that discontent and envy, hatred and malice might thrive unchecked in our body politic." Ogden had learned that Americans had the duty to help others when they needed help, and sacrifice for the greater good when called upon, as their troops had done when called upon in Europe. "The privilege of self-sacrifice is as great and the need is greater than it was in 1917," he would conclude in the same speech years later.

Now, in January 1919, preparing to travel to Germany to join the Occupation Army, Hugh Ogden believed he had drawn enough inspiration in the heroic actions of the Rainbow Division to seek a higher legal calling when he returned to civilian life. He was more determined than ever that the law would work for all people; men or women, wealthy or poor, Brahmin or immigrant. He would do what he could to uphold the principles that drove him to become a lawyer in the first place—careful deliberation, wise counsel, unwavering honesty, and a devotion to the truth.

He could not predict exactly how this new commitment would affect his future. He just knew it would.

Boston, January 12-13, 1919

It was bitter cold as Frank Van Gelder brought the *Miliero* into port just after 11 A.M. on Sunday, January 12. Sunbeams reflected silvery off the choppy gray-black water, producing brilliant light but generating little heat. The temperature was in the teens, and a stiff wind whistled across Boston's inner harbor, rattling the pilings that supported the long walking pier that extended from the wharf. According to weather reports, the mercury would drop to 2 degrees Fahrenheit by nightfall.

The *Miliero* carried 1.3 million gallons of molasses. Van Gelder's crew would pump six hundred thousand gallons into the Commercial Street tank to fulfill Arthur Jell's order for the Cambridge distillery, and then steam to USIA's Brooklyn plant to unload her remaining seven hundred thousand gallons. At 11:20 A.M., tank supervisor William White gave Van Gelder the go-ahead, and the captain ordered the discharge pumps to begin off-loading the *Miliero*'s cargo. Despite the severe cold, the molasses flowed smoothly through the pipe into the monstrous tank, an unexpected though not entirely unusual bonus, part of the "queer behavior" of molasses that Van Gelder had seen throughout his career.

The dock was deserted and peaceful this Sunday morning. No freight trains chugged along Commercial Street, no horse-drawn wagons or motorized trucks crowded the wharf area, no stevedores shouted as they hoisted large wooden crates, no farmers herded squealing animals onto ships, no chickens shrieked as they met their demise at the slaughterhouse across the street. The only sounds were the pulsating hum of the hydraulic pumps pushing the molasses through the intake pipe, the low tones of conversations between the *Miliero* crew members as they went about their work, the distant squawk of the gulls circling overhead, and the occasional whinny or snort from the horses in the nearby city stables.

The unloading progressed smoothly all day Sunday, throughout the night, and into the next morning. Van Gelder's log book showed that the pumping was completed at 10:40 A.M. on Monday, January 13, 1919, well after the Sunday-morning quiet had given way to the rush of a new workweek on the wharf. It had taken just under twenty-four hours to pump more than a half million gallons of molasses from ship to tank. "We had no trouble with this delivery," Van Gelder would say later. "We finished the next morning (Monday) and it was a normal discharge."

By 11 A.M. Monday, as the wharf grew crowded with horses, wagons, delivery men, railroad cars, livestock, beer barrels, and shipping crates, Van Gelder had maneuvered the *Miliero* across the inner harbor and pointed it seaward, full-speed ahead toward New York.

Behind him, mere feet from the Clougherty house, where Bridget hung laundry; mere feet from the Engine 31 headquarters where George Layhe and his buddies worked; from the city stables and the North End Paving Yard; from the freight houses and Boston Elevated railroad trestle; from the spot where little Maria Distasio and Pasquale Iantosca collected firewood and scooped molasses into their pails; from the pump-pit where Isaac Gonzales had once slept; from the wooden fence where the American Anarchists had tacked up their placards threatening to dynamite area targets—mere feet from all of this—stood the fifty-foot-tall Commercial Street tank, gleaming in the late-morning sunlight.

Van Gelder was well into open water before the loudest of the sounds started from inside the tank, but William White heard them as he stood in the pump-pit. The firefighters heard the noises, too. So did the teamsters delivering beer barrels to the dock. The warm molasses that had just flowed from the *Miliero*'s hold was mixing with the cold, thick molasses that had been congealing inside the tank for weeks, producing a bubbling churn that vibrated against the tank's walls. The men on the Commercial Street wharf heard those walls groaning, had heard them groan many times before, usually immediately after a delivery, but it is unlikely that they knew that when warm and cold molasses mix, the reaction triggers a fermentation process that produces gas. And in a near-full tank, that gas increases the pressure against the steel walls.

There was one other thing these men could not have known. With the addition of the *Miliero*'s latest delivery, the tank was now filled to near capacity with 2.3 million gallons of molasses that reached a height of forty-eight feet, nine inches, and weighed *26 million pounds*.

Never in Boston's history had an aboveground receptacle held more.

PART II

Waves of Terror

⚜ SIX ⚜

BEFORE ...

Boston, Wednesday, January 15, 1919, 4 a.m.

Martin Clougherty walked home from the Pen and Pencil Club on this damp Wednesday morning with elation and wistfulness as his companions, both tugging at him like lovers competing for his affections.

His elation was easy to understand. Since acquiring the club outright three years ago, he had succeeded in amassing nearly $4,000, more than enough to purchase a nice home in Revere, or other points north of Boston, for him and his family. He finally could move his mother, sister, and brother out from the shadows of the elevated railroad trestle, away from the unending noise and the pervasive grime, far from the stench of horse manure and slaughtered chickens. It was time to leave the North End, and Martin finally had the means; he would meet with his accountant that afternoon to hammer out the details of selling his club and his mother's house.

Martin's wistfulness was nearly as strong, but more complicated to define. There were the usual feelings of anxiety that came with leaving familiar surroundings for parts unknown. He would miss the boys at the Pen and Pencil Club. He had built a successful business from scratch and considered many of the bar's patrons his friends. He enjoyed the rich conversation he overheard while he tended bar, often joining in as he mixed and poured drinks. The spark he felt when the club was jumping, the camaraderie that warmed him as surely as a shot of top-shelf whiskey—Martin wondered if he would ever again experience those feelings.

The loss would soon extend beyond Martin's world, and perhaps that was the true cause of the sad nostalgia that played around the edges of his otherwise good spirits. Prohibition was coming. In a matter of days, maybe *a single day*, one of a handful of states vying for the honor would become the thirty-sixth state—representing three-quarters of the nation's forty-eight—to ratify the Constitutional amendment that would prohibit the legal sale and consumption of alcoholic beverages. There would be a one-year grace period to allow manufacturers, distributors, and tavern and restaurant owners to prepare for the economic impact of the law, and then Prohibition would be in full effect.

It was a foregone conclusion that by January 1920, the United States would be dry.

No longer would Americans be able to experience the warm glow of a tavern on a snowy evening, or the taste of a cold beer as the summer sun baked the city streets. No longer would working men be able to unwind with a drink after a dusty day of hauling cargo on the docks, nor would journalists enjoy swapping raucous opinions about Wilson's peace plans while ordering double shots of brandy to fuel the debate. Martin thought that Prohibition would make it more difficult to make friends, meet women, conduct business, and enjoy life. These thoughts alone were enough to dampen anyone's enthusiasm.

Martin reached his home, and once inside, scribbled a note to his sister, Teresa, asking her to wake him at 12:30 P.M., which would give him more than enough time to get ready for the 1:30 P.M. meeting with his accountant.

Amid his conflicting emotions—the elation about moving, the melancholy about leaving the club, the uncertainty of Prohibition— Martin was clear about one thing: Life as he knew it was about to change.

He climbed the stairs to his bedroom and was fast asleep in moments.

11:55 a.m.

Today should be a quiet day at the molasses tank, a rarity, William White thought. The *Miliero* had discharged her huge shipment two days ago, and no new molasses deliveries would arrive for at least three months. Within the next few days, and continuing for weeks afterward, White would be busy. He would supervise the process of filling railroad tank cars with molasses and transporting them to the USIA Cambridge distilling plant. He would fill out enough paperwork to bury his small office that sat next to the pump pit. Today was a bonus day, a "middle day," the calm between the *Miliero*'s arrival and the frenetic production cycle that followed a major delivery.

White was thankful for the pause, even more so when his wife, Sarah, had called a few moments ago from South Station asking if he could meet her at the Jordan Marsh department store to help her choose some dresses she wanted to buy. She suggested that they could have lunch at a downtown restaurant following the brief shopping trip. White, who usually ate at his desk, thought he deserved a lunch-hour away from the tank, and saw the invitation as a good opportunity to indulge his wife. Besides, the weather had warmed considerably in the two days since the *Miliero*'s delivery, with temperatures soaring from 2 degrees to 40 degrees Fahrenheit. It was another good reason to venture downtown and walk around a bit.

He grabbed his coat and hat and set out to meet Sarah, happy for the break in his routine in the middle of the workweek.

The thought crossed his mind that the tank would be left unattended while he was gone, but no harm—he would be back in his office within an hour.

12:41 p.m.

Pasquale Iantosca and Antonio Distasio crouched behind the giant molasses tank and watched the two adults scold Antonio's sister, Maria. The children's parents had told the youngsters to collect firewood from around the molasses tank while they were home for lunch from the Paul Revere Elementary School on Prince Street. Pasquale complained to Antonio that he knew his father would be watching him from the window of their home across the street to make sure this chore was done, a task made all the more difficult with the two sweaters Pasquale's parents forced him to wear to keep from catching cold. Antonio smiled when he looked at his friend; Pasquale was so bundled up that he had a hard time moving, and beads of sweat were forming on his forehead on this mild winter day.

Hiding behind the tank, both boys were frightened and restless as they watched two big railroad workers wagging their fingers at Maria, whom they had spotted gathering wood between a railroad freight car and the molasses tank. The men were shouting at her to leave the area.

Antonio felt sad that his sister was suffering alone and he left his hiding spot next to the tank to help her. Little Pasquale—Pasqualeno

—remained where he was, hunched between the tank and a railroad freight car.

Antonio emerged from behind the tank and circled to his right. He watched as Maria turned toward him, and away from the men who were scolding her. Then everything happened fast.

The railroad workers screamed and Maria swung her head back to face them, her long hair trailing across her face. Antonio saw that the men were no longer yelling at Maria. Their mouths agape, their eyes wide, they were focused on something *behind* his sister, fixed on the spot that he had just vacated, where Pasqualeno still hid. Terror darkened the men's faces, and, in the same instant, Antonio glimpsed a blur of movement to his left and saw a shadow falling across his sister . . .

❖❖❖

Peter Curran walked his two-horse team into the Commercial Street wharf yard, the fifteen hogs he had just picked up from the New England Beef Company on nearby Clinton Street squealing and snorting in the wagon behind him. He backed the wagon carefully into the Bay State Railway shed, coaxed the hogs out of the truck and onto the platform, and presented the receiving clerk with the bill of lading. As the two men talked, Peter Curran felt the ground shake and heard a roar. The hogs squealed louder and huddled closer, becoming a single mass of pink-brown flesh jiggling on the platform. Curran turned to look, convinced by the tremor and the noise that a Commercial Street elevated train had jumped the track and plunged to the street below . . .

❖❖❖

U.S. Navy gunner's mate Robert Henry Johnston stood on the deck of the *Bessie J.* talking to two other sailors about the work the men had completed that morning. Since the armistice had been signed, the Navy—in this case, Johnston and his mates—was stripping a number of small boats of their ordnance and armaments. These smaller craft pulled alongside the *Bessie J.*, and all morning, Johnston had been removing guns and ammunition so that the boats could be decommissioned. They had just taken a breather and were about to eat lunch, when Johnston, facing the Commercial Street wharf, heard a rumble and began shouting at the top of his lungs . . .

✤✤✤

Twenty-year-old Walter Merrithew, a freight clerk for the Boston & Maine Railroad Company, walked under the covered platform at the Number Three freight shed on the Commercial Street wharf. He saw Ryan, the deaf mute laborer employed by the railroad, stacking crates and preparing them for shipment. Merrithew didn't envy the fellow, unable to hear a word or make a single sound. Ryan worked hard, but could never join in the banter with the fellows on the docks and loading platforms, an activity Merrithew considered the best part of the job. Even now, Merrithew could hear boisterous laughter from the cellar of the freight shed, where other men were storing boxes and barrels that had arrived from ships and would be transported by train up and down the East Coast. It was laughter that Ryan could not hear and could not share.

Merrithew paused for a moment in the doorway, his bulk cutting the light. Ryan looked up as the shadow crossed his face. At that moment, Merrithew heard a long rumbling sound behind him, similar to the passing of an elevated train over Commercial Street, only louder.

Then something happened that Merrithew would never forget. The deaf mute, the boy Merrithew had never heard utter a sound, pointed a trembling finger in Merrithew's direction, but *beyond* him, and let out a long, painful screech that sliced through to Walter Merrithew's soul ...

✤✤✤

Babe Ruth was complaining again and the boys at the Engine 31 firehouse found it laughable. The Boston Red Sox star, who had led his team to a World Series victory over the Chicago Cubs in October, was threatening to retire to his forty-acre farm in nearby Sudbury if his demands for a big salary increase were refused by the team. Ruth earned $7,000 in 1918, four or five times more than most firefighters, for playing a *game,* Bill Connor scoffed as he dealt a hand of lunchtime whist. Plus, the Sox ace had earned another $1,100 for his winning World Series share. "We should all be so lucky," he said to his fellow players around the table—firefighters Fred McDermott, Nat Bowering, and Paddy Driscoll—and to George Layhe and the stonecutter, John Barry, both of whom were watching the friendly card game.

The firefighters played whist almost every lunch hour, and Barry enjoyed the visits, found that the hour passed pleasantly. Sometimes he joined the games, but mostly he filled his pipe, relaxed, and talked with the guys, about sports, like today, or about politics or what was happening around the city. Today he had felt a chill outside, despite the warm-up in temperature, so he welcomed the warmth of the firehouse during the noon hour.

Connor had just finished dealing another hand when the men heard a tremendous crashing noise, a sound Barry later described as a "roaring surf" and one Connor likened to a runaway two-horse team smashing through a fence. Driscoll, who was closest to the window, jumped from his chair and looked out onto the wharf. "Oh my God!" he shouted to the other men, who were already scrambling. "Run!" . . .

❖❖❖

Royal Albert Leeman, a brakeman for the Boston Elevated Railroad, stood in the front vestibule of the third car of the passenger train bound for North Station. He was working the 12:35 shuttle train out of South Station, traveling on elevated tracks above Commercial Street, a trip he had made hundreds of times before. The train, filled with midday shoppers and workers, had just made its stop at the Battery Street station and was chugging up to the big left-hand bend in the track near Copp's Hill, traveling between fifteen and twenty miles per hour, on its way to North Station. Leeman looked out at the molasses tank and the harbor through the closed vestibule window as the train began its turn, its steel wheels screeching and straining against the rails. A moment later, he saw a black mass bearing down on him, *pushing* toward the elevated track, darkening the sky. As Leeman blinked in disbelief, his ears filled with the scream of tearing steel and, behind him, a thunderclap-like *bang!* Then he felt the overhead trestle buckle and his train start to tip . . .

❖❖❖

A few moments later than she was supposed to, Teresa Clougherty tiptoed across the room and gently shook her brother, Martin, awake. He had less than an hour to get ready for his meeting. Their mother, Bridget, had lunch ready downstairs. Teresa turned away from the bed, caught movement through the window from the harbor area, and just as Martin murmured, "I'll be right down," she heard a deep growling sound, felt the house shaking, and was thrown to the floor ...

✻✻✻

Boston Police patrolman Frank McManus approached the call box on Commercial Street to make his regularly scheduled report to head-quarters. It was the kind of day Frank McManus had been waiting for—warm and quiet. The temperature had climbed past 40 degrees, which was practically a heat wave after the previous few days. Aside from the danger of saboteurs during the war, and the noise the Italian anarchists were making even now, there was nothing he disliked more about walking the waterfront beat than the bone-chilling wind and dampness that numbed his fingers and toes, and burnished his face raw. Today, though, was like the arrival of an early spring, and there was an extra buoyancy in the activity around the wharf that McManus attributed to the unusually fine weather. Horses stepped lively as their teamsters drove them onto the wharf to deliver produce, beer, and leather goods. City workers sat outside the paving yard buildings, eating lunch and talking, and McManus heard occasional laughter carry across the street.

McManus picked up the call box and began his report to head-quarters. A few words into it, he heard a machine-gun-like rat-tat-tat sound and an unearthly grinding and scraping, a bleating that sounded like the wail of a wounded beast. McManus stopped talking, turned, and watched in utter disbelief as the giant molasses tank on the wharf seemed to disintegrate before his eyes, disgorging an enor-mous wall of thick, dark liquid that blackened the sky and snuffed out the daylight.

McManus froze momentarily, wanting to flee but unable to move. Then he recovered enough to bark into the phone words that sounded unbelievable even to him, let alone the dispatcher at the other end:

"Send all available rescue vehicles and personnel immediately—there's a wave of molasses coming down Commercial Street!"

SEVEN

ENGULFED!

January 15, 1919, 12:45-5:00 p.m.

Midday turned to darkness as the 2.3 million gallons of molasses engulfed the Boston waterfront like a black tidal wave, 25 feet high and 160 feet wide at the outset.

Several years would pass, and a raging debate would ensue, before people knew *why* the tank had burst, but almost instantly they saw that the power of the molasses was more devastating than any crashing ocean wave. Its crushing weight unleashed a terrible force that pulverized the entire waterfront and a half-mile swath of Commercial Street. Worse, too, unlike an ocean wave, whose momentum is concentrated in one direction, the wall of molasses pushed in all directions after it escaped the confines of the tank, so that it was more like four *separate* walls of viscous liquid smashing across the wharf and into the street. Add to that the speed with which the molasses traveled— thirty-five miles per hour initially—the fact that the tank itself disintegrated into deadly steel missiles, and that thousands of fastening rivets turned into lethal steel bullets, and the result was destruction in a congested area equal to that of even the worst natural disaster.

The molasses tore the North End Paving Yard buildings into kindling, ripped the Engine 31 firehouse from its foundation and nearly swept it into the harbor, destroyed the wood-framed Clougherty house, crushed freight cars, autos, and wagons, and ensnared men, women, children, horses, dogs, rats, wood, and steel. The molasses wave crashed across Commercial Street into brick tenements and storefronts, rebounded off of the buildings, and retreated like the outgoing tide, leaving shattered windows and crushed walls in its wake. Rolling walls of molasses, fifteen feet high, scraped everything in their paths, carrying a wreckage of animals, humans, furniture, produce, beer barrels, railroad cars, automobiles, and wagons, and smashing them against other buildings, into the street, or sweeping them into the harbor.

This landscape photo, taken from atop a nearby building, shows the massive damage caused by the molasses wave. The top of the tank can be seen in the top quarter-center of the photo, just below the white building on the harbor. Flattened buildings that had been part of the city-operated North End Paving Yard are seen in the foreground.

(Photo courtesy of Bill Noonan, Boston Fire Department Archives)

Molasses inundated cellars of businesses and residences along Commercial Street and in the freight sheds on the wharf, smothering men who were working below ground level. Electrical wires were torn down from their poles, smoking and sputtering, until they sank into the molasses. A one-ton piece of the steel tank sliced through a column of the elevated railroad, causing the tracks overhead to collapse nearly to the street. Thousands of rivets that fastened the steel plates had torn away as the tank collapsed, becoming deadly projectiles that sprayed the waterfront like machine-gun fire—the *rat-tat-tat* sound McManus heard—ricocheting off brick and stone and embedding themselves in wood buildings. In minutes—in *seconds*—the landscape in the North End inner harbor area resembled a bombed-out war zone.

Rescue teams of police, firefighters, doctors, and nurses from the nearby Haymarket Relief Station were on the scene quickly, stunned by the unthinkable scene before them. "Molasses, waist deep, covered the street and swirled and bubbled about the wreckage," a *Boston Post* reporter wrote. "Here and there struggled a form—whether it was animal or human being was impossible to tell. Only an upheaval, a thrashing about in the sticky mass, showed where any life was ... Horses died like so many flies on sticky fly paper. The more they struggled, the deeper in the mess they were ensnared. Human beings— men and women—suffered likewise."

Police and fire rescue teams worked feverishly, along with more than a hundred sailors from the *USS Nantucket* and the *Bessie J.*, to free those who were trapped. Firefighters crawled out on ladders stretched across the molasses to pull victims from the quicksand-like morass, careful not to get sucked in, clearing molasses from the breathing passages of the living, dispatching the dead to the mortuary for identification.

Rescuers were too late to save Maria Distasio, who had stood directly in the path of the mountainous wave and perished immediately from asphyxiation. A firefighter spotted her tangled hair swirling in a sea of dark molasses and pulled out her small, broken body. Her brother, Antonio, survived, though he suffered a fractured skull and a concussion when he was thrown against a lamppost; a firefighter managed to snatch him up before the molasses swallowed him. The third child, Pasquale Iantosca, disappeared. None of the dozen or so city workers whom patrolman McManus had seen minutes earlier survived. They had been smothered, buried by debris, or swept into the harbor.

Five minutes after the tank disintegrated, the North End waterfront had been obliterated, property ruined, lives snuffed out. The question now was: How many were dead and how many could be saved?

❖ ❖ ❖

As the elevated railroad car tipped and settled back onto the tracks, Royal Albert Leeman cracked his right shoulder against the window. He reached up and pulled the emergency cord. His train had just cleared the wreckage, rounding the bend seconds before the weight of the molasses and the large piece of the tank had buckled the support trestle behind him. Leeman had stopped the train about three

The massive piece of the steel tank that caused the overhead tracks to buckle is shown at the bottom of the photo. Workers used torches to cut up the steel before carrying it away. The building's windows were shattered by the molasses that slammed into the wall like a tidal wave. Note that the windows above the "molasses line" are not shattered, which plaintiffs argued was clear evidence that no concussive force normally associated with an explosion took place.   (Photo courtesy of Bill Noonan, Boston Fire Department Archives)

car lengths beyond the damaged track; had the train arrived just a moment later, it likely would have plunged onto Commercial Street.

Opening the vestibule door, Leeman jumped off the train, glanced behind him and down at the horror. The destruction the molasses had caused in just *minutes* made him shiver. There was nothing left of the waterfront. All the buildings were flattened, and it appeared that every square inch of ground was covered with molasses. Closer, he could see the elevated trestle, broken and twisted, the track sagging nearly to the ground.

Leeman moved fast, first a few yards north to the trackside guard shack, where he issued instructions to the railroad worker to stop the train coming from North Station. Then he ran back, south, past his stopped train, made his way carefully across twisted track and support beams, and scrambled beyond the broken trestle until he reached undamaged track on the other side. Then he ran again, full speed down the track, for another hundred yards. The next northbound train that had originated at South Station was approaching, the one behind Leeman's, and it was just beginning to pick up some speed after stopping at the Battery Street station to discharge passengers, about a half-mile before Copp's Hill.

Leeman stood in the center of the track, waving his arms frantically, screaming, "Stop—the track is down! The track is down!" Through the vestibule glass, he saw the look of disbelief on the engineer's face, knew the engineer couldn't hear him, but Leeman held his ground, standing on the track high above Commercial Street, the shredded track and snapped trestle behind him, a three-car train bearing down on him. Finally, Leeman heard the shriek of steel wheels on rail, saw the train slowing down to stop. The engineer opened the vestibule door and stepped out. Leeman turned and pointed northward, behind him, and shouted again: "The track is down—almost to the street. You can't go any further. The goddamn molasses tank burst!"

He sat down on the tracks then, heart pounding, his entire body shaking. He looked down at the terrible, alien scene below him, the landscape covered with dark brown ooze that swallowed humans, animals, vehicles, and structures with equal ferocity. Raising his head, Leeman saw fire trucks and horse-drawn medical vehicles already approaching the wreckage.

He had just saved a train from crashing to the street below, and in minutes would help the shaken engineer lead his passengers to safety.

⁂

Martin Clougherty was sinking, drowning . . . *smothering*, but he didn't know why or how. Awakened by his sister, Teresa, he had rolled over in bed, saw her heading toward the doorway, heard her scream, *"Something awful has happened to the tank!"* and then felt his bed overturn. He had had the sensation of falling overboard, had felt his head go under, and it was only then—when the liquid rushed into his nose and mouth, when he could taste it—that he realized he was immersed in molasses. He felt himself sliding downward, out of control, as though riding the churn of the most violent river rapids or being

While horrified spectators look on, rescuers try desperately to save the occupants of the Clougherty house, which was torn from its foundation and smashed against the elevated railroad trestle by the molasses wave. Bridget Clougherty, sixty-five, was buried by debris and timber, and died from terrible injuries one hour after crews pulled her from the wreckage. Her son, daughter, and a boarder living in the house survived the disaster. (Photo courtesy of Bill Noonan, Boston Fire Department Archives)

swept over a waterfall. Flailing, he battled the suction, struggled to lift his head out of the clammy molasses, used his powerful arms to break the surface, and finally, he breathed fresh air and actually *tread molasses* as he rode the pounding wave that dumped him into the middle of Commercial Street. The ride stopped then and Martin stood in chest-deep molasses, wood and debris pressing against his back and neck. He cleared his eyes and mouth, looked around and was stunned to see that his house had been swept into the street, smashing into the elevated railroad trestle, and splintering into pieces.

He struggled frantically to pull himself from the molasses, which clung to his pajamas and his hair like wet wool. He spotted what looked like a raft, waded through the thick molasses until he reached it, and heaved himself aboard. He realized the raft was his bed-frame, but for now it provided him with a refuge from which to collect his bearings. Taking in the destruction around him, he called for his family, but no one answered. Then he saw a thin hand to his right, protruding from the molasses like a white stick. He lay down on his bed-frame-raft, stretched his arms out and pulled the hand up . . . up, with all of his strength, the quicksand-like molasses fighting him the whole way. A head emerged from the dark sea and he saw that it was his sister, Teresa. She was choking and gasping, but alive, thank God. "Hold on, sis, I've got you—I've got you," Martin cried, and with one mighty tug, he yanked her onto the makeshift raft. He wiped molasses from around her eyes and from inside of her ears, while she choked and coughed it from her breathing passages. Then he hugged her with his strong arms, their molasses-soaked clothing making a *whapping!* sound as their bodies came together. She was crying and he held her close, whispering in her ear, "Okay, it's okay." Then he looked into her eyes and said: "Stay here, you'll be safe on the raft. I'm going to look for Ma and Stephen."

He rolled off the bed-frame, splashed back into the black ooze, and waded forward, pushing aside molasses-covered timbers and debris in a frantic effort to locate his mother and his mentally retarded brother.

�֍✖֍

Giuseppe Iantosca recoiled from the second floor kitchen window of his home, which looked out over Commercial Street. Giuseppe had been keeping an eye on his son, Pasquale, easily tracking him in his bright red sweater as he gathered firewood by the molasses tank. Then Pasqualeno had suddenly disappeared—a dark wall had consumed him as though he had never existed. The wave bore down on Giuseppe, too, and before he could cry out or move his feet, the older man felt the house tremble and he was thrown from the window and onto the floor. As he fell and struck his head, he saw his wife and children tumble to the floor, and then he blacked out. He awoke a short time later, bruised and shaken, saw his daughter comforting his wife, Maria, even as his wife was sobbing and screaming uncontrollably in Italian: "My son is lost! Pasqualeno is lost!"

✖֍✖

Walter Merrithew barely had time to turn after the deaf-mute, Ryan, had screeched. Instantly, Merrithew had found himself in the middle of black muck, his eyes squeezed shut, preparing to die. For now he had survived. He was pinned up against the back wall of the freight shed, his feet three feet off the floor, by a wall of debris—timbers, freight cars, automobiles, a suffering horse struggling silently in the molasses. To his left, in the corner, the freight shed wall had opened up and he could see the harbor. He believed it was only a matter of time before the pressure from the mountain of debris burst the wall and carried him into the water. When that happened, he would either be pulled to the bottom of the harbor to drown amidst a tangle of wood and metal, or he would be injured when he tumbled into the water, with a chance to swim to safety.

Something had to give soon. The weight of the debris against his chest was crushing him, and his foot was somehow trapped, so that he could not move. He heard noises then, caught movement through the pile, and wiped away the molasses that had begun to crust around his eyes. Ryan, the deaf mute, was pulling debris away! Ryan was trying to shout again, calling for survivors, but Merrithew only heard a strangled whistle from the man's throat, an eerie *wheeeeeeee, wheeeeeeee,* as Ryan worked.

"Back here!" Merrithew shouted. "I'm alive back here." He knew Ryan could not hear him, but maybe the railroad clerk would sense a motion, a vibration, *something* that would indicate to him that a person was buried alive back here, at least until he cleared away enough of the mess and could actually see Merrithew trapped against the back wall. Merrithew's hands were free, although wedged tightly against his body. He managed to bring them up directly in front of his face, and waved them back and forth with the hope that Ryan would notice the movement through the small openings in the wreckage. "I'm here, back here," Merrithew shouted again.

No answer from Ryan—just the *wheeeeeeee, wheeeeeeee,* as he kept working.

Hurry, Merrithew thought. Damn it, *hurry!*

❧·❧·❧

The fifty-six-year-old stonecutter John Barry heard moaning in the darkness, felt searing pain across his back and legs, smelled and tasted the sweet molasses as it tried to flow into his nostrils and mouth. He was pinned face down, his cheek mashed into the sticky molasses, only his left arm free. He used the arm as a sweeper to keep the molasses from smothering him. He tried moving other parts of his body, but other than his neck, which he could twist, he couldn't budge. Whatever was pressing on his body was crushing the life out of him. It hurt to breathe, whatever breath he *could* draw seemed insufficient to fill his lungs, and he had to be careful not to inhale a mouthful of sticky molasses.

The darkness was total. The moaning continued, but he couldn't tell from which direction, or from how far away. He heard a skittering sound. A rat? Oh, God, Barry hated the filthy rodents. Terror gripped him as he imagined a fat, hungry, gray water rat chewing at his face while he lay helpless, trapped in the blackness, buried alive. He called for help, his voice raspy. Could anyone hear him? Did anyone know he was there? He felt on the brink of madness, and with a mighty, panic-filled effort tried to lift his body, but to no avail. He had worked as a stonecutter since he was fourteen years old, but with all of his strength and his skill, he couldn't lift a hammer or a blade or a chisel to help himself—he could barely lift his head to keep from smothering in molasses. John Barry knew he was going to die, here, buried under the firehouse in this dark stinking space, anonymous and unable to move, a pool of molasses ready to swallow him, rats ready to tear him apart, his screams falling on deaf ears. He would soon join two of his children who had perished from influenza last fall. But what would become of his other ten? Would they become wards of the state when their father was gone?

He began to itch all over and couldn't do anything to stop it. He felt his body bleeding and could not stanch his wounds. His chest and back burned like they were on fire. He summoned up strength and cried for help again, and this time heard his voice resonate in the darkness. And then, a miracle: a *response!* He recognized the voice of firefighter Paddy Driscoll, trapped under here with him, one of the moaners he had heard. "Keep up your courage, John," Driscoll said, his voice cracking. "They'll get us out."

John Barry tried to answer aloud, but could not. His initial shout for help had drained him of energy. Overcome with exhaustion and emotion, his broken body wracked with pain, he could barely manage a whisper: "I hope they hurry, Paddy," he choked. "I hope they hurry."

He lay sobbing in the darkness, tears streaming down his face, mixing with the molasses that stained his cheeks and threatened to drown him.

✢✢✢

Lying just a few feet away from John Barry, though unaware of how close he was to the stonecutter, firefighter Bill Connor realized that there was only one way he and his buddy, Nat Bowering, could remain alive until rescuers reached them. Connor had just extricated himself out from under a steam column-radiator that had pinned him face-down in the molasses. He had managed to turn over onto his back, and there was Bowering, right alongside him, trapped by what once was a firehouse support beam resting across his midsection.

Connor looked up, and no more than a foot above his face were heavy joists and a wooden floor. He surmised that the full force of the molasses wave had slammed into the firehouse, torn it from its foundation, and caused the second story of the three-story building to pancake down on top of the first, creating this eighteen-inch crawl space in which they were now trapped. The molasses was rising—slowly, but rising—and it had reached their chins. Connor could see light, and the harbor beyond, through a small opening in the wall at Bowering's feet. "For God's sake, keep that hole clear in front of you," Connor said. "Kick that shit away so the molasses can flow out."

Bowering pumped his feet furiously, clearing the hole of sticks and wood and debris. "They will never find us here, Bill," Bowering cried. "There is no possible chance for us."

"Our only salvation is for you to keep that hole open," Connor snapped back.

As the senior man of the two, Connor knew *he* had to remain calm, had to be the leader, the one that issued the instructions, until help arrived. Though the light was faint, Connor could discern that a col-lection of odd timbers, chairs, tables, the firehouse piano, and, sev-eral feet away, a billiard table, was supporting the second floor, now just inches above them, allowing them to remain alive in a cocoon of debris in this hideous dark place. Both men had bumped their heads hard on the collapsed first-floor ceiling trying to keep their noses and mouths above the molasses.

Molasses clung to him, to his clothes and his skin. It wormed its way under the collar of his shirt and into his hair. He tried in vain to wriggle his body to prevent molasses from seeping into his waistband,

The Boston Firehouse near the harbor, home of the Engine 31 fireboat, was pushed from its foundation by the molasses wave and nearly swept into the water. The second floor of the building pancaked onto the first, trapping for hours stonecutter John Barry and several firefighters, including George Layhe, who was pinned beneath debris. Layhe tried desperately to keep his head above the rising molasses, but his stamina gave out as rescue crews attempted to reach him, and he dropped his head back into the molasses and drowned. (Photo courtesy of Bill Noonan, Boston Fire Department Archives)

crawling down his pants, clinging to his private parts, like an army of insects that just kept coming. Bill Connor wanted to scream, but he fought the urge. He needed to block out thoughts of everything else except survival. After Paddy Driscoll had yelled at them to run, Connor had seen this black *wall* rushing at them, and it reminded him of boiling oil, curling toward them like a tidal wave. He hadn't even *thought* of molasses at first. He and Bowering reached the door, both of them got their hands on the knob, but before they had time to open it, the molasses had surrounded the firehouse and snuffed out the light entirely.

That was all Bill Connor remembered for a while. When he came to, here he was, facedown under the building, a radiator across his back, Bowering trapped beside him.

"Kick again," he said to Bowering. His buddy complied, his heavy boots knocking more sticks and debris from the hole to allow the molasses to flow out. Connor couldn't reach the hole—he would have had to crawl over Bowering to do it, and that would have been nearly impossible in the narrow space. This must be what it's like to be in a coffin, Connor thought, to be buried alive.

He heard a voice, a new voice, faint but clear. It came from the pool table, just barely visible in the weak light that trickled through the hole at Bowering's feet. "Oh, my God," the voice said. "Help me, Oh God."

Connor recognized the voice. It was George Layhe, his good friend, the man who joined the fire department on the same day as he did. "George!" he shouted. "George, it's Bill. Stay calm, George. They'll get us out."

"Oh, Bill, we're gone," George Layhe replied.

Connor could make out the pool table in the gloom, but couldn't spot Layhe. Then he realized that Layhe was pinned *under* the pool table, desperately trying to keep his head out of the molasses, which had to be rising faster and higher away from the opening in the wall. "George, hang in," he screamed. "Hang in, they're coming, George!"

"I don't think I can," Layhe replied, his voice weak. "Oh, Bill, it's too late. I'm gone—my God, I'm gone."

"There goes poor George," Nat Bowering wailed.

"Shut up, Nat!" Connor shouted to Layhe again: "Stay with me, George!" No response. "George, answer me!"

But Layhe remained silent.

✢✢✢

Suffolk County medical examiner, Dr. George Burgess Magrath, had
no idea what to expect when he arrived on the scene at around 1:30
P.M., but the destruction on and around the Commercial Street wharf
shocked him. He had been performing an autopsy at the nearby
North Mortuary on Grove Street, when he received word at 1 P.M.
that the molasses accident had occurred. He suspended the autopsy,
drove to the scene with his assistant, donned a pair of hip-high rubber fishing boots, and ventured into the carnage to lend his assistance.

He had been practicing medicine since graduating from Harvard
Medical School in 1898, and had served as medical examiner of Suffolk County for the past twelve years, but nothing could have prepared him for what he saw at the Commercial Street waterfront. He
had not served with the Army overseas, but had read of the ghastly
deaths and seen photos of the destruction, and could not have imagined a wartime scene worse than what he witnessed here. The entire
waterfront had been leveled. Every building in the North End Paving
Yard and all of the Bay State Railway freight sheds lay in ruins. The
large plate glass windows on the Bay State office building had been
shattered and the furniture inside split apart, pieces of desks and
chairs and cabinets swamped by the thick molasses. Boston's only trolley freight terminal and most of its big steel trolley-freight cars had
been destroyed. Freight wagons had been crushed, railroad boxcars
split open, automobiles and trucks bent and broken as though they
were children's toys. The steel trestle that had supported the elevated
railroad tracks had buckled like wet cardboard, and the overhead
tracks dangled toward the ground.

Horse-drawn and mechanized rescue vehicles and firefighting
equipment covered the waterfront and Commercial Street area, ven-
turing as close as they could without getting stuck in the molasses,
still knee-deep an hour after the initial wave. Firefighters, police officers, and hundreds of sailors and soldiers from the ships moored
in the harbor swarmed over piles of molasses-drenched debris in a
desperate search for survivors, more often making the grim discovery of bodies. Priests from the nearby North End parishes slogged
through molasses in their long black cassocks and white collars, helping rescuers remove debris, comforting the injured, and performing

Rescuers with stretcher (foreground, right) negotiate mounds of debris to reach victims. *(Photo courtesy of Bill Noonan, Boston Fire Department Archives)*

last rites on the dead and mortally wounded. Rescuers loaded the injured onto wagons and into trucks for transportation to the nearby Haymarket Relief Station; many were swathed in white bandages that stood out in stark relief against the black molasses that saturated their clothing.

Dr. Magrath could see how the molasses wave had rolled over the waterfront, like a giant breaker at the seashore, scooping and scouring everything in its path, leaving destruction behind as it receded. He saw several poor souls being pulled from the molasses, later saying their bodies "looked as though they were covered in heavy oil skins ... their faces, of course, were covered with molasses, eyes and ears, mouths and nose filled with it. The task of finding out who they were and what had happened to them began by washing the clothing and bodies with sodium bicarbonate and hot water."

Closer to the waterfront, near the site of the former city stables, Magrath watched in chilled horror as police officers shot dozens of horses

*Photo shows the Clougherty house smashed under the overhead trestle. In the back-
ground are destroyed structures that were part of the North End Paving Yard.*
(Photo courtesy of Bill Noonan, Boston Fire Department Archives)

who were trapped in the molasses. Most had been knocked down and
were struggling in vain to lift their large heads and break free from the
viscous liquid, snorting to clear their nostrils of the thick molasses;
others had been knocked down and injured by falling timbers and
steel. The sound of these gunshots reverberated across the waterfront,
and Magrath flinched as each animal was put out of its misery.

A police officer spotted Magrath wading through the molasses and
directed him to the smashed Clougherty house, which lay in splinters
up against the overhead trestle in the middle of Commercial Street.
Rescuers had recovered the broken body of sixty-five-year-old Bridget
Clougherty from beneath the wreckage and needed Magrath to pronounce her dead. Magrath made his way to what was left of the three-
story wooden house, now little more than a pile of splintered rubble.
A crowd had gathered on the rise of Copp's Hill Terrace and looked

down silently at the destruction. The onlookers watched—respectfully, Magrath thought—as he examined the late Bridget Clougherty. Her ribcage and chest had been crushed, and Magrath knew before his examination that massive internal injuries had caused her death. He carefully attached an identification tag to her body, and ordered it transported to the morgue. Magrath learned that her two sons, Martin and Stephen Clougherty, and a daughter, Teresa, had all been injured, and had been taken to the Haymarket Relief Station for treatment, along with two boarders who lived in the house.

With his work at the Clougherty house finished, Magrath moved across Commercial Street, the molasses tugging at his boots with every step, to the area where the tank once stood. Steel plates from the tank's wall lay broken and partially submerged in the molasses. But Magrath saw that the tank's large circular roof had fallen almost straight down, basically intact, and now lay right-side-up atop the concrete foundation, in sharp contrast to the violence and destruction on the waterfront. It was as if the molasses had spewed out in all directions from *under* the roof, carrying the tank's walls in all directions, but the roof had settled gently onto the ground below.

Near the roof, Boston mayor Andrew Peters stood shin-deep in molasses, and, with a crowd of reporters and rescue workers gathered around him, Magrath heard him react to the disaster in a firm, strong voice: "Boston is appalled at the terrible accident that occurred here today … An occurrence of this kind must not and cannot pass without a rigid investigation to determine the cause of the explosion—not only to prevent a recurrence of such a frightful accident—but also to place the responsibility where it belongs. Such an investigation has been instituted this afternoon by corporation counsel [city law office] at my direction." Magrath took note that the mayor used the word "explosion" and clearly implied that the collapse of the tank had not been an accident.

When the mayor finished, Magrath decided the best place for him to be was back at the morgue. The bodies would be arriving soon, and would continue to arrive well into the night, and probably for many days afterward. He would officially pronounce dead more victims from this disaster than any single event since he had become medical examiner in 1907. He wanted to make sure things were ready at the

Photo shows scene in the immediate aftermath of the flood, from approximately where the tank stood. In the foreground is the top of the tank (vent pipe extending), which hit the ground virtually intact. Firefighters opened hydrants in a largely unsuccessful effort to clear the molasses, which began to harden quickly, and they eventually had to pump seawater directly from the harbor. In the background, on the elevated tracks, is the train that was stopped just in time by engineer Royal Albert Leeman, whose own train barely escaped derailment as the main trestle buckled. Leeman's action probably saved scores of lives.   *(Photo courtesy of Bill Noonan, Boston Fire Department)*

mortuary, so he left the waterfront by 3 P.M., aware that his day was just beginning.

By leaving early, Dr. Magrath missed a statement issued by USIA attorney Henry F. R. Dolan, one of Boston's most prominent attorneys, shortly after Mayor Peters finished speaking. Dolan's message was similar to the mayor's, though his language was much stronger. Dolan went on the offensive, blaming "outside influences" for the tank's collapse, most likely North End anarchists who planted a bomb to advance their radical agenda. "We know beyond question that the tank was not weak," Dolan said. "We know that an examination was made of the outside of the base of the structure a few minutes before its collapse. We know, and our experts feel satisfied, that there was no fermentation because the molasses was not of sufficient temperature to ferment. The company contends that there was no structural weakness, but we do venture the opinion that something from the outside opened up the tank."

✣✣✣

Arthur P. Jell arrived at the waterfront shortly before 2 P.M., shaken by both the level of destruction in front of him and the short telephone conversation he had had a half-hour earlier with USIA headquarters in New York. His bosses had instructed him to remain silent, to let the company attorney, Dolan, issue any statements about the disaster, and, above all, to ensure that no city inspectors or law enforcement officials confiscate USIA property—specifically, pieces of the tank. USIA engineers, based in Baltimore, would be in Boston tomorrow, Thursday, January 16, to begin the process of collecting the remnants of the tank and transporting them to safe storage.

Jell approached the police ropes, about 150 feet from where the tank had been located, his mouth agape at the incredible scene before him. He had not believed it at first when William White called to tell him about the tank, how White had returned from lunch with his wife to discover the catastrophe that had occurred while he was away. White had described the extent of the damage, but no explanation could have prepared Jell for *this*.

He tried to duck under the ropes but was stopped by a Boston police officer. Jell explained his reason for wanting to reach the tank site, but the officer rebuffed him. A rescue operation was under way and unauthorized persons whose presence might hinder it could not pass. Jell turned and walked away without a fight. Rescuers were concentrating on removing the dead and injured from the molasses; no salvage work had begun yet. He doubted anyone would remove the tank pieces today.

He would return tomorrow with USIA engineers and take control.

✣✣✣

As the frantic rescue teams worked to save victims trapped in the hardening molasses, doctors and nurses were scrambling to help others in the nearby Haymarket Relief Station. Located about a half mile from the disaster scene, the small hospital, an adjunct to the large Boston City Hospital in the South End, was transformed into a triage facility as the wagons rolled in with the injured. Fortunately, the hospital was in the midst of a shift change when the molasses tank collapsed, so doctors, nurses, and orderlies from both shifts were at the relief station when the injured began arriving. The relief station, with twenty-five permanent beds, was quickly swamped with more than forty victims, the overflow relegated to temporary cots that were jammed into small hospital rooms.

Hospital personnel removed molasses from the patients' breathing passages and cut off molasses-soaked clothing so they could learn the gender of the victims and the extent of their injuries. "Those already on duty were soon covered from head to foot with brown syrup and blood," the *Boston Post* reported. "The whole hospital reeked of molasses. It was on the floors, on the walls, the nurses were covered with it, even in their hair."

Dr. John G. Breslin had been superintendent of the relief station for two years and had never seen chaos like this. He tried to remain calm, to prepare his doctors and nurses for the worst, but no one could have foreseen the terrible trauma the victims' suffered, nor the difficulties the molasses presented as the staff tried to treat the injured. Within an hour, the wheeled stretchers became immovable because the hospital corridors were covered with congealing molasses. Corridor floors and walls became so slippery with molasses that dripped from the clothing of the injured that attendants found it necessary to repeatedly swab the entranceways with hot water. Doctors and nurses were smeared with the liquid after the first few victims were treated, and the heads of patients who lay in bed were soon encircled by rings of brown molasses that flowed from their hair and clothes onto the white linen pillowcases.

Clergy members arrived at the relief station, and then shortly thereafter, the relatives of victims—men, women, and children— began to stream into the small hospital and seek information about their loved ones, their sobs filling the hallways and small waiting areas. Some relatives begged Dr. Breslin for information about their family members; others who had seen their husbands, brothers, fathers, and sons wracked with pain pleaded with him to treat their loved ones first. Breslin heard awful moaning from a nearby room and stepped inside. A nurse stood at the foot of the bed while a woman dressed in a hat and coat comforted the man lying motionless beneath the sheets, his arms folded on his chest, his pallor as white as the bedclothes. His hands and face had been washed, but Breslin noticed the molasses smears that stained the pillow behind his head. The man's moaning was the only indicator that he was still alive.

"This is Margaret McMullen," the nurse said softly. "This is her husband, James, who works for Bay State Railroad. I told her she could see him for just a moment if she could remain composed." Breslin nodded, knowing he should get back out to the main entrance and direct traffic, but he couldn't pull his eyes away from McMullen, away from his parchment-like skin, bleached so white that Breslin thought he might see *through* the man if he looked long enough.

Breslin heard the wife speak to her husband. "You are one of the unfortunate ones," she said.

"Yes," he said. "I am here but I don't know how long. Keep up the courage and I will make a battle for you all."

"Where were you?" Margaret McMullen asked her husband, a catch in her throat. "Where were you when it happened?"

"Right next to the tank," McMullen rasped. "I was trying to run some kids off, a little girl collecting firewood. I think she's dead."

"How do you feel? The pain?"

Breslin saw McMullen move his hands from his chest down his body. "I am all to the bad, hon, from here down. From here down. And I am so thirsty."

"Mrs. McMullen," the nurse said in a hushed tone. "Time to go now."

"Yes," she said, bending to kiss her husband on the forehead, clutching his face between her hands. "I must go now, my love. I will be back later tonight."

"Please hon," Breslin heard the man say. "Bring me something to drink when you come back. They give me some water here, but water doesn't help. I'm so thirsty."

Breslin and the nurse stepped out of the room. "Injuries?" Breslin asked.

"Compound fractures of both bones in both lower legs," the nurse said. "Fragments and splinters in wounds, considerable trauma. He'll need an operation." She added, looking directly into Breslin's eyes:

"The wound is badly soiled." He knew these injuries meant that severe infection was likely imminent. If that happened, surgeons would need to amputate both legs to save McMullen's life. Breslin nodded to the nurse and she walked away to treat other patients.

Moments later, Margaret McMullen emerged from her husband's room, her face drawn, eyes red from crying, clutching at the front of her overcoat as though to steady her hands. Head down, she walked shakily toward the front door of the relief station. Breslin thought she would go home for a few moments, take care of her children, perhaps get a bit of rest, and then return for the grueling, sorrowful vigil at her husband's bedside. James McMullen was forty-six years old, and if he survived, there was a good chance he would never walk again.

Breslin thought: What the hell had happened on the waterfront?

And how bad was it going to get?

✣ ✣ ✣

For the third time in as many hours, John Barry watched the rescue worker wriggle toward him, pulling himself forward on his elbows, inch by inch through the molasses-drenched dirt and debris. The scruffy-faced fireman needed to use his elbows, because both hands were occupied; one carried a syringe filled with morphine, the other a bottle of brandy. Twice before, this man had crawled to Barry and injected morphine into his spine to relieve the astonishing pain that wracked the stonecutter's body. Barry was still pinned, facedown, under the firehouse, head facing left, his right cheek squashed into the molasses, his free left hand wiping molasses from his face, the searing pain returning to his back, chest, and legs now that the previous morphine injection was wearing off. Barry longed for the needle again, not just to relieve the pain, but to provide the drug-induced haze that would transport his mind away from this hell. He had stopped screaming hours ago, more from total exhaustion and the morphine than anything else. But still, terror gripped him, squeezing his throat until he was reduced to shallow and ragged breaths. He would become too weak to wipe the molasses away, and it would clog his nostrils and smother him. He would never get out—the unbearable pain would not end and the unbearable fear of being buried alive would not end, and he would die in the dirt.

His only comfort, as the fireman crawled closer, was that the dark-

Firefighters worked in shifts for four hours clearing debris from around and under the wrecked firehouse to reach their trapped colleagues. Firefighters Bill Connor and Nat Bowering, as well as stonecutter John Barry, were freed.

(Photo courtesy of Bill Noonan, Boston Fire Department Archives)

ness was no longer total. A while ago, two hours or more—though Barry felt like it had been an eternity—workers had cut a hole in the floor of the firehouse twenty feet away from where Barry lay trapped. Light had poured down through the hole and then traveled weakly into the crawl space, casting the tunnel in an eerie gloom. Since then, workers had used key-hole saws to cut away additional sections of floor, allowing more light into the crawl space. Barry could now see the stubble on the firefighter's jaw and the intensity in his dark eyes as he struggled toward him. "Almost there, John," the rescuer said, squirming closer. "Almost there."

Barry heard them cutting right above him now, and he heard timber and wood crashing, too. As workers cut away the floor and moved debris, the building settled further—it was falling around him, Barry thought. "Look *out*, for God's sake, or the building will kill the whole of them," he heard a man shout from above his head, though Barry could not see him yet. The rescuers still needed to remove more floorboards and debris to reach him. Barry was weeping again, distraught that the firehouse would collapse and kill him seconds before crews pulled him to safety.

The firefighter reached Barry now, rested the syringe on the stonecutter's upper back.

"Are you ready, John?" he asked softly. "Do it," Barry said, squeezing his eyes shut. He felt the burning pain immediately as the needle plunged into his spine for the third time. He heard himself cry out, a big, wracking sob, but only once.

"There you are, John," the firefighter said. "No more needles for now." Then he drew the stopple on the brandy, and stuck the bottle into Barry's mouth. "Drink all you can, John, but don't bite it," he said. Barry drank, coughed, drank some more, and felt somewhat revived. The firefighter was close to him, so close that Barry could smell his foul breath. But the firefighter was free, and, in moments, would crawl backward out of this stinking crawl space. Barry was still pinned by timbers and a large hot water heater that lay across his back, as helpless as a baby and completely dependent on others to save him.

The firefighter jammed the bottle into Barry's mouth again for one more swig, then Barry swung his free arm, indicating he had had enough. "Hang in, John," the man said, capping the brandy bottle. "We're almost there." Barry's benefactor began crawling backward to safety, his shoulders and face shrinking as he retreated.

Barry felt the morphine kick in, the pain subside a bit, the thick fog surround his head and eyes. He thought he heard distant voices—"one more ... one more ... careful!"—though perhaps he was hearing them only in his own head. He dozed, dreamed that he was sitting in his living-room chair smoking his pipe, then heard voices again, closer this time. "That's his leg—his leg's out!" Awake now, but drowsy, lying in a pool of molasses, he heard the rhythmic swish-swish of a saw inches above his left ear. Then suddenly, *miraculously*, he felt the enormous weight being lifted from his back and legs, relieving the pressure. Seconds later, he could move his head and lift his face out of the muck. "Easy, John, easy," he heard the voices saying, but he didn't recognize them. Then he heard louder voices, feet clomping on wood, felt hands on his body and felt himself being hoisted into the air. A cool breeze hit him then, salty, from the harbor, and he could breathe again and see gray water and gray sky, and then he was being lowered again, gently, onto a stretcher, his back and legs shrieking with pain. He caught sight of a priest and a group of firemen. He heard himself crying, then laughing, then crying again, tasted tears and molasses, felt molasses running down the sides of his face, down his chest, down his legs. His drenched shirt pressed against his chest as he lay on the stretcher, this time flat on his back, staring at the darkening late afternoon sky. Then they lifted the stretcher with him in it, and he felt himself moving forward; he saw the flash of legs and boots and faces and helmets as he went by, saw men looking down at him, some shaking their heads, others shouting words of encouragement.

He heard one voice, one question that puzzled him: "Who's the gink with the white hair?" the voice said. He had heard it clearly, cutting through the shouting, through the smell of molasses and freshly sawn wood, through his own pain and the morphine haze.

John Barry didn't know. But as the exhausted stonecutter slipped into sleep atop the molasses-covered stretcher, he found himself hoping that the white-haired man had not suffered too much.

✲✲✲

Late afternoon January darkness enshrouded the waterfront when they finally pulled firefighter George Layhe's lifeless body out from under the firehouse around 5 P.M. Earlier, workers had rescued firefighters Bill Connor, Nat Bowering, and Paddy Driscoll, all of whom suffered injuries and were taken to the Haymarket Relief Station after they were helped from the crawl space. When John Barry was finally rescued, poor Layhe lay by himself under the firehouse. The firefighter work teams had to be especially careful extricating their fallen comrade; with the weakening of the building after so much of the floor had been cut away, one false step could bring the whole structure down, perhaps killing additional men. The arrival of dusk increased the possibility of missteps and made the task even more risky.

But the firemen helping with the rescue efforts insisted that the work continue until each of their brothers was removed from under the firehouse. They had lived and worked together in that house, and now the house had claimed one of its own, one of their own. There would be no break until George Layhe could be laid to rest with dignity.

Now, steadying himself on a shaky plank of split wood, fire department deputy chief Edward Shallow snapped a salute as four beleaguered firemen carried George's body across the pile of wreckage, placed it gently on a stretcher, and lifted the stretcher into the ambulance that would take Layhe's body to the morgue. They had found the thirty-seven-year-old fire department marine engineer wedged under the pool table and the piano, his legs crushed by timbers. Layhe, unable to move, had struggled desperately to keep his head above the rising molasses, and managed to do so for perhaps as long as two hours, before his stamina gave out. He finally dropped his head back into the molasses and drowned. Chief Shallow thought that Layhe "looked like a colored man" when rescue teams lifted him out from under the firehouse, his hands, face, head, and clothing completely covered with the dark molasses. Eyes scanning the dark waterfront, Shallow knew that Layhe was one of many good men who had died today. He believed Layhe had been the only firefighter; miraculously, the others in the Engine 31 station had survived, and he had accounted for the other men in his command. But his crews were now searching the molasses and the destroyed remains of waterfront buildings for the bodies of other men, women, and children who were not so lucky. Police had already called for electric lights, deciding that the search would continue well into the night. Shallow expected to be on the scene until midnight at least, with one break in the next few minutes—when he would call Elizabeth Layhe and deliver the news about her husband.

The fire chief turned and walked away from the ruined firehouse. There would be time to think about rebuilding, but later, much later; after rescuers had completed the grim task of unearthing and identifying the dead, and after clean-up crews disposed of the molasses and restored the face of the waterfront. It could take months. Surveying the damage, Shallow thought that it would take even longer for the shock to wear off in the North End neighborhood and across the city, for people to recover from this disaster and feel safe again, for things to return to normal.

Firefighters tried to wash the molasses away with fresh water, but would later find that briny seawater was the only way to "cut" the hardened substance. In the background is the damaged elevated railroad structure.

(Photo courtesy of Bill Noonan, Boston Fire Department Archives)

As he waded through the knee-deep molasses that slathered the wharf, Shallow heard a single gunshot ring out from the direction of the city stables, its echo carrying on the cold, evening air.

The Boston Police had put another molasses-enmeshed horse out of its misery.

Returning to normal would take a long time, indeed, Shallow thought.

✲ ✲ ✲

Giuseppe Iantosca stood alone at the bottom of the stairs that led to the door of his home sandwiched between Charter and Commercial streets. He needed to gather his thoughts before heading inside to see his wife, Maria. He had no more information about Pasquale now than he did nearly four hours ago, when he started searching for his little boy minutes after the tank collapsed, minutes after Giuseppe had regained consciousness from his own fall. No one had seen their son, and Giuseppe feared that God had taken Pasquale from them. The police would not let him past their ropes, so he could not even search for his boy among the piles of splintered wood, bent metal, and smashed railroad cars. In frustration, he had spent the last few hours questioning people along the perimeter of the destruction, using hand gestures and broken English to describe Pasquale, asking whether they had seen him, begging for information about him. In the mass confusion, most onlookers were searching for news about their own missing loved ones, and had neither the inclination nor the patience to listen to Giuseppe's halting speech and confusing questions. Many had walked away before he could finish speaking.

Giuseppe's own eyes had told him the horrible story. He had seen the giant wave of molasses consume his ten-year-old son; first Pasquale was standing there and then he was not. Now he could be anywhere. The molasses could have carried him under a building or flung him into the harbor. But the police would not let Giuseppe onto the wharf to find him. He had tried at several different checkpoints, but they had stopped him and ordered him roughly to go home and await news from the authorities. He felt like he had failed Pasqualeno when his son needed him most.

Now, standing very still in the darkness outside of his home, Giuseppe listened, praying that he would hear Pasqualeno's thin, excited voice calling to him, the boy's enthusiastic greeting when Giuseppe returned from work. Giuseppe would give his own life to hear his son once more.

But all he heard were scattered gunshots from the wharf as the police put down more trapped horses.

He drew a deep breath, and thought he would faint from the overwhelming, sickeningly sweet smell of molasses that hung thick in the air. Did the disaster only happen hours ago? He felt as though he had been walking, searching, for many days. He recalled Maria's hysterical screams after the tank had burst, her words filled with heartache, and it seemed to him as though they had been spoken a long time ago. *My son is lost! Pasqualeno is lost!*

Exhausted and disconsolate, he trudged up the dark stairs and stepped into the house. Maria was waiting for him, her black eyes rimmed red from crying. Neither of them spoke—he had come home alone, and that said everything. He reached for her then and brought her close, enfolded her in his arms, whispered to her gently as she trembled like a wounded bird, felt her broken heart beating against his own, the two of them sharing the unspoken fear that, like Pasqualeno, they, too, were lost.

⇜ EIGHT ⇝

"I AM PREPARED TO MEET MY GOD"

Night, January 15, 1919—The Haymarket Relief Station

Veronica Barry clutched her sister Mary's arm as the two women left the chaotic hallways of the Haymarket Relief Station and slipped into the quiet dimness of their father's room. John Barry lay motionless in his bed, moaning softly, a single lightbulb near his head casting a pale yellow glow across his upper body. His two daughters inched closer, Mary leading, Veronica at her elbow as they reached the foot of the bed. Veronica heard her sister gasp, "Father! What . . . ?" and she felt Mary go limp against her, nearly falling to the floor, before Veronica caught her under her arms. Veronica dragged Mary to a chair next to the bed, propped her up, lifted her head, gently slapped her face. "Mary, Mary, wake up, please wake up," she said. Mary groaned, her eyes fluttered open, she looked at her sister in horror.

"Mary, what is it? What's wrong?" Veronica asked.

"Is it father?" Mary asked. "Is it father? Look at him. I don't *know* him."

Veronica swung around then, gazed at her father, so she could see what Mary had seen, though a part of her was afraid to look. It took her eyes a moment to adjust to the pale light, but within a moment, as she moved closer to her injured father, she saw what had shocked her sister's system.

John Barry's upper torso was uncovered. His neck, shoulders, and chest were black from severe bruising, his abdomen and arms covered with lacerations. He looked as though he had been beaten repeatedly. The horrible extent of these injuries made her despair about what she could *not* see beneath the sheets; she knew from the doctor that her father's legs and back were badly damaged. Veronica looked at her father's face, now drawn and haggard. And his hair, which had been dark brown when he left the house early this morning, had turned snowy white. The strong fifty-six-year-old stonecutter looked like a broken seventy-six-year-old man, lying helplessly in the bed.

Her father moaned, stirred slightly, but did not waken. Veronica stared at him, the man who had become a stranger since morning—his disfigured body, his aged face, his white hair. She knew rescuers had pulled her father from under the firehouse, but that didn't seem to tell the whole story.

"What happened under there?" she whispered, tears welling in her eyes.

✣ ✣ ✣

Neither Kittie Callahan nor her cousin, Mary Doherty, could ever remember seeing John Callahan cry. Now, though, tears streamed down John's face, as the forty-three-year-old paver for the City of Boston writhed in pain from a fractured pelvis. Molasses streaked his face and congealed around his mouth. The black liquid spilled onto the pillow beneath his head, and his wife, Kittie, could see that his hair was saturated with molasses.

"I need water to wash the molasses off," John Callahan whispered. "Please wash me off." As Mary Doherty moved to leave the room and get water, John said, "No, please, I want Kittie to go."

With his wife out of the room, John motioned Mary Doherty closer. "I am in terrible agony," he said, "in my ribs and my body. I feel like I am all squashed. I don't think I will make it. I don't want her to know right now. She needs to be strong for little John."

"John, what happened?" Mary asked.

"I was reading a paper before lunch when the tank burst. It came on me like a wave at the sea. It crushed me and pinned me to the ground. I was buried in six feet of molasses. I was able to clear my mouth and find an air pocket and scream. Firefighters dug me out. They brought me here. I had $10 and a set of rosary beads when they brought me in. Promise me that Kittie will get them."

"But, John, they may be able to do something."

"No. I am feeling terribly—I can't stand the suffering much longer. I'm sinking fast. Now promise you'll take care of Kittie."

"I promise, John," Mary Doherty said.

✣ ✣ ✣

Twenty-one-year-old Ralph W. Martin, a teamster and driver for Dolan Meats and Provision, was hanging practically upside down when his mother and father, Catherine and Michael, visited him at the relief station. Firefighters had unearthed Ralph from beneath a pile of debris at the wharf. Now, rigged up in a traction device called a Bradford Frame, his feet were high in the air, held fast by ropes and pulleys, and his bandaged head rested on the pillow, almost as if he were standing on his head. Michael and Catherine stood on either side of Ralph's bed, noticing the molasses on his ears and his face.

"Please, Mom, Dad," Ralph sobbed. "Please. The pain is terrible. You have to ask them to change my position so I can get relief." Michael watched as Ralph clutched at his mother's dress, gritted his teeth, rolled his eyes.

"Ma and Pa," Ralph said. "I guess I'll be all right, do you think? Will I? It's tough, but we'll beat it."

Neither parent spoke, but Michael Martin thought that he had never seen a person suffering as much as his son was now. There was no way he could beat pain like this.

✤✤✤

Peter Francis's son, William, raced to the Haymarket Relief Station from nearby Scollay Square in time to hear a priest from St. Mary's Church in the North End administering last rites to his father.

"I am prepared to meet my God," William heard his father say. "There are other men hurt worse than I am, and I would ask you to attend to them first." Peter Francis moaned in pain, a sure sign to his son that he was seriously injured. "He was a man who never complained," William said. "I knew by his groaning that he was injured too badly to ever recover." Years later, though, it was not his father's moans that haunted William, but the grinding of the hardening molasses in his father's clothes every time he moved.

Peter Francis died minutes after his son's arrival at the relief station.

✤✤✤

Death's pall clung to the relief station throughout the night, as the screams of dying men echoed off corridor walls stained with blood and molasses. James McMullen, John Barry, John Callahan, and Ralph Martin, all with terrible injuries, fought to stay alive, and there were others who did the same. Patrick Breen, a forty-eight-year-old teamster for the City of Boston Paving Department, who was hurled into Boston Harbor by the molasses wave and rescued by sailors aboard the USS *Nantucket,* hung by a thread with pneumonia and infection that had developed from fractured ribs and a serious leg injury. Peter Curran, whose team of hogs had been crushed by the molasses, was dragged from the flood and now lay at the relief station with broken ribs, back and chest injuries, and a severe shock to the nervous system from which doctors were not sure he would ever recover.

Others were identified and shipped to Dr. George Burgess Magrath's North Mortuary deep into the night. William Brogan, fifty-seven, a teamster for the paving department, stayed alive long enough for his wife, Ellen, to reach him at the relief station, before he succumbed to a fractured skull. His wife's last memory of him was the pain in her husband's eyes as he pawed at the bandages that swathed his head, as though tearing them off could ease his suffering. John Seiberlich, sixty-nine, a blacksmith for the City of Boston, suffered a fractured skull and a compound fracture of the femur when the wave caught him about fifty feet from the tank. He died at the relief station shortly thereafter. And the oldest flood victim—even older than Bridget Clougherty and John Sieberlich—seventy-eight-year-old Michael Sinnott, a messenger who was caught on the wharf during lunch hour, died at just past 11 P.M. on January 15, from multiple injuries, including a fractured skull, a fracture of the tibia, and severe shock.

By the time the terrible day had ended—a Wednesday that had begun with the buoyancy and high spirits that accompany a January thaw in New England—the death toll from the molasses flood had reached eleven; nine men, plus the widow Clougherty and little Maria Distasio. Another group of victims lay seriously injured and wracked with pain in the relief station, their fate hanging in the balance, largely dependent on their bodies' ability to fight off infection.

There was also a third group: the missing. Had they been swept into the harbor? Crushed by tons of debris? Swallowed up and drowned by molasses, their bodies trapped in ooze, the chances of recovering them were impossible until cellars and freight sheds had been pumped out. As midnight approached, the cloyingly sweet smell of hardening molasses hung heavy in the Boston air, and the waterfront rats scurried across the wreckage, looking to taste and feed without becoming trapped. Rescuers tried to work, but the electric lighting was inadequate to illuminate the area. No real progress would be made until first light.

It would be then, too, that North End residents would witness the totality of the carnage on the waterfront.

January 16, 1919

News of historic proportions was on the verge of breaking on January 16, 1919, news that would change the economic and social face of America, and the world's geopolitical landscape.

A Prohibition amendment to the U.S. Constitution, one that would ban the manufacture, sale, and consumption of alcoholic beverages, needed the approval of just one more state legislature for ratification. Thirty-five of the forty-eight states had ratified the soon-to-be enacted 18th amendment—one short of the three-fourths majority necessary for approval—only the sixth amendment to the Constitution since the Civil War and the first since 1913. Now the states of Nebraska, Minnesota, and Missouri were racing to become the thirty-sixth state to ratify the Prohibition amendment, a historic achievement that was expected within a day or two, perhaps within hours.

Half a world away, President Woodrow Wilson, who had made history by becoming the first American President to set foot on European soil while in office, was hoping to make it again outside of Paris at the famed chateau of Versailles. There, Wilson and the other "big four" leaders—British prime minister David Lloyd George, French premier Georges Clemenceau, and Italian prime minister Vittoria Orlando—were seeking to negotiate a peace treaty to end the Great War and prevent future wars. As part of the treaty, Wilson would put forth his "fourteen points," aimed to prevent the secret alliances and treaties that had pulled the world into war in 1914. Further, in their efforts to build a lasting peace, Wilson and the other world leaders would craft, as part of the treaty, a blueprint for a new League of Nations, an unprecedented alliance of countries that would work together "to promote international cooperation and to achieve international peace and security."

Nonetheless, both Prohibition and the peace talks were dwarfed by the coverage Boston newspapers gave to the molasses disaster, emblazoning banner headlines and displaying large photos of the flood across their front pages and throughout their news sections, in their Thursday, January 16, editions.

"Huge Molasses Tank Explodes in North End; 11 Dead, 50 Hurt," screamed the front page of the *Boston Post*, adding in a nightmarish subhead, "Giant Wave of 2.3 Million Gallons of Molasses, 50-feet High, Sweeps Everything Before It—100 Men, Women and Children Caught in Sticky Stream—Buildings, Vehicles, and 'L' Structure Crushed." The *Boston Globe* countered with a banner headline, "Molasses Tank Explosion Injures 50 and Kills 11," and a graphic subhead: "Scene of Ruin and Desolation in North End ..." plus, "Death and Devastation in Wake of North End Disaster ... Buildings Demolished, Sticky Mass Floods Streets." The *Globe* let Boston residents know what happened in this report:

> Fragments of the great tank were thrown into the air, buildings in the neighborhood began to crumple up as though the underpinnings had been pulled away from them, and scores of people in the various buildings were buried in the ruins, some dead and others badly injured.
>
> The explosion came without the slightest warning. The workmen were at their noontime meal, some eating in the building or just outside ... once the low, rumbling sound was heard no one had a chance to escape. The buildings seemed to cringe up as though they were made of pasteboard.

In its first-day report, the *Post* led with the following account:

> A 50-foot wave of molasses—2,300,000 gallons of it—released in some manner yet unexplained, from a giant tank, swept over Commercial street and its waterfront from Charter street to the southerly end of North End park yesterday afternoon.
>
> Ensnaring in its sticky flood more than 100 men, women, and children; crushing buildings, teams, automobiles, and street cars—everything in its path—the black, reeking mass slapped against the side of the buildings footing Copp's Hill and then swished back toward the harbor.
>
> Eleven persons—a woman, a girl, and nine men—were the known

Sailors at bottom left from the USS Nantucket, *which was in port when the flood occurred, aided in the rescue efforts as crews cleared tons of debris to reach trapped victims.*   *(Photo courtesy of Bill Noonan, Boston Fire Department Archives)*

dead at midnight. More than 50 injured were in hospitals and at their homes. Some of them may die. Dead horses, cats, and dogs had been carted away in team after team.

In its inside pages, the *Post* described the destruction in the colorful newspaper language of the day:

A rumble, a hiss—some say a boom and a swish—and the wave of molasses swept out. It smote the huge steel girders of the "L" structure and bent, twisted, and snapped them, as if by the smash of a giant's fist. Across the street, down the street, it rolled like a two-sided breaker at the seashore. Thirty feet high, it smashed against tenements on the edge of Copp's Hill. Swirling back it sucked a modest frame dwelling [the Clougherty house] from where it nestled beside the three-story brick tenements and threw it, a mass of wreckage, under the "L" structure.

Then, balked by the staunch brick walls of the houses at the foot of the hill, the death-dealing mass swept back towards the water. Like

The swath of destruction caused by the molasses wave extended for hundreds of feet down Commercial Street. Note the smashed vehicle against the stone wall at right. The mass of debris burying the Clougherty house can be seen in the center of the photo, beneath the trestle.   *(Photo courtesy of Bill Noonan, Boston Fire Department Archives)*

eggshells it crushed the buildings of the North End yard of the city's paving division ... To the north it swirled and wiped out practically all of Boston's only electric freight terminal. Big steel trolley freight cars were crushed as if eggshells, and their piled-up cargo of boxes and merchandise minced like so much sandwich meat.

Meanwhile, the cause of the disaster continued to be a source of debate carried out in the press. State chemist Walter Wedger, and U.S. inspector of explosives Daniel T. O'Connell, believed strongly in the "collapse theory"—that the tank disintegrated because of a combination of structural weakness and fermentation inside the tank. USIA attorney Henry F.R. Dolan continued to argue "beyond question" that outside influences, "evilly disposed persons," were responsible for destroying the tank, insisting that the fifty-foot receptacle was structurally sound.

As the clean-up continued—as workers first tried to remove hardening molasses with chisels and saws, and finally used millions of gallons of briny seawater to cut the congealing liquid; as the injured were ministered at the relief station and the search continued for additional victims amidst the debris on the waterfront—Boston newspapers, and even the *New York Times*, continued to carry reports of the disaster on their front pages. They listed the names, ages, and occupations of the dead and the injured. They ran sidebars of people who escaped the wave by ducking under railroad cars. They published small stories explaining that people who were feared lost were actually alive and well.

For a week after the flood, the molasses tragedy became the *only* news in Boston, the talk of the city, the focus of activity in the North End.

Meanwhile, rescue teams kept searching for bodies.

Thursday, January 16, 1919, 8 p.m.

While clean-up and recovery efforts were continuing, church bells throughout Boston pealed in celebration. Nebraska had just become the thirty-sixth state to ratify the Prohibition amendment, providing the three-fourths total necessary to amend the U.S. Constitution; after a one-year grace period, the actual law banning alcohol in the United States would go into effect on January 17, 1920.

It no longer mattered to U.S. Industrial Alcohol. Its 2.3 million gallons of molasses covered Commercial Street and filled the basements of homes and businesses in the area. Its attempt to convert its molasses distillation process from industrial alcohol for munitions to grain alcohol for rum—its attempt, in effect, to outrun the oncoming Prohibition amendment—had ended in disaster.

USIA's days in Boston were numbered.

Friday, January 17, 1919

Two days after the disaster, with the water of Boston Harbor stained brown from the molasses that had been washed into it, more than three hundred workers covered the waterfront, combing through wreckage for the bodies of the missing, clearing debris so the search could proceed more smoothly, and wielding acetylene torches to cut the steel pieces of the tank into manageable sizes that could be carried away. The city provided about 125 of those workers, Boston Elevated another hundred, and the Hugh Nawn Construction Company, builders of the tank's foundation, supplied another hundred. United States Industrial Alcohol had supplied no workers and, indeed, its first representatives had not visited the scene until Friday, when Vice President M.C. Whittaker arrived from New York, engineers William F. Cochrane and John F. Barnard traveled north from Baltimore, and treasurer Arthur P. Jell made his way over from USIA's East Cambridge distilling plant.

Whittaker and his men met with Thomas F. Sullivan, commissioner of Public Works for Boston, and a heated argument ensued that could be heard outside the building in which they met. Sullivan angrily disapproved of the fact that USIA had delayed so long before sending representatives to the scene, and was providing no clean-up assistance. Whittaker finally agreed to hire up to 150 men to assist with the clean-up. In addition, engineers Cochrane and Barnard would supervise the removal of the steel tank pieces to a scrap metal yard in Roxbury, a few miles away. The pieces would either be transported by wagon if they could fit, or for larger sections, dragged by teams of horses fitted with ropes and harnesses. Arthur P. Jell remained on the waterfront for several hours that day, but there is no evidence that he contributed to the discussion during the meeting.

After the brief exchange between the city and USIA officials, a member of the press cornered Whittaker outside.

"Can you give some cause for the accident?" the reporter asked.

"No. If I could, I wouldn't have to work for a living," Whittaker snapped back.

✤✤✤

Meanwhile, at about 3 P.M., Ralph Martin, the twenty-one-year-old teamster and driver for Dolan Meats and Provision, died from infection at the Haymarket Relief Center, his parents by his side. He was conscious up to an hour before his death, begging his mother and father for some relief from the pain.

Peter Curran, whose team of hogs was destroyed in the flood, was luckier. Despite three fractured ribs, a severely bruised thigh, a bruised chest, a wrenched back, an injury to his left eye, and what doctors described as "severe nervous shock," he was released from the hospital at about the same time as Ralph Martin died. He would be bedridden for a month and incapacitated until May.

Saturday, January 18, 1919

Chief Justice Wilfred Bolster of the Boston Municipal Court, renowned in legal circles for his sound judicial temperament, tromped through the molasses-covered debris, inspecting the ruins and surveying the horrific destruction on the waterfront with a sense of shock. The North End Paving Yard had been destroyed, reduced to a pile of kindling. The steel girders and trestles and tracks of the elevated railroad structure had been bent and broken into a misshapen mass that would take weeks, or months, to repair. Men and women, hundreds of them, swarmed over the wreckage like ants, their steps tenuous due to the dangerous footing. Some were Red Cross and Salvation Army workers assisting the rescuers, others were firefighters and sailors carefully removing wood and steel in their search for the dead, the more hopeful among them searching for survivors. Scores of other men were wielding brooms, chisels, shovels, or high-pressure hoses in their efforts to remove the molasses from the street and the wharf area. Across Commercial Street, the fire department's hydraulic pumps were groaning as they worked to siphon thousands of gallons of molasses from the cellars of stores and tenements. In all of his fifty-two years, Wilfred Bolster had never witnessed such a scene.

As the judge who would next month conduct the criminal inquest into the terrible disaster, Bolster needed to get a complete feel for the scene. He had already interviewed the Boston Public Works superintendent and the USIA lead engineer, William Cochrane, to learn as much as possible about what had happened on Commercial Street.

Beyond his judicial responsibilities, though, Bolster loved Boston and felt compelled to see the tragedy that had befallen his city. He was a distinguished graduate of Harvard Law School, had served on the Boston School Board, and had been chief justice of the Municipal Court since 1906. Boston had been grotesquely altered by the waterfront catastrophe that had taken place this week. Bolster took this as a personal affront as much as a municipal tragedy.

As he plodded across the molasses-covered waterfront, avoiding piles of splintered wood and side-stepping the fire hoses that curled through the wharf debris, Judge Wilfred Bolster knew only one thing: Someone was responsible for what had happened here, and someone would pay.

Sunday, January 19, 1919

James McMullen, the Bay State Railroad worker who had shouted at Maria Distasio for trespassing at the tank, died at approximately 10 A.M. from infection. His wife, Margaret, who had been at his side from the beginning, said he was delirious and complained about his ferocious thirst right up until his death.

One hour later, Patrick Breen, the teamster for the City of Boston Paving Department who had been hurled into Boston Harbor by the molasses wave and rescued by sailors, died alone, from pneumonia as a result of his injuries. His daughter, Margaret, and cousin, Charles Breen, had left their bedside vigil for a few hours to get some rest.

✣ ✣ ✣

John Barry was alive and home before the end of the day Sunday, January 19, and whereas he merely feared death while he was trapped under the firehouse four days ago, now he *wished* for it. He hadn't been able to get a good look at himself in the hospital—each time he moved a nurse would order him to lie back and rest—and the morphine had masked much of his pain. But now he could see and feel, and he thought that death would be a welcome alternative.

The timbers and heavy water-heater that had pinned him for hours had damaged his torso, injured his back and legs, and crushed his spirit. His pain was indescribable. His entire body, from his neck down, was black from bruising. His thighs and knees were torn and lacerated, and his spine felt as though it would snap at any moment. Boils covered his arms and chest; the doctor had already visited once to slice them open and drain the pus, and he showed John Barry's daughters how to clean the boils in the future. His girls, he knew, still couldn't bear to look at him. Their strong, powerfully built father had, within days, become a broken, pitiful old man with snow-white hair.

As wretched as he looked and felt today, as much as he believed that dying would be better than the suffering he was experiencing now, John Barry still had no way of knowing how profoundly his life would change. His back and legs would never heal completely. He would remain bedridden for weeks, and even after he did manage to get out of bed, he would never be able to stand fully erect.

When he did return to work for the city, he would shuffle paper in the office, keeping track of the paving jobs—John Barry, a strapping picture of health, a man who had never been treated by a doctor prior to the molasses disaster, would also never again be physically able to cut stone for a living.

The molasses flood would not claim John Barry's life, but it would claim his health, his livelihood, and, eventually, his self-worth. He had no way of knowing all of this on January 19, 1919, no way of knowing how much he would suffer in the years to come.

Monday, January 20, 1919

John Callahan, the City of Boston paver who sent his wife out of his room and confided to her cousin that he was "sinking fast" on the night of the molasses disaster, died five days later from shock and pneumonia. The time of death was 4 A.M. John Callahan died alone— his wife, Kittie, had not yet arrived from their South Boston home.

Later That Day, Boston City Hospital

It was just after noon, but already, it had been a long day for Martin Clougherty. His mother's funeral had just ended, a simple, but well-attended affair. He suspected that the throngs who had paid their respects had come not so much as a testament to the family's popularity, but more out of curiosity about the bizarre and violent manner in which his mother had died.

Now, Martin stood at the bedside of his sleeping brother, Stephen, who had been transferred to Boston City Hospital yesterday from the Haymarket Relief Station. His thirty-two-year-old brother, a man with the mind of a seven-year-old, had been a far cry from his pleasant, docile self when Martin first arrived to visit him. He had been frightened to death, begging Martin to stay with him, fearing that the hospital personnel were conspiring to harm him. "The nurses are getting ready to poison me and throw me out the window," Stephen had cried, "just like I got thrown out the top window of our home."

Martin had learned that sailors from the USS *Enterprise* had pulled his brother from the molasses and placed him in the ambulance that took him to the relief station. His brother's hands and arms had been cut and bruised, but beyond that, he had no serious injuries. *Physical* injuries, Martin corrected. There had definitely been a serious diminishment of his brother's mental condition. Normally, he could tease and joke with Stephen. But Martin had known as soon as he had walked into his brother's room that something had changed. He could see it in Stephen's eyes first, the sheer terror, and then his brother had begun talking about the hospital staff's plotting to kill him. Martin had calmed him, speaking softly and gently stroking his forehead, until Stephen had fallen asleep. How he would react when he awoke was anyone's guess.

Martin had to think about Stephen's future. Before the accident, Stephen had handled simple chores around his mother's house and, despite his feeble-mindedness, was enjoyable to be around. Immersed in routine and familiar surrounding, his brother could manage day-to-day living without constant care and direction. But what now? Stephen had clearly taken a turn for the worse. He was terrified and paranoid. How long would these feelings last? What if they were permanent? Stephen had no familiar surroundings to come home to. Their mother was gone. Their *home* was gone.

Martin himself had been affected by the disaster more than he had imagined possible. He missed his mother, but it was more than that. His own injuries were minor, but his nerves were on edge nearly every moment and he had not been able to sleep since the disaster. He was staying with friends, and on two occasions already, they had mentioned to him that he cried out during the night. If the tragedy was affecting Martin this much, keeping him awake at night and in a state of anxiety during the day, he could only imagine how it was affecting Stephen. His brother often had trouble separating fantasy from reality. How much would his ordeal change him? And could Martin care for him if Stephen's mental condition became much worse?

He would have to deal with this eventually, but first things first. As Martin looked down upon his sleeping brother, he wondered how he would tell Stephen that their mother was dead.

Late That Afternoon, the Waterfront

They pulled out ten-year-old Pasquale Iantosca's battered, molasses-covered body from behind a railroad freight car as late afternoon dusk enveloped the waterfront and a raw wind whistled off the harbor. The boy's arms, legs, pelvis, and chest were broken and his face was disfigured beyond recognition. The molasses had driven the railroad car into Pasquale, carried them both about fifty feet, and smashed both up against the wall, the railroad car crushing the little boy instantly. Rescuers knew Pasquale was missing, and when they pulled the boy out, one ran to get Pasquale's father, Giuseppe, at his Charter Street home.

When Giuseppe arrived, he recoiled in horror upon seeing his son's body. He couldn't recognize the boy's face. His first instinct was to cover his own face with his hands and weep, but Giuseppe would not do this in front of the rescue workers. He composed himself, saw that the dead boy was wearing a red sweater, bent down, lifted the sweater, and saw the second red sweater underneath. It was Pasquale. The black corduroy pants and the high brown shoes were also Pasquale's.

Giuseppe gently hugged little Pasqualeno's shattered body close to him, felt his son's broken bones squirming under the sweaters, tried to imagine the boy's pain and fear in those last seconds. Giuseppe prayed to God that Pasquale had died quickly, that he was dead before the railroad freight car had smashed his body against the wall of the building.

In a few moments, Giuseppe felt hands on his shoulders and men pulling him to his feet. One man carefully took Pasqualeno's body and placed him tenderly into the back of a Red Cross ambulance that would take him to the morgue. The other rescuers turned away to continue their work and give Giuseppe his privacy. Giuseppe stood motionless and watched the ambulance drive north on Commercial Street. His heart was broken, but at least little Pasqualeno was no longer lost. And his wife, Maria, would be grateful. Their son would have a funeral.

January 26, 1919

Eleven days after the tank burst, firefighters fished the body of thirty-seven-year-old truck driver Flaminio Gallerani from the water underneath one of the Bay State Railroad freight houses. He had been making a delivery to Bay State on January 15, and the molasses wave lifted him and his four-ton 1915 Packard truck into the water. The vehicle was smashed to pieces, and Flaminio drowned in a combination of water and thick molasses. Luckily, during the time Flaminio's body was in the water, only his hands were eaten by sea animals—they had left his face alone. This made it easier for Flaminio's nephew, Frank Gallerani, to identify his uncle's body.

�֍ �֍ ✖

With the discovery of Flaminio Gallerani's body, the molasses flood had claimed nineteen lives. Authorities were still reporting one man missing: a thirty-two-year-old Italian immigrant named Cesare Nicolo, who drove a team and wagon and delivered goods to the waterfront. Witnesses had seen Nicolo near the Boston & Worcester Railway freight station on the Commercial Street wharf, just before the molasses tank collapsed. His wife, Josie, had visited the scene each day since the January 15 disaster, begging in vain for news about her husband.

Meanwhile, workers continued the massive recovery and clean-up effort. Police and firefighters, city workers and sailors, laborers and volunteers continued to haul away wreckage, claw through debris, operate hydraulic pumps, remove ruined goods from Commercial Street cellars, and man seawater-shooting fire hoses to cut congealed molasses. The disaster also was spreading, literally, as molasses was tracked across the city by rescue workers and onlookers when they returned home; molasses covered subway platforms and seats inside the trains and trolleys, stuck to the handsets of pay telephones, and floated in the water-troughs around the city where horses would stop for a drink.

But as bad as the situation was, rescue crews were already expressing their thanks that the tragedy had not happened in summer. In the warm weather, when school was out, there would have been twenty-five to thirty children playing in the North End Park, all of whom would have been drowned by the wall of molasses. And in the summer, the health risks from pests and rodents would have been as devastating as the flood itself; rats by the hundreds and flies by the *millions* would have descended upon the waterfront, attracted by thick, sweet liquid that spread across the wharf and Commercial Street. Insects were scarce in late January, but the rats were still a nuisance—in warm weather, their sheer numbers would have made them unstoppable.

As rescue workers pondered the unthinkable scene around them, as they sullenly shook their heads when Josie Nicolo asked about her missing husband, as they wondered whether the waterfront would ever return to normal, most of them had one question uppermost in their minds:

How could this have happened?

NINE

DARKENING SKIES

February 1919

Bostonians must have been bewildered, even angry, when they picked up their morning newspapers on Saturday, February 8, 1919, less than a month after the molasses tank collapsed, and read that a seething Judge Wilfred Bolster was blaming *them* for the disaster.

Not only them. He chided the Boston Building Department for its cursory examination of USIA's plans to construct the tank and for the "incompetent" people who reviewed those plans. He scolded USIA and Arthur P. Jell for failing to verify the tank's safety and relying solely on the assurance of the manufacturer.

But in his inquest report filed in the office of the clerk of the Superior Criminal Court, Bolster blasted the public for its failure both to adequately fund its city inspection departments and to insist on qualified people to staff them. "The chief blame rests upon the public itself," Bolster declared. "This single accident has cost more in material damage alone than all the supposed economics in the building department. Laws are cheap of passage, costly of enforcement. They do not execute themselves. A public which, with one eye on the tax rate, provides itself with an administrative equipment 50 percent qualified, has no right to complain that it does not get a 100 percent product—and so far as it accepts political influence as the equivalent of scientific positions which demand such attainment in a high degree, so long it must expect breakdowns in its machinery."

Still, Bolster acknowledged that the public's "error of judgment" was not negligence, and that the only party that could be held criminally responsible for the tank disaster was U.S. Industrial Alcohol. "The only assignable crime involved is manslaughter, through negligence," Bolster said. "My conclusion from all this evidence is that this tank was wholly insufficient in point of structural strength to handle its load, insufficient to meet either legal or engineering requirements. This structure being maintained in violation of the law, the lessee has incurred the penalty which is absolute. I have therefore ordered process against the United States Industrial Alcohol Company."

Based on Bolster's inquest report, District Attorney Joseph Pelletier presented evidence to a grand jury the following week. "The evidence tends to show that the huge tank collapsed by reason of faulty construction and not because of an explosion," he said.

Five days after hearing the evidence that Pelletier presented, the grand jury issued its report. It agreed that the structure did not comply with the law, and that the building department gave USIA authority to put up the structure in a way "not permitted by the law."

In addition: "The Grand Jury concurs with the expression of Chief Justice Bolster that no matter of expense of qualified employees should deter the city from making a most thorough examination of all plans and materials submitted before issuing a permit."

However, on the larger issue of criminal negligence, the grand jury ruled that there was insufficient evidence to justify, or return, an indictment for manslaughter. There would be no criminal charges brought against anyone in the molasses flood case.

Two days later, on February 14, MIT professor C.M. Spofford, who had been hired by Boston Elevated to examine and test pieces of the tank, reported that the steel plates were of "insufficient thickness" to withstand the pressure of molasses, and that there were not enough rivets to fasten the tank sufficiently. "In my judgment, the tank was improperly designed and its failure was due entirely to structural weakness," Spofford stated in his report. "The stresses due to the static pressure of the molasses alone were so great that the whole structure was in a dangerous condition."

USIA dismissed the assertions of Bolster, Pelletier, and Spofford, and instead was heartened and emboldened by the grand jury's failure to issue indictments. In a brief statement, its last until civil proceedings began in 1920, the company reiterated its belief that evilly disposed persons had used dynamite to blow up the tank, and that USIA bore no responsibility for the disaster.

❖ ❖ ❖

The Boston molasses disaster was the first in a series of events that disrupted the equilibrium of the city and the country in 1919, events that generated first uneasiness, and then fear and disillusionment, across the land. The euphoria that had accompanied the armistice in November 1918 had dissipated, and Bostonians and Americans struggled to make sense of a nation that seemed to be spinning out of control in February and March of the new year.

It was a year that began with returning soldiers and sailors flooding the civilian labor market even as government war production contracts were being canceled. In addition, with the wartime shortage of labor in 1917 and 1918, blacks from the South had migrated to northern industrial cities seeking jobs, a practice they continued after the war ended. Now, blacks, whites, and returning veterans were battling for fewer jobs, all in the midst of rising prices and a soaring cost of living.

As a result, labor unrest was sweeping industry and government from coast to coast. In Massachusetts, a violent strike erupted in the textile mills of nearby Lawrence, and soon after, more than twelve thousand telephone workers employed by the New England Telephone and Telegraph Company walked off their jobs. Both groups were seeking higher wages, a forty-eight-hour workweek, and stronger collective bargaining rights. The telephone operators, who earned $16 per week, demanded $22, and finally settled for $19 after a one-week strike. Despite its short duration, the strike alarmed and disrupted the business community—it was an ominous sign of discontent among American workers.

There were more. Boston Police, who were beginning their contract negotiations with the city, rejected a $100 annual raise, and also rejected a compromise $140 raise (10 percent), adopting the slogan, "$200 or nothing."

Elsewhere, thirty-five thousand dressmakers in New York struck for a forty-four-hour week and a 15 percent pay increase, and more than sixty thousand workers struck in Seattle, bringing the seaport city to a standstill. This "general strike," the notion that a city could be paralyzed by work stoppages, made Americans uneasy, even more so when a labor newspaper in Seattle editorialized, "We are undertaking the most tremendous move ever made by Labor in the country . . . We are starting on a road that leads—no one knows where."

Historian Francis Russell noted that inadequate working conditions and rising prices both frightened and galvanized workers. "Wherever one turned, in industry or transportation or public service, there seemed to be a strike or threatened strike," he said. "To add to the malaise, prices, instead of falling, continued to rise. The value of the 1914 dollar had dropped to only forty-five cents. Food costs had gone up 84 percent, clothes, 114 percent. For the average American family, the cost of living was double what it had been five years earlier, and income had lagged behind. Professional classes, from clergymen and professors to clerks, state and city employees, firemen and police, found themselves worse off than at any time since the Civil War."

The uncertainty bred by these woeful economic conditions, coupled with the strikes and threatened work stoppages, focused the public's attention on—and fueled its fear of—domestic radicals such as Socialists, IWW, and anarchists, who were often blamed for the social unrest. In mid-February, the Bureau of Immigration deported between seven thousand and eight thousand aliens "as rapidly as they can be rounded up and put on ships." The mayor of Seattle, Ole Hanson, toured the country following the strike in his city, warning of the Red menace in the United States. A Lawrence, Massachusetts, Citizens' Committee announced plans to "wage war on Bolshevism" and root out labor agitators. A radical labor leader was arrested in Cleveland in connection with a conspiracy to kill President Wilson.

The domestic tension affected international diplomacy as well. President Wilson, fresh off successful negotiations in Paris for both the Treaty of Versailles and the League of Nations, faced strong opposition on the League from Republicans in the Senate, led by Henry Cabot Lodge of Massachusetts. GOP senators believed that the League would jeopardize American sovereignty and become "an impediment to the independence of this country." Lodge and other Republican senators wanted the Treaty and the League of Nations severed in their ratification discussions; President Wilson believed that they were inextricably linked.

Wilson decided to make Boston the first American city that he would visit following the Versailles peace conference, and sailed from Paris in mid-February. It would be his first visit to Boston as president, and his goal was to speak directly to the people to promote the League in the state in which the leading Republican, Lodge, had been its staunchest and most vociferous opponent.

The day before Wilson's arrival, Secret Service agents and members of the New York Police Department arrested fourteen Spanish anarchists in Manhattan and charged them with conspiracy to assassinate the president. Acting on an anonymous tip, the agents raided a Lexington Avenue home, expecting to find loaded bombs that the anarchists were planning to set off in Boston. Neither bombs nor explosives were found, and the anarchists were not carrying firearms, but agents said they found documentary evidence that proved that radicals had planned to kill the president using dynamite.

While Wilson's ship, the *George Washington,* was at sea, an anarchist shot and wounded French premier Georges Clemenceau in Paris. One of the three shots that struck him pierced a lung, but Clemenceau later recovered.

The attempted assassination and the anarchist plot cast a grim pall over Wilson's return to America and led to extraordinary security precautions for his Boston visit. Warships escorted the *George Washington* through the harbor when it arrived at the city's Commonwealth Pier on Monday morning, February 24. Once Wilson set foot on Boston soil, a contingent of Secret Service, troops, police, and detectives guarded him and his entourage for the entire length of his visit. A solid line of troops, led by the Massachusetts State Guard Cavalry, maintained vigilance on horseback along Wilson's parade route, as he made his way to Mechanics Hall to deliver his remarks.

More than five hundred thousand people lined Boston's streets to cheer the president, and Bostonians greeted Wilson warmly, but there was something disquieting about Secret Service agents armed with rifles lining the rooftops, and windows being ordered closed during the president's drive by. His visit to Boston was brief and nothing untoward occurred, but Francis Russell noted, "the fear remained, a fear that Secretary of Labor William B. Wilson gave voice to when he warned an apprehensive middle-class audience that 'recent events at Lawrence, Seattle ... and other places were not industrial, economic disputes in their origin, but were results of a deliberate, organized attempt at a social and political movement to establish Soviet Governments in the United States.'"

Two days after President Wilson left Boston, Italian anarchist Luigi Galleani, himself awaiting deportation, delivered an incendiary speech in Taunton, Massachusetts. The next evening, in the nearby town of Franklin, four Italian anarchists, all ardent Galleanists, blew themselves up in what police believed was a botched plot to destroy the mill of the American Woolen Company where they worked and where a strike was in progress. Federal authorities arrested three other men in the conspiracy on March 1. The newly sworn-in U.S. attorney general, A. Mitchell Palmer, promised a nationwide crackdown on "aliens and Bolsheviks, radicals, and anarchists" who were roaming the country, disrupting its peace, and terrorizing its people.

April 9, 1919

Martin Clougherty made the most difficult decision of his life with little fanfare and a clear conscience.

For nearly three months, his mentally deficient brother, Stephen, had been living with a cousin. But Stephen's condition had deteriorated so profoundly that the normally docile young man had been hallucinating and prone to violence. The latest incident had occurred yesterday, when the afternoon shadows had fallen across his bedroom. Stephen screamed inconsolably, babbling that the building was about to collapse and crush him and that he would be smothered in molasses. Martin had witnessed the panic attack and had made the decision on the spot to commit Stephen to the Boston State Hospital for the insane in the city's Mattapan section.

He had no choice. Stephen had been visibly upset since he had been rescued from the molasses on January 15, but now he was uncontrollable.

This afternoon, Martin had accompanied his brother to the hospital and signed the commitment papers. He stayed with Stephen while they prepared his room. When the nurse tried to take his temperature, Stephen Clougherty hurled the thermometer across the floor.

Martin retrieved the thermometer, apologized to the nurse, and touched his brother's shoulder. He left then, promising Stephen that he would visit soon.

April 28–May 1, 1919

As May Day approached, anarchists grew bolder. Angry about economic conditions and Galleani's impending deportation, they mailed package bombs to some of the nation's most prominent and influential citizens, most especially those who had spoken out against aliens, radicals, IWW members, and labor leaders.

On April 28, a package containing a homemade bomb was sent to Seattle mayor Hanson, who, after the general strike in his city, had railed against "scoundrels who want to take possession of our American Government and try to duplicate the anarchy of Russia." Hanson was in Colorado, fulfilling a speaking engagement, when the parcel arrived. Luckily, his assistant opened the package from the wrong end; the bomb failed to go off and the assistant summoned police. Another bomb, sent to the home of Georgia's former senator Thomas Hardwick, co-sponsor of the 1918 deportation bill, did find a target, exploding as the Hardwicks's maid opened the package, blowing off both of her hands.

The Hardwick bombing made headlines across the nation, and on April 30, orders went out to all post offices to be on the lookout for suspicious packages. In all, inspectors discovered thirty-four "May Day" bomb packages in the mail before delivery, addressed to people such as Attorney General Palmer, Postmaster General Albert S. Burleson (who had banned radical literature from the mail), U.S. Supreme Court Justice Oliver Wendell Holmes, Judge Kenesaw Mountain Landis (who had sentenced Big Bill Haywood and other IWW leaders), Commissioner General of Immigration Anthony Caminetti, and multimillionaires John D. Rockefeller and J.P. Morgan. Not a single bomb harmed its intended victim. No one was killed, and the Hardwick maid was the only person to suffer serious injury. Postmaster General Burleson attributed the outcome to the vigilance of his department's employees.

Americans were outraged, and newspapers clamored for action. The *New York Times* called it the "most widespread assassination conspiracy in the history of the country." Law enforcement responded with immediate crackdowns. Police and citizens, including ex-soldiers and ex-sailors, rousted and disrupted radicals who gathered to commemorate May Day in Cleveland, New York, and Boston, according to historian Paul Avrich. The worst of these disturbances occurred in Boston, where parading radicals in Roxbury were set upon by indignant bystanders, "chased through the streets, beaten, trampled, and kicked." Shots were exchanged, a police captain died of a heart attack during the melee, and all told 116 demonstrators were arrested, including followers of Galleani.

Tried before Judge Albert F. Hayden at the Roxbury Municipal Court, fourteen demonstrators were found guilty of disturbing the peace and sentenced to several months in prison. After sentencing, Hayden blasted "foreigners who think they can get away with their doctrines in this country . . . if I could have my way I would send them and their families back to the country from which they came."

As it had been for the past three years, Boston remained *the* hotbed for Italian anarchist activities. In the spring of 1919, the nerves of citizens and police were frayed and the city had become a powder keg. Bostonians wondered when and what kind of spark it would take to set off an explosion.

May 12, 1919

Nearly four months after the molasses disaster, the body of Cesare Nicolo was pulled from the water, out from under the wharf near the Boston & Worcester Commercial Street freight station. His wife, Josie, identified his body.

The flood had claimed its twentieth victim.

Monday, June 2, 1919

Malcolm Hayden, the twenty-year-old son of Roxbury District Court Judge Albert F. Hayden, was walking home just before midnight when a touring car traveling in the other direction sped past him, nearly climbing the sidewalk and sideswiping him as it turned the corner and raced away down Blue Hill Avenue. The car had appeared suddenly out of the darkness, from the direction of the Hayden home on Wayne Street. In the few seconds that he saw the vehicle as it flashed by him, Malcolm wondered why the roof was up, considering the late-night humidity. A heat wave had gripped Boston for the past week. The temperature had approached 100 degrees today, and even now, had to still be pushing eighty. A beautiful night for a walk *or* a drive, Malcolm thought, until the careening automobile had missed him by inches.

The car disappeared and the night stillness returned. The street was dark and deserted at this hour, the only sound the snap of Malcolm's shoes on the pavement as he continued down Wayne Street. He had enjoyed dinner and drinks with friends (how many more such nights would they enjoy with Prohibition approaching?) and he was so tired he expected to be asleep in minutes. He was alone now on the street and would be alone when he reached his house; his parents and sister had been away for the past week at the family's summer home in nearby Plymouth.

Malcolm was two hundred feet from his front door when the midnight quiet was shattered by a deafening explosion ahead of him. He felt the searing heat from the blast sweep across his face, and the explosion's concussive force pound his eardrums and knock him off his feet. From the ground, he watched the front of his house crumble, the second-level piazza shudder and crash to the lawn.

Scrambling to regain his feet, the first thought that entered Malcolm Hayden's head—before he consciously wondered why the Haydens had been targeted and by whom—was how thankful he was that the house was empty.

As his neighbors streamed onto the street in their nightclothes, Malcolm sprinted toward his house to see how much damage the bomb had done.

❖❖❖

Had he left the saloon and arrived home two minutes earlier, Malcolm Hayden would have been blown to pieces. The entire front of the Hayden house had been destroyed by the bomb that had been placed against a main support column, just under Malcolm's bedroom window. The blast also had blown out windows and ripped shingles from the roof of the house next door. Both homes, among the finest in Boston's Roxbury section, sustained thousands of dollars in damage.

What the Wayne Street neighborhood would find out the next day was that the dynamite bombing of the Hayden house was part of an organized anarchist conspiracy unleashed in Boston and six other major cities, including Washington, D.C., when powerful bombs exploded almost simultaneously, all going off within an hour of midnight, all planted at the homes of prominent persons who were involved in antiradical or anti-anarchist activities. This included United States Attorney General A. Mitchell Palmer, whose home in the fashionable northwest section of Washington, D.C., was destroyed while he and his family slept on the second floor. The bomb, planted under the steps of Palmer's home, destroyed most of the dwelling and smashed in windows of houses as far as a block away, but miraculously did not injure Palmer, who was reading near a front window of an upstairs bedroom and was showered with glass, or his wife, asleep in a rear bedroom.

Within minutes an army of policemen, firemen, and federal agents were at the scene, according to historian Paul Avrich. At the same time, policemen and soldiers were placed at the homes of other officials in possible danger, including Franklin D. Roosevelt, then assistant secretary of the Navy, who lived in Palmer's exclusive neighborhood.

While searching the scene around Palmer's house, police made a remarkable discovery: The bomb had blown to bits the man who had planted it. Police believed that the bomb exploded prematurely before it could be planted under the house. Fragments of the bomber's body were scattered all over the neighborhood. An intact Italian-English dictionary was also discovered near the Palmer house. While police never identified the dead bomber, Avrich concluded that the evidence pointed to Carlo Valdinoci, a dedicated follower of Galleani. Avrich also surmised that both Nicola Sacco and Bartolomeo Vanzetti, militant anarchists, were involved in the conspiracy.

At each bomb site—Boston, Washington, New York, Cleveland, Philadelphia, Pittsburgh, and Paterson, New Jersey—police also found leaflets, printed on pink paper, bearing the title *Plain Words* and signed by "The Anarchist Fighters." The leaflet, in style and content, resembled the *Go-Head!* flyer that police had found near the Boston waterfront at the time of the molasses disaster. The message of the text was indeed plain enough: "There will have to be bloodshed; we will not dodge; there will have to be murder; we will kill, because it is necessary; there will have to be destruction; we shall not rest until your downfall is complete and the laboring masses have taken possession of all that rightfully belongs to them . . . Long live social revolution! Down with tyranny."

In Boston, Judge Hayden was defiant, acknowledging that he was targeted because of the stern sentences he imposed on the May Day rioters, and his harsh anti-anarchist comments in the courtroom. "I cannot be intimidated," he said the morning after the explosion destroyed his home. "It was not done to intimidate me, but to intimidate the whole community. We have got to defeat the Bolshevists; we have got to deport them. They should not be allowed in this country. They should all be deported at once. I do not believe they know what they want. It is force, force, force. That's all they want."

True to his word, Hayden was not intimidated. When police arrested a Russian anarchist, Ernest Graudat, and charged him with being one of the bombers of the judge's Roxbury home, Hayden presided over Graudat's arraignment.

✢✢✢

The brazen nature of the June 2 bombings sent another wave of fear and anger rippling across the country, particularly after the Secret Service announced that they believed the same group of anarchists had sent the May Day bombs through the mail. "These obviously coordinated explosions, their shocking, outrageous character, the bloodthirsty language of the leaflets, fueled passions that had been building for months and gave powerful impetus to the unfolding Red Scare," noted Paul Avrich.

Nor did federal spokesmen allay the panic. The Department of Justice declared the bombings to be part of an organized, nationwide conspiracy to overthrow the American government. Further explosions were predicted. A campaign had been launched, as one official put it, to start a "reign of terror in the United States." Attorney General Palmer said those, "who can not or will not live the life of Americans under our institutions ... should go back to the countries from which they came." The day after the bombings, he said: "The outrages of last night ... will only increase and extend the activities of our crime detecting forces. We are determined now, as heretofore, that organized crime directed against organized government in this country shall be stopped."

Palmer wasted little time. He beefed up the Justice Department, especially the Bureau of Investigation, whose General Intelligence Division was supervised by J. Edgar Hoover. This set the scene for the notorious "Palmer raids" during the fall of 1919 and winter of 1920, in which more than three thousand aliens would undergo deportation proceedings, and eight hundred, including many anarchists, would be evicted from the country.

Most Americans supported Palmer's actions, but many abuses oc-curred. "Arrests were made without warrant, men were beaten with-out provocation," said Avrich. "The raids were carried out with utter indifference to legality. Thousands of aliens were taken into custody and subjected to brutal treatment." But a law journal cited the more popular view that national safety was the priority: "There is only one way to deal with anarchy and that is to crush it, not with a slap on the wrist, but a broad-axe on the neck."

Bostonians, for the most part, shared the majority view, especially when Boston Police announced that the city was the nation's "Bolshe-vist headquarters" and that some of the Boston Anarchists were in-volved in the June 2 explosions in other cities. "I would ask every citizen—man, woman, and child—to be mindful of his duty and to re-port anything of a suspicious nature that he might discover," Police Superintendent Michael Crowley requested. "Secret meetings in any part of the city must be watched closely, and information regarding such gatherings should be communicated to police."

As the summer of 1919 approached, the terror and suspicion that gripped the nation was felt most acutely in Boston, where residents believed that anarchists had burrowed deep into the fabric of their city, and worse, that they were capable of anything.

July 7, 1919, Washington, D.C.

Lt. Col. Hugh Walker Ogden sat in the prestigious Cosmos Club lounge, his pen poised above a sheet of the club's stationery. The club was located on Lafayette Square, the social headquarters for Washing-ton's intellectual elite, in the former Dolly Madison House, named af-ter the wife of the fourth president. It had a shabby elegance, and a comfortable charm, and it suited Ogden well.

He had a simple note to write to his friend Horace Lippincott at the University of Pennsylvania, but the occasion had him reviewing his past and pondering his future. He had spent the last two years preaching and instilling discipline—into soldiers at the front, into the Rainbow Division's command structure, and for the last two months, into the Army's court-martial procedures as part of a review committee appointed by the secretary of war. The committee had just recommended that court-martial procedures remain stringent, despite criticism that penalties handed out during the European war were often too harsh for the crimes that soldiers committed. He and his two colleagues, both major generals, believed that relaxed court-martial standards would lead to a breakdown in overall discipline, morale, and battlefield unity.

Now, days after the commission had issued its report and three weeks before his discharge and his return to private practice in Boston, Ogden believed discipline in civilian life was crumbling. The country was in turmoil, its fundamental values being battered by anarchists, labor unionists, and other radicals. The sense of order he had relished as a soldier, the order he *craved*, had given way to a frightening chaos across America.

He had been in Washington during the bombing of Attorney General Palmer's house and had read about the damage to Judge Hayden's home in Boston. It angered him that two sentinels of law and order could come so close to death, without provocation, simply by virtue of their positions. He had been anxious for months to return to civilian life and make a fundamental difference as a lawyer, make a contribution that extended beyond mundane corporate work and encompassed some of the moral *nobility* of his military service; today, in a country whose moral compass appeared to be broken, it appeared that his commitment was needed more desperately than ever.

Ogden's review of his recent past was not without a sense of satisfaction. He had just been awarded the Distinguished Service Medal for "exceptionally meritorious services" as judge advocate with the Rainbow Division. "He rendered valuable services and exhibited ability of a high order throughout the operations of the division," the citation read. "Later assigned to the Bureau of Civil Affairs for the Third Army, he performed his task with marked success."

As a Distinguished Service Medal recipient, he was in good company. The medal was confirmed by an Act of Congress in July 1918, and awarded to those who distinguished themselves with outstanding service "in a duty of great responsibility" in a combat or noncombat role. At the direction of the president of the United States, the first recipients of the medal were the commander of the Allied armies, including General John J. "Blackjack" Pershing, "as a token of gratitude of the American people to the commander of our armies in the field."

Ogden thought the news of his Distinguished Service Medal award was worth sharing with Lippincott and the University of Pennsylvania community. "The enclosed War Department order just published containing the citation for my DSM may be of interest to my friends," he wrote simply on Cosmos Club stationery, no embellishment or other comment needed.

Ogden loved soldiering, loved serving his country, and he felt that it was his duty to set a good example. He believed he had accomplished this during his service in France and Germany, and with the work he had done in Washington, D.C. The Distinguished Service Medal seemed to him fitting confirmation of and recognition for his contributions, and an appropriate way to close an important and rewarding chapter in his life.

Ogden sealed the envelope to Lippincott and headed for the door of the Cosmos Club. It was time to go home to Boston, to a city and a nation that he no longer recognized, and begin the next chapter.

August 1919

United States Industrial Alcohol reported to authorities in mid-August that two of its molasses steamers had vanished without a trace —and without any distress calls—en route from the Caribbean to the northeast. Both steamers had full loads, and USIA assumed both had sunk to the bottom of the ocean. The disappearances were bizarre and unprecedented.

Though it was never proven, the company blamed the disappearance of both vessels on anarchists. USIA executives said that only the sudden and powerful explosion of bombs could have obliterated any evidence of the ships and prevented either captain from issuing a call for help.

USIA said the destruction of its ships was a continuation of the attacks against the company by anarchists, attacks that had begun with the bombing of its Boston molasses tank seven months earlier.

September 1919

September would be the darkest month of all.

It had been eight months since the molasses flood had ushered in a year of turmoil: a year when labor battled business; when the cost of living rose and workers demanded that their wages rise, too; when anarchists preached and practiced violence in the name of justice; when xenophobia exploded and isolationist declarations boomed through the halls of Congress.

A torrid and turbulent summer in Boston had provided a preview of a bleak September. Even as record heat and humidity smothered the city, tensions smoldered among the workers and the general public.

In late June, anarchist leader Luigi Galleani was deported to Italy as scheduled, along with eight associates. The anarchist leader had escaped arrest when federal agents, after questioning the men, were unable to prove their suspicions that Galleani had orchestrated the June bombings.

On July 4, five thousand New England fishermen began a job stoppage that would last more than a month, tying up shipping and driving the price of fish skyward. Then in mid-July, a storm of protest greeted Boston Elevated's announcement that fares would increase to ten cents. Two days later, the trains and streetcars stopped running when more than seven thousand members of the Carmen's Union went on strike for four days until their demands for an eight-hour day and payment of seventy-three cents per hour were met.

Nationally, rail workers threatened to strike in August and paralyze the nation's transportation system unless Congress took actions to deal with the high cost of living and increase wages. President Wilson asked Congress to defer its planned five-week summer recess to consider the demands and hammer out legislation to avert a nationwide rail shutdown.

The widespread summer storminess set the stage for September, which started on a hopeful enough note. President Wilson left Washington, D.C., on September 4 for a thirty-city, twenty-five-day, eight-thousand-mile tour of Midwestern and Western states to generate support for the Treaty of Versailles and the League of Nations, a journey described as "longer than (his trip) to France and back and more strenuous."

But the country's brief optimism and promise over Wilson's commitment to peace were dashed on September 9, when the national spotlight focused on Boston once again.

Nearly 1,400 Boston police officers went on strike after the 5:45

P.M. roll call, angry that their wage demands had not been met. That night, riots broke out across the city, and mobs smashed windows, looted more than fifty stores, and threw stones at striking police officers. "Wave of crime sweeps city," the *Boston Herald*'s headlines shouted the next day. During a second night of rioting, three men were killed and another fifteen injured. In all, eight people died in the strike, seventy-five were injured or wounded, and an estimated $300,000 worth of property was stolen or destroyed. Mayor Peters called in the State Guard to restore order in downtown Boston and surrounding neighborhoods.

The unprecedented strike of public safety officers shocked the nation and drew angry denunciations. Massachusetts governor Calvin Coolidge flayed the striking policemen, calling their actions a "deliberate intention to intimidate and coerce the government of this Commonwealth ... No man has a right to place his own ease or convenience or the opportunity of making money above his duty to the state." Supporting the use of troops to restore order, The *Boston Herald* added in a blistering editorial: "The police of Boston, having mutinied, stood by and saw the hoodlums loot the city, in some instances abetting the violence and disorder ..." Speaking in Montana on September 11, an outraged President Wilson said that for the policemen of a great city to go on strike, "leaving the city at the mercy of thugs, was a *crime against civilization.* The obligation of a policeman was as sacred and direct as the obligation of a soldier."

Unsurprisingly, in sharp contrast to Coolidge and Wilson, AF of L President Samuel Gompers told a Congressional committee that the Boston police strike benefited police across the country, "because it has moved city officials everywhere to devise plans for better pay for members of police forces."

The Boston police walk-out acted as a catalyst for steelworkers, who, on September 20, declared strikes against the major steel companies. More than three hundred thousand workers in Pittsburgh, Chicago, Cleveland, and Youngstown, Ohio—demanding higher wages, shorter hours, and better working conditions—struck against Carnegie, Bethlehem, and U.S. Steel. Workers were looking to abolish the grueling twelve-hour workday, and improve what they saw as dangerous safety conditions in the mills and squalid living conditions in company-controlled steel towns. Riots marked the opening days of the strike, as workers threw bricks and rocks at state police, local officers, and replacement workers brought in by the companies. One striker was killed and seven wounded on the first day of striking when guards in Newcastle, Pennsylvania, fired into a mob of rioters who attacked nonstriking workers attempting to get into the mill.

The steel strike would last for months, pitting powerful men like Elbert H. Gary, the chairman of U.S. Steel, against John Fitzpatrick, chairman of the Conference Committee of twenty-four steel unions. In a fiery speech in October to the Illinois Federation of Labor, Fitzpatrick declared: "Out of this strike is going to come a consciousness on the part of the workers that they are a real force and factor in this industry ... that even if the United States Steel Corporation can set itself up as bigger than the United States Government, there is still a greater power here, and that power rests with the workers themselves ..."

But the companies held firm against worker demands, broke the strike, and effectively ended significant union influence in the steel industry until the mid-1930s.

✤ ✤ ✤

With the Boston Police and steel strikes dominating headlines across the country, President Wilson continued stumping for the League of Nations in the western United States, even as he communicated with his cabinet about the worsening labor situation. The stress of trying to accomplish both tasks proved too much. After thirty-seven major speeches in twenty-two days, he was suffering from severe headaches. At 2 A.M., on the night of September 25, he was found sitting motionless in the drawing room compartment of his private railway carriage outside of Pueblo, Colorado, "ashen and drooling slightly from the left side of his mouth."

The president had suffered a nervous collapse from sheer exhaustion. He canceled the remainder of his speaking tour and his train sped back to Washington, where his physician ordered "absolute rest."

On October 2, Wilson suffered a massive stroke from which he would never fully recover, and was incapacitated for the next seven months. His illness would be the beginning of the end of America's involvement in the League of Nations, which the Senate would ultimately reject, and delay America's further participation in world politics. Undoubtedly, it was also the end of Wilson's plans to run for a third term, leading to an overwhelming victory for Republican Warren G. Harding in the 1920 election.

❖ ❖ ❖

One other incident occurred in September 1919 that received little notice in the press, its overall impact dwarfed by events that were tearing at the country's fabric.

On the night of September 14 and the morning of September 15, fire roared through United States Industrial Alcohol's Brooklyn manufacturing plant. No one was injured, but the processing facility, where molasses was distilled into alcohol, was destroyed. Flames also consumed the five steel molasses storage tanks on the site, badly charring the outside walls. Though the tanks' rivets held strong and molasses did not escape, USIA's factory was so badly damaged that the company shut down its Brooklyn operations.

Millard Fillmore Cook, Jr., the superintendent of the plant since 1912, the man in charge when police found a bomb on the premises in June 1916, was transferred to supervise USIA's plant in Peoria, Illinois.

USIA's internal investigation later showed that the fire was set by someone using an "incendiary device." It was clear evidence, the company claimed, that anarchists had attacked USIA yet again in 1919, a pattern that had begun with the destruction of the Boston molasses tank in January.

Police never apprehended anyone for the Brooklyn fire.

December 1919

On December 1, USIA shut down its manufacturing facility in East Cambridge, Massachusetts, nearly four years after the Commercial Street tank was built and eleven months after the molasses catastrophe changed everything.

The company fired nearly all of the 125 people who worked at the plant.

Arthur P. Jell was transferred to New York City headquarters, where he became assistant treasurer and vice president of USIA.

December 11, 1919

Stephen Clougherty died in the late morning at the Boston State Hospital for the insane in Mattapan, a troubled and frightened man who finally surrendered to the demons that had tortured him every day since rescuers pulled him from the molasses.

His brother, Martin, thought Stephen's death was a blessing. Martin had visited Stephen twice a week for most of his confinement in the asylum, and every day since the thirty-two-year-old retarded man had been placed on the danger list. Each time Martin visited, he found that Stephen had deteriorated both physically and mentally. Stephen had started out nervous, agitated, and prone to hallucinations. Then he contracted tuberculosis, which doctors attributed to his overall weakened condition. It appeared that Stephen had neither the strength nor the will to fight off the disease.

From that point, Martin witnessed his brother's rapid decline with anger and sadness. Stephen was a man in age and physical appearance only; he had been no more than a boy, really. He had been a good-natured sort, friendly, smiling, almost docile, willing to do simple chores and taking life as it came day by day. But the molasses had killed him, as sure as if it had smothered him on January 15. Martin found himself again enraged by the disaster, but whose fault was the tank's collapse? Who was responsible for killing his mother, and now, his brother? He had had such big plans for them, and for himself, plans to leave the city, to move out from under the shadow of the overhead rail tracks, and into a clean and quiet suburban neighborhood. Now those dreams were shattered.

Near the end, his brother, Stephen, alternated between quiet sobs and utter silence, a husk of a man, catatonic much of the time. He died without making a sound.

His was the twenty-first and final death attributed to the Boston molasses flood.

December 21, 1919

Four days before Christmas, at 5 A.M., the *Buford* set sail from New York harbor for Russia, carrying 249 deportees, including renowned anarchists Emma Goldman and Alexander Berkman. J. Edgar Hoover, who was a special assistant to Attorney General Palmer, watched the ship pull away. Hoover had strongly advocated the Goldman and Berkman deportations, branding them as "beyond doubt, two of the most dangerous anarchists in this country." The *Cleveland Plain Dealer* echoed the feelings of the vast majority of the general public: "It is to be hoped and expected that other vessels, larger, more commodious, carrying similar cargoes, will follow in her wake." With the deportations of Luigi Galleani in June, and now Goldman and Berkman, the Justice Department had succeeded in expelling three of the most influential anarchists from the United States during 1919.

The year's economic deterioration, unprecedented labor union militancy, and increasingly daring and violent anarchist attacks rocked postwar America, sowed fear across the land, and fueled hatred toward so-called Bolshevist agitators and foreigners, whom many Americans blamed for the mayhem and chaos.

United States Industrial Alcohol would rely on these twin emotions of fear and hatred as the foundation of its defense when one of the largest civil lawsuits in the nation's history began in 1920. The suit would finally determine who was to blame for the Boston molasses flood, a tragedy that had killed twenty-one people, injured 150 others, destroyed property, and foretold a year of turbulence and disruption.

USIA had escaped criminal prosecution when the grand jury declined to indict any of its executives for manslaughter.

But the victims and their families still demanded justice.

PART III

David vs. Goliath

Colonel Hugh W. Ogden, Boston's "soldier-lawyer," ruled against United States Industrial Alcohol, finding the company liable for the molasses disaster.

(From the Collections of the University of Pennsylvania Archives)

"ONE OF THE WORST CATASTROPHES"

Boston, Monday, August 9, 1920

It was midafternoon of the hottest day of the year, and waves of heat shimmied like dancing specters off Boston's baked downtown streets. Sweating beneath his stiff, high collar, Hugh W. Ogden toiled in his 75 Federal Street office, high above the city, putting his business affairs in order. Through the open window, Ogden saw veins of lightning crackle across a purple-black sky to the north, heard the low rumble of summer thunder miles away, and smelled fresh rain mixed with sea salt on the warm wind that blew in from the harbor.

For the last three days, the weather pattern had been the same. Sweltering mornings and early afternoons, then violent thunderstorms lashing the streets when the heat of the day reached its apex around 3 P.M. Yesterday, hailstones had damaged crops in communities far north of Boston, and lightning set ablaze several wood-frame buildings in nearby suburbs like Lynn and Somerville. Ten people had collapsed from the heat. One sea captain who had piloted a steamer from Costa Rica declared that Boston was hotter than the tropics.

Ogden was hoping for a break in the temperature tomorrow. He would begin presiding over hearings in the molasses flood case at Suffolk County Court House in downtown Boston, and the old building held the heat like a cauldron. Superior Court Judge Loranus Eaton Hitchcock had asked Ogden to serve as an "auditor," an impartial master who would hear evidence on liability, and possible damages, and issue a report on his findings. Depending on the nature of his report, the case could then move on to a full civil trial in front of a jury.

The court believed that, due to the complexity of the case, and the number of plaintiffs and potential witnesses, justice would be better served if a tough, fair-minded legal expert could first whittle down the essence of the arguments and find the nub of truth—or at least make it less cumbersome for a jury to arrive at its *own* truth. Ogden

163

had agreed to serve as auditor, for a nominal stipend, after Judge Hitchcock had assured him that he would only need to carve out about six weeks from his schedule to fulfill the responsibility. Today, he would finish organizing his affairs for the next month and a half and referring his regular caseload to colleagues he respected.

Private practice had been good to Ogden since he arrived back in Boston as a decorated veteran one year ago. He focused on equity and corporation law, and found that his talents were well-suited to working alone. He was bold, aggressive, shrewd, opinionated, intuitive, compassionate, unorthodox, and he often took the measure of a man's character before he took his case—a combination of contradictions that would leave him unfulfilled at a large law firm, where making money was the number one priority. Ogden liked making money as much as anyone, but he would never take a case *just* for money. In fact, he often took cases *pro bono*; the factors that mattered most to him were the quality of the individual he was representing, the merits of his client's case, and his ability to help his client achieve justice. He loved private practice, and many of his clients had become his friends.

For a year, he had looked for a way to do more, to go beyond the *pro bono* work, beyond his contributions as a member of the Boston Chamber of Commerce and the ecclesiastical work he did for the Episcopal Church, and to find an honorable way to share his talents for a greater cause.

So when Judge Hitchcock had called, Hugh Ogden had answered. If he could help find the truth in the molasses case, six weeks of his time would be no sacrifice at all.

�֍ ✦ ✖

Ogden had never been part of, let alone presided over, a case so massive—but then again, almost no one had. The Boston legal community was abuzz about the Superior Court's decision to consolidate the 119 separate legal claims against United States Industrial Alcohol into a single legal proceeding, creating in effect, if not by strict legal definition, the largest class-action suit to date in Massachusetts history and one of the largest ever in U.S. legal annals.

The Superior Court had decided to consolidate the cases during the preliminary filing stage, at the request of U.S. Industrial Alcohol.

USIA had argued that the plaintiffs' claims were similar, and, more practically, the courtroom simply wasn't large enough to hold all the lawyers. More than 125 attorneys had crammed the courthouse, and many of Boston's finest legal minds had been part of the overflow that spilled and shuffled into the hallway. The rest could barely move without bumping into each other. The comical scene symbolized the complexity of the case and the difficulty of trying them all individually. During a trial, there would have been no room for the lawyers, let alone witnesses, stenographers, and members of the press and public. USIA had recommended that the cases be consolidated and that two lead lawyers be appointed to represent each party; the court had agreed.

Ogden believed that the consolidation made sense, but he also suspected that USIA had another motive for requesting the unprecedented co-joining action. If the company's lawyers could successfully discredit just one witness or refute one piece of documentary evidence, the defense could undermine all the plaintiffs' claims, and their cases against USIA would tumble like a house of cards. Had the cases remained severed, one "poisoned" plaintiff witness would not taint the other claims.

The basic arguments for USIA and the plaintiffs could be simply stated, though Ogden knew this fact alone would not necessarily ensure a swift proceeding. The plaintiffs would claim that the molasses tank had been structurally deficient, built without safeguards, and carelessly located in a busy, congested neighborhood. They would seek financial damages for the victims' families and for property owners. USIA would argue in defense that anarchists operating in Boston during the time of the disaster had dropped a bomb inside the tank just after noon on January 15, 1919, and the resulting explosion had destroyed the tank and caused the deaths, injuries, and property destruction. The company would also argue that the North End waterfront area, on the periphery of the neighborhood, had been used for years for commercial purposes.

If USIA could prove its case, the company almost certainly would be absolved of any legal liability. Ogden had already heard that USIA was spending more than $50,000 on expert witnesses to buttress its case—including scientists, metallurgists, academics, and explosion experts.

The anarchist argument intrigued Ogden, since he believed that it was plausible; whether it was provable was another question. The year 1919 had been the most chaotic and violent one he could remember. And while things had calmed somewhat in the early months of 1920, the spring had brought more disturbing events.

In early March, an anarchist named Andrea Salsedo, whom authorities believed was one of the key Galleanists behind the rash of bombings in June 1919, was arrested, and held in custody for two months while government agents questioned him. There had been rumors that Salsedo had cooperated with authorities and furnished the names of other prominent anarchists, but these had never been confirmed. Incredibly, when agents left him alone for a few moments in early May, Salsedo apparently jumped to his death from a fourteenth-story window. His fellow anarchists had protested loudly that Salsedo had first been beaten for information, and, after he had divulged all he knew, had then been hurled from the window, a claim that had never been proved and that Ogden found impossible to believe.

On April 15, two employees of the Slater and Morrill Shoe Company were shot dead and robbed of the company's payroll in South Braintree, Massachusetts. Two men armed with handguns did the shooting, and the killers were picked up by colleagues in a getaway car, escaping with more than $15,000. On May 5, police arrested two avowed anarchists for the murders, Nicola Sacco and Bartolomeo Vanzetti. The pair gave false or evasive answers about their political beliefs and their whereabouts at the time of the murder, though both later protested strenuously that they believed they had been arrested for deportation purposes and had no inkling of the seriousness of the charges against them. Sacco and Vanzetti were now awaiting trial for the South Braintree murders. Vanzetti alone was also indicted, and later tried and convicted, for a Christmas Eve 1919 hold-up in Bridgewater, Massachusetts, and he was scheduled to be sentenced for *that* crime in about a week.

Ogden had the unsettling feeling that the controversial Salsedo suicide, coupled with the Sacco and Vanzetti arrests, could set the anarchists in motion once again.

If it did, the uproar would provide timely energy to USIA's argument that anarchists had destroyed the Boston molasses tank in 1919. But Ogden knew that the court had asked him to preside over the molasses case precisely because he would not get caught up in any uproar. He would issue his report based strictly on the evidence in this case.

Any new anarchist activities, if they did occur, might infuse *energy* into USIA's case. But *evidence* was something altogether different.

Now that there were only two small teams of attorneys working the case, Ogden's courtroom would be sufficiently large to house them. Whether it would be big enough to contain their egos was still open to debate.

Ogden knew both lead attorneys—Damon Everett Hall for the plaintiffs and Charles Francis Choate for the defense—and thought it would be much more entertaining to be a third-party observer rather than the jurist caught in the crossfire between two of the most brilliant, powerful, resourceful, sharp-witted, and indefatigable lawyers in the state. Both were wealthy men whose lineages ran deep, whose ancestors arrived on American soil years before the Revolution. Both were men who believed they were *entitled*, that winning was practically a birthright.

Ogden liked Hall better as a man. Choate may have been the more intellectual barrister, but Ogden thought that his fellow Harvard Law School graduate's aristocratic gentility often camouflaged a condescending air of superiority. Hall, a graduate of Boston University, was no less astute than Choate, but enjoyed a good legal street fight at the same time. He had a tough streak, an edge, a poker player's willingness to take risks, even a sense of sarcasm in the courtroom that Ogden found appealing. Hall and Choate were both men of means, both well-respected attorneys, both scions of Boston's oldest money, but Hall seemed more comfortable with average men, a trait Ogden believed he himself shared with the plaintiffs' lawyer. Choate was diligent and honest enough, but also facile, bombastic, and often reluctant to get his hands dirty, traits Ogden found distasteful. The two men had chosen sides well in this case; it strained Ogden's imagination to envision Choate representing poor Italian immigrants and

Irish city workers in their fight against a major national corporation. Conversely, Hall would relish the task, viewing himself as a guardian of the common man's rights.

None of this would matter tomorrow, of course. Once Ogden set foot in the courtroom and ascended to the bench, he would subjugate his personal feelings about both men, and rely on the rule of law and his own strength of judgment and fairness.

Ogden finished his work and prepared to leave the office, which for at least the next six weeks, would no longer be his regular workplace. He might stop in occasionally after the molasses hearings had concluded for the day, but he expected the testimony to consume most of his time. He had even informed Hall and Choate that he was willing to continue the hearings until 10 P.M. any time it was necessary, to give laborers a chance to testify without jeopardizing a day's pay, or worse, their jobs. Both lawyers had grumbled before grudgingly conceding Ogden's point and agreeing to the unusual schedule.

The lightning flashed in the northern sky and the thunder rumbled closer. Ogden hoped for a torrential late-afternoon rainstorm to cool the city.

❖-❖-❖

One other prominent Boston attorney would play a role in how history would mark the molasses case. Dudley H. Dorr, owner of two Commercial Street buildings destroyed by the flood, became trustee for the consolidated cases brought by the plaintiffs. On July 1, 1918, Dorr had joined forces with Boston attorney Richard Hale to form Hale & Dorr, which would one day become Boston's largest and most prestigious law firm. For now, Dorr's participation in the biggest civil suit in Massachusetts history—the Great Boston Molasses Flood case —meant that the court proceedings were officially catalogued as *Dorr v. United States Industrial Alcohol.*

August 10–September 8, 1920

"This was one of the worst catastrophes which has visited the City of Boston in my remembrance," declared attorney Damon Hall in his opening statement for the plaintiffs. "We have all been accustomed to make fun of cold molasses, but this experience, which occurred in the heart of Boston at noon in January, 1919, taught us that cold molasses has death-dealing and destructive powers equal to the tornado or the cyclone when it is suddenly unloosed."

Hall's statement came on Wednesday, August 11, the second day of the hearings; day one was a succession of scheduling and procedural details that needed to be ironed out at the outset of any major trial or hearing. The lengthiest haggling had come during discussion of the court's start time. On Monday mornings, Damon Hall's train arrived in Boston from his suburban Belmont home just before 11 A.M., and his colleague, Endicott Peabody Saltonstall, arrived at 10:30 A.M. Thus, Ogden agreed that Monday proceedings would begin at 11 A.M. Since all the lawyers would stay in Boston overnight during the week, Ogden ordered court to begin at 9:30 A.M. Tuesday through Friday. "I feel a little pressure to get started and moving on this case," Ogden told the attorneys. Henry Dolan, one of USIA's lawyers, urged Ogden not to hold hearings on Saturdays. Ogden agreed reluctantly: "These gentlemen who have families at the shore, I think would go on strike if we tried to sit on Saturday," the auditor lamented.

After the procedural issues had been decided on Tuesday, Ogden adjourned the session, and Hall began his opening statement first thing on Wednesday. Hall was not a large man, but he commanded attention in the courtroom.

"Now I have no doubt that your Honor had occasion to see many of the devastated areas of France," Hall said to Ogden. "If you take a little section of one of those devastated areas, and put in it dead men and dead horses, and then cover it with molasses, you get some idea of what this (scene) looked like a few minutes after this occurrence ... on January 15, 1919, shortly before one o'clock, a time when fortunately a good many people who otherwise would be using Commercial Street were at their lunch ... (this) giant reservoir constructed in the heart of a busy section, for the purpose of holding a heavy fluid, suddenly gave way, deluged the surrounding territory, took twenty-one lives, and did property damage amounting to hundreds of thousands of dollars."

Hall said he would not use his opening statement "to place my finger upon the negligence, or unlawfulness, or whatever you call it, which was responsible for this accident ... and I shall not, at this time, attempt in any way to advance any theories as to the cause of this accident." That, Hall declared, would become apparent during his questioning of witnesses and in his closing arguments. In his opening, he would "stick to the facts" to outline his case. But in Hall's skillful hands, the facts themselves carried more than a whiff of accusation.

"It is important for your Honor to know the size of this steel container," he said. "The height of the steel reservoir was fifty feet, but it is very difficult to appreciate figures on their own. But the height of the tank, from the surface of the foundation to the top of its roof, was fully twice the height of this courtroom. The elevated (railroad) structure is about thirty feet in height. So this tank towered above the elevated structure for twenty feet. The diameter of this steel reservoir was ninety feet, or a diameter equal, substantially, to *twice* the length of this courtroom. It was an enormous reservoir, built and intended to contain an enormous amount of molasses."

Hall painted a similar picture when he described the weight of the molasses in the tank. "When we speak of 2.3 million gallons of molasses, it is impossible for the mind to work readily to conceive what that means," he said, "and so I want to just use one or two illustrations to show the weight of molasses in that reservoir at the time this thing occurred. Two million, three-hundred thousand gallons of molasses is something over 26 million pounds ... thirteen thousand tons. One of our big Mogul locomotive engines weighs about a hundred tons. So that this steel reservoir contained on the day of the accident a weight of molasses equal to 130 hundred-ton locomotive engines ... or thirteen thousand Ford automobiles, which weigh about a ton each."

Hall described the suffering of the victims—the violent deaths of Bridget Clougherty, Maria Distasio, and Pasquale Iantosca; the valiant struggle of George Layhe before he succumbed under the firehouse; the pain-wracked torment of John Barry as he lay pinned a few feet from Layhe, awaiting rescuers. He listed the property that the molasses waves destroyed, including the elevated railroad, whose "enormous support pillars were doubled up as if they were willow trees" by the combined weight of the molasses and the steel pieces of the crushed tank. The molasses wave swept through the North End Playground, Hall said, "a place that was frequented in summer by thousands upon thousands of the dwellers of the North End; men, women, and children, particularly the women and the children who went to that playground to escape the heat of the city."

When Charles Choate interrupted Hall's opening by noting that the accident occurred in the dead of winter, Hall snapped back: "That is true, but you kept your tank there in July, as well as in January, and . . . there was coasting and skating on the North End Playground by the children of the city in the cold weather."

Hall implored Ogden to tour the North End site to get a genuine feel for the area, to see how the 2.3 million gallons of molasses "let loose . . . the tank folded back and fell and the molasses went in all directions . . . north, south, east, and west, demolishing structures as if they were houses of cards . . . flooding cellars and destroying goods. Men who were eating their noon-day lunch were overwhelmed and drowned . . . a woman and two children were crushed. That is a picture of what occurred that day . . . when a structure, erected in such a locality, designed to be used as this reservoir was used, when it suddenly gives way, carrying with it death and destruction . . ."

As he had promised, Damon Hall finished his opening statement without mentioning a cause or blaming anyone for the molasses flood—yet, in his colorful choice of words, the passion of his language, and the graphic flavor of his descriptions, he left no doubt whom he held responsible for the disaster.

✤✤✤

USIA's lead attorney, Charles Choate, would not begin his opening remarks for several weeks, until after Hall had called some preliminary witnesses to describe the scene of devastation on the waterfront after the giant tank let loose.

On August 16, 1920, a week after the molasses flood hearings had begun, while Hall was questioning witnesses in Boston, Bartolomeo Vanzetti was sentenced in a Plymouth courtroom for a December 24, 1919, hold-up in Bridgewater, Massachusetts. The anarchist was sentenced to twelve to fifteen years, "one day thereof solitary imprisonment and the residue of said term confinement of hard labor," although he had no previous criminal record and no one was hurt in the hold-up.

After the sentence, Vanzetti was sent to state prison to await trial with his fellow anarchist, Sacco, on the South Braintree murders.

Their anarchist comrades, who had been relatively quiet for most of the summer, began to stir again.

✳✳✳

On Thursday, September 2, Charles Choate took center stage in Hugh Ogden's courtroom to deliver opening remarks in what he believed was a winning strategy for USIA. It would take him most of the day, plus a second morning, Wednesday, September 8, when court resumed after the Labor Day holiday.

Choate got off to an inauspicious start when he arrived late, and before launching into the substance of his remarks, apologized to Ogden. "I know that your Honor's mind will be open to a fair consideration of the facts (although) your Honor's views have almost universally been opposed to mine," Choate said. Ogden replied that neither Choate's tardiness nor his differences with the auditor would have any bearing on the molasses case. "I sometimes think I have fatal facility for encountering men whose views are opposed to mine," he said. "I am not offended in the slightest."

Unlike Hall, Charles Choate's opening argument *did* provide a window into the heart of the defense's case. "What was there to have caused a tank containing a perfectly harmless substance, in common commercial use, to go down with every indication that its breaking was caused by some tremendous explosive force?" Choate asked. The tank was built "by reputable people, who were skillful in this kind of work ... it was carefully painted and kept in perfect condition ... there is no suggestion of a defect or deterioration in the tank which could account for the fracture in any way."

No, Choate argued, the molasses disaster was not due to any accident, or structural defect, and once those causes were eliminated, "your mind is drawn *irresistibly* to the conclusion that the tank could not have collapsed without the operation of some agency which, in an instant of time, multiplied the pressure on that outside shell hundreds or thousands of times."

Choate said USIA would show evidence of persons in the vicinity of the tank—"we can't pretend to name them"—whose activities included "dynamite outrages in this immediate community ... One was the explosion at Judge Hayden's house. Others were the placing of bombs in police stations and the stealing of dynamite from storehouses."

Choate reminded the court that anarchists had placed inflammatory posters along fences near the molasses tank, and that the "federal cordon was withdrawn" around the tank once the armistice was signed ending the Great War. "At the time of the accident no one connected with the defendant was on the premises," Choate argued. "There was a flight of steps that led to the top of the tank which was necessary to permit the gaugers of U.S. Customs to make their measurements and keep their records . . . it was an easy thing for a person to go up those stairs, get onto the top of the tank, and drop down an explosive device through one of the four manholes."

Choate said the defense would present evidence that USIA was involved "almost exclusively in the production of alcohol for making munitions" during the war, "and that fact was well known to the general public and evilly disposed persons alike."

Choate then offered a glimpse of the company's "expert witness" defense, revealing that USIA had hired metallurgists to conduct an experiment with a "replica tank" filled with molasses. "They used dynamite ignited by a fuse of the kind I have described, dropped it to the bottom, and that experiment disclosed fractures and ruptures and twisting and bulging of the plate that exactly agrees with what occurred here," Choate said. "This study was conducted by scientific men of high repute . . . and shows, as conclusively as circumstantial evidence can show, the cause that produced this catastrophe."

Much of the damage around the tank, Choate argued, was caused not by the flow of molasses but by the concussion of a dynamite explosion. "It was sufficient to break glass at a considerable distance, to throw and shatter all kinds of wooden and metal objects, to rend and shatter them into kindling wood, to spatter—and I used that word with a purpose—to *spatter* molasses to the places where the wave of molasses never reached at all . . . the appearance of things about the tank point to the action of an explosive, and could only attend the action of an explosive."

Apparently concerned that Ogden would not be fully aware of what was at stake for USIA in the case, Choate stressed its importance: "There has seldom been a case tried in this County . . . that involved more important issues of law, or involved a larger sum of money than in the aggregate is involved here, because the damages that are claimed by these plaintiffs run into many hundreds of thousands of dollars."

Why would they be entitled to anything, Choate argued, when it was clear that "for a person who had an evil purpose, and the opportunity to reach the top of the tank . . . it would have required no more than five pounds of dynamite—probably less—to have accomplished everything that happened there? And that dynamite could have been carried—as it has been carried scores of times when these outrages have occurred here in this community at about this time—in a pipe of comparatively short length, not over a foot long and not over three inches in diameter."

With certainty and righteousness ringing in his words, Choate concluded: "There was some explosive agent introduced into that tank which so increased the pressure by its explosion that the rupture was due to that—and not to the static pressure of the molasses itself."

✢ ✢ ✢

Damon Hall and Charles Choate had drawn the battle lines with passion and precision in Hugh Ogden's courtroom. The civil suit would determine who, if anyone, was responsible for the terrible disaster on Commercial Street in January 1919, and what should be done about it. Most of those who had been killed were the breadwinners for their wives and children, families who were now struggling to survive. Many of the injured had been out of work for months and now had little or no means of support. Some would never return to work.

A victory for Hall and the plaintiffs, if they could prove that the tank collapsed due to USIA's negligence, would provide some financial relief for these people, even if lives could not be restored or injured bodies made whole. But if Charles Choate and his team could convince Ogden that the climate of unrest and violence in Boston and America in 1919 had incited anarchists to destroy the tank with dynamite, the victims of the molasses flood would likely wind up with nothing.

New York City, September 16, 1920

Charles Francis Choate was a brilliant and respected member of the Massachusetts legal community, a professional and a gentleman, a man about whom a colleague would one day say, "there was, there is, no better, braver, stronger man." Such a man, a lover of the law, would be angered by the use of violence as a means to achieve results, would be appalled if innocent people were injured or killed because of that violence.

But in the places none of us like to visit—the darkest corners of the mind, the coldest reaches of the heart—Charles F. Choate must have felt a sense of perverse satisfaction when he received word on the afternoon of September 16 that someone, most likely an anarchist, had detonated a deadly bomb on Wall Street in New York City. As awful as the noontime explosion had been, killing nearly forty innocent people, the tragic event instantly enhanced the credibility of the opening argument Choate had delivered just days earlier, *affirmed* his circumstantial thesis, offered a timely and deadly reminder that violence was still a way of life for anarchists.

The Wall Street bombing was the most deadly anarchist action in America. In addition to the dead, more than two hundred people were injured, and property damage exceeded $2 million. The blast originated on the north side of Wall Street in front of the Subtreasury building and the U.S. Assay Office, directly across the street from the banking house of J.P. Morgan and an excavation where the New York Stock Exchange was building an annex. It was lunch hour, and an endless stream of office workers had just started pouring into the streets from buildings in the neighborhood.

"Suddenly, a cloud of yellowish, black smoke and a piercing jet of flame leaped from the street outside the Morgan offices," reported the Associated Press. "Then came a deafening blast. A moment later, scores of men, women, and children were lying prostrate on the ground and the streets were covered with debris from thousands of broken windows and torn facades of adjacent buildings. Ten minutes later, the stock and curb exchanges, the financial pulse of the world, had closed. Panic and confusion reigned in the heart of New York's financial district."

Thousands of office workers fled in terror from adjoining buildings; scores fell and were trampled in the rush. The noise of the explosion had been heard throughout lower Manhattan and across the river in Brooklyn, "and brought thousands of the curious to the scene." Downtown hospitals went on full alert, and makeshift medical stations were set up in the lobbies of nearby buildings, where nurses and doctors treated the less seriously injured. The few police on duty in the district were unable to cope with the crowds and downtown police stations were notified to send additional men. Subtreasury officials, fearing looters might try to rob the building—which the blast had seriously damaged—requested the assistance of military authorities at Governor's Island, and officials dispatched a company of troops to guard the building.

Overnight, authorities launched a widespread investigation extending into every section of the country. Attorney General A. Mitchell Palmer called the blast "part of a gigantic plot" to overthrow the capitalist system. Extra guards were placed at all government buildings in Washington, D.C. William J. Flynn, chief of the Bureau of Investigation, went to New York the next day to oversee the investigation. He told the press that his agents had collected convincing evidence that the bombing was planned by a group of anarchists who perpetrated the "bomb outrages" of June 1919. The motive, Flynn believed, was revenge for the prosecution of Sacco and Vanzetti, and for Salsedo's death earlier in the year, which anarchists still insisted was not a suicide.

Among the evidence Flynn cited were several circulars found by a letter carrier in a mailbox on the corner of Cedar Street and Broadway, a few blocks from the scene, with the following message printed in red ink:

Remember.
We will not tolerate.
Any longer.
Free the political prisoners
Or it will be sure death
For all of you.

AMERICAN ANARCHIST
FIGHTERS

The signature, combining those of *Go-head!* ("The American Anarchists") and *Plain Words* ("The Anarchist Fighters"), convinced Flynn —most likely correctly—that Galleanists had been behind the Wall Street bombing. Later, Flynn announced that the anarchists had left the bomb in a horse-drawn wagon that they had hitched to a pole on Wall Street, "with the timing device set a few minutes ahead." Three minutes later the bomb exploded. The horse and wagon were blown to bits.

A massive manhunt ensued. Detectives and federal agents visited nearly five thousand stables along the Eastern seaboard in a vain effort to trace the horse, according to historian Paul Avrich. Police did find the maker of the horseshoes, a blacksmith in Manhattan's Little Italy section, "who recalled that the day before the explosion a (Sicilian) man had driven such a horse and wagon into his shop and had a new pair of shoes nailed to the hooves."

Though the bomber was never found, Avrich has surmised that the Wall Street explosion was the work of Galleanist anarchist Mario Buda, a close comrade of Sacco and Vanzetti—"the best friends I had in America"—who believed he was retaliating against America's financial power structure in retaliation for the September 11 murder indictments of his friends for the South Braintree killings. "The victims of the blast," Avrich noted, "far from being the financial powers of the country, were mostly runners, stenographers, and clerks. Buda was surely aware that innocent blood might be spilled. He was a man, however, who stopped at nothing."

Avrich traced Buda's movements from New York to Providence, where the anarchist secured a passport from the Italian vice-consul, and a few weeks later sailed back to Italy. By the end of November, he was back in his native Romagna, "never again to return to the United States."

Several days after the Wall Street bombing, Boston mayor Andrew Peters received a threatening letter, mailed from New York, accusing him of having the "blackest and yellowest" government in the country and warning him that he was being watched, and that a "better job" would be done in Boston than was done in New York. The letter was signed "The Reds." Peters turned the letter over to police, but said he intended to take no special precautions to protect himself.

However, in Boston's financial district, Secret Service agents guarded federal buildings, including the subtreasury, the post office, the Federal Reserve bank, and the Internal Revenue offices. "The financial section of Boston is plentifully supplied with plainclothesmen and a large number of uniformed men are patrolling the streets of that district as a precautionary measure against attempted repetition of the New York bomb outrage here," the *Boston Herald* reported. Police officials gave orders for officers to act against "loiterers or suspicious looking persons or vehicles," and to examine any vehicle, "motor drawn or horse drawn that may have a suspicious aspect." Guards were also placed around the perimeter of the Massachusetts State House on Beacon Hill.

Once again, Boston was a city on alert, this time against an enemy that was difficult to identify and one that could strike from almost anywhere, at anytime.

✲✲✲

There is no mention in the historical record of whether extra guards were placed around Boston's courthouses. But in Hugh Ogden's courtroom, the Wall Street bombing, just five weeks into the molasses hearings, could not have failed to create an impression among all parties.

Neither Hall, Choate, nor Ogden referred to the New York City tragedy specifically in open court, but each must have pondered one question in connection with the molasses case, from vastly different perspectives—Hall with distress, Choate with the moral outrage of one who is pained to be right about man's capacity for evil, and Ogden with the quizzical conjecture of all good arbiters:

If anarchists could explode a bomb at high noon in the heart of New York City's financial district in September 1920, couldn't they have done the same thing at the same time of day in the heart of Boston's commercial waterfront district in January 1919?

More than anything else, the outcome of the molasses case depended on the answer to this single question.

~ ELEVEN ~

FACTOR OF SAFETY

Late September 1920

As New York recovered from the Wall Street tragedy, and law enforcement authorities offered their theories on the explosion, Charles Choate was taking his expert witnesses through their own bomb story in Hugh Ogden's Boston courtroom.

Choate's strategy was to impress Ogden with the brainpower and credentials of the distinguished men he would call to the stand, one after another, a parade of academicians and professionals who would validate USIA's thesis that an "evilly disposed person" had dropped an "infernal device" into the molasses tank, causing it to explode. Choate called engineering professors George E. Russell of the Massachusetts Institute of Technology and George F. Swain of Harvard, as well as Lewis E. Moore, engineer of the Massachusetts Public Utility Commission, all of whom testified as hydraulic and structural experts. Each proffered the same conclusion: that the tank was structurally safe, although admittedly, the "factor of safety" of the tank's walls was materially less than they would have provided. (The factor of safety is a number that describes the maximum amount of pressure the walls could withstand without buckling; a factor of safety of 3 would mean that the tank could withstand a force equivalent to three times the total pressure exerted on its walls by the contents inside.) Choate also questioned nationally renowned metallurgist Albert Colby, who spent *three weeks* on the stand testifying about the tensile strength of steel, its properties at different temperatures, and its ability to withstand the changing stress levels created by fermenting molasses.

In addition, Russell, along with Choate's other expert witnesses—professor A. H. Gill of MIT's chemical department and state police chemist Walter Wedger—testified that they had conducted tests, both at MIT and at USIA facilities in Baltimore, using a smaller replica of the Commercial Street tank. At MIT, they had filled the thirty-foot model tank with water; in Baltimore, they had used molasses. The blast ripped a hole in the side of the tank and damaged the steel walls in a fashion similar to the way the actual steel plates had been damaged after the real tank collapsed.

Choate scored a courtroom coup by convincing the fifty-nine-year-old Wedger, an eleven-year veteran of the State Police Department of Public Safety, to testify for USIA. Wedger had broad and lengthy experience in dealing with explosives, and his reputation was impeccable. He had responsibility for enforcing all state regulations governing the handling of explosives and inflammable material, including the inspection of buildings where they were stored. He was also the first person called to the scene to investigate explosions, fires of suspicious origin, and illegal explosives of "any kind found anywhere, all over the state." Prior to his work with the state, he had served as superintendent and chemist for a fireworks manufacturing company. Wedger had been trained at MIT, but most of his working knowledge had been passed on by his father, who was a distinguished chemist and pyrotechnist killed in an explosion in 1895. "For more than forty years, I have studied explosives and inflammables," Wedger said.

Now this longtime explosives expert, an eminent state police chemist, perhaps *the* most knowledgeable person in Massachusetts on the effects of dynamite, TNT, and nitroglycerine, stated under oath what USIA needed Ogden to hear. Wedger, who had initially stated publicly, and under oath at Judge Bolster's 1919 inquest, that there was no evidence of any explosion on Commercial Street, reversed that opinion when Charles Choate put him on the stand:

Choate: State again what your opinion is as to the cause that produced the accident.

Wedger: I should say it was caused by an explosion.

Choate: And what kind of explosive?

Wedger: It might be most any kind of high explosive—dynamite or nitroglycerine.

Choate: Suppose a person had taken dynamite in some sort of a container to the top of that tank, with the fuse wound around the container, and lighted it with his pipe, or cigarette, or cigar, and dropped it through the manhole at the top, so that the burning end of the fuse had immediately gone under the molasses, would that [molasses] have put out the fuse?

Wedger: No, sir.

Choate: How much dynamite or nitroglycerine would be required [to destroy the tank]?

Wedger: Anywhere from five to fifteen pounds; twelve or fifteen pounds.

Choate: How large a package, or container, would be required to hold that amount?

Wedger: Ten pounds would require a pipe three inches in diameter, about two-and-a-half feet long.

Choate had drawn first blood. He had succeeded in eliciting sworn testimony from a distinguished and disinterested law enforcement expert, an unpaid witness, one whose word was above reproach, that the Commercial Street molasses disaster had been no accident.

But USIA's advantage didn't last long. Under cross-examination, Damon Hall filleted Walter Wedger, using against him his own inquest testimony, and reducing the cool, experienced state police chemist to a near-incoherent state, a man who at best appeared befuddled and a parser of words, and at worst, came across in court as an outright liar.

First, Hall asked Wedger to describe a "common explosion scene" and then took him through the day of the disaster, when the chemist visited the scene about an hour after the tank collapsed. At any explosion, Wedger said, the concussive force of the blast shatters windows and glass "for many hundreds of feet" from the actual bomb; broken glass, Wedger said, "is one of the almost inseparable evidences" of a dynamite or nitroglycerine explosion.

Hall: So, given that, did you find any of the common evidences of a dynamite explosion [at the molasses scene]?

Wedger: I did not.

Hall: Nowhere on that day were you able to find that cardinal evidence [broken glass] of a dynamite or high explosive explosion [sic], were you?

Wedger: I did not find it.

Hall: Did you see any effect that day, such as you would expect to find where a high explosive has been used?

Wedger: No, sir.

Hall: Did you see any evidence in any of the parts [of the tank wall] that were collected ... from which you could make up your mind that dynamite or any other high explosives had caused the failure?

Wedger: Did not, no sir.

Next, Hall reminded Wedger that he had collected a sample of both the "old" molasses that had been stored in the tank and the "new" molasses that the *Miliero* had pumped in days before the explosion. Since the new, warmer molasses had been pumped into the tank from the bottom, it pushed up against the colder molasses already in the tank. Wedger had conducted his test in a similar way. Hall quoted Wedger from his 1919 testimony during the inquest: "I took some of the molasses to the State laboratory and gave it a test to see just about what it contained and its purity, and inside of an hour after it reached there, I noticed bubbles coming from the top of it, fermentation taking place ... I then connected up a quart bottle of molasses to a pressure gauge, and in twenty-four hours, I got a pressure of half a pound; in forty-eight hours, I got a pressure of a full pound."

Fermentation is the process by which sugar, or molasses, is converted to alcohol by microscopic yeasts that thrive in the absence of oxygen, a process used commercially to produce wine. Wedger acknowledged that, as the yeasts grew in number inside the tank, they would also produce carbon dioxide gas as a by-product of the fermenting process. The pressure from the gas would seek a release of some sort.

Hall: Did you testify under oath at the inquest that the upper layers (of molasses) would effectively act as tamping agents, and pressure [inside the tank] running into very high figures would develop?

Wedger: I don't remember that I said or made any such statement.

Hall: You do not? Did you say that the upper mass of molasses was so leathery [because it was cold] that in your opinion it was an effective tamping which prevented the escape of the gas?

Wedger: It would act more or less as a tamping owing to its higher viscosity, but it would not prevent the escape of gas through it.

Hall: Wouldn't it? Let me read what you said under oath about the matter: "That gas has to go somewhere. It tries to get up through these several feet of leathery substance and it takes a long time for it to get up through there, and at the same time it exerts a certain fermenting pressure." Do you remember that testimony?

Wedger: Yes it seems to me that I do.

Hall: Then owing to the cold weather, in your opinion, that mass of molasses was so leathery that it would hold back the escape of the gas and cause a fermenting pressure on the *sides* of the tank?

Wedger: There would be some amount of pressure on the sides of the tank ... but it would not fully prevent its ultimate escape [through the molasses] ... a certain amount of pressure on the sides of the tank, yes. I don't know how that could be figured.

Hall: Do you remember saying to the grand jury that if the tank had the proper factor of safety that any pressure which might be exerted against the sides by this gas in the process of fermentation, that there would not be "*any* chance for the thing to give way?"

Wedger: I do remember that that was the way I felt about it.

Hall had succeeded in getting Wedger to admit two critical points under oath. The fact that the state police chemist had discovered no broken glass at the Commercial Street scene (beyond the windows that had been smashed by the molasses wave itself), meant that the customary "cardinal evidence" of a concussive explosion was lacking. Second, because the cold molasses most likely blocked or trapped the carbon dioxide gas fermenting below (between the warm and cold layers of molasses), the gas would almost certainly exert pressure against the sides of the tank looking for escape.

Having elicited those concessions from a key defense witness, Hall dispatched of Wedger with a flourish:

Hall: Did you *ever*, until your testimony this morning, express to anybody—Judge Bolster, your superior, the State Police or anybody else—that the cause of the Commercial Street tank collapse was dynamite, or some other high explosive of that nature?

Wedger: I had not fully formed my opinion until he [Charles Choate] asked the question.

Hall: This morning, then, for the first time in your life, you either formed or expressed the opinion that dynamite was the cause of this disaster.

Wedger: I had thought it over.

Hall: But you formed or expressed it for the first time this morning?

Wedger: It is the first time I have been asked for an opinion.

Hall: And the first time you have ever formed the opinion?

Wedger: Well, I couldn't form one until he told me what to form it on.

Hall: I see. Well then, your answer, sir, is based upon his [Choate's] *hypothesis* only?

Wedger: Why, absolutely so.

Wedger's woeful performance was magnified by the fact that Charles Choate and USIA were relying almost entirely on expert witnesses to prove their case—and Wedger was the only one of these who was not being paid by the company. Choate was not calling a single representative of USIA to vouch for the tank's sturdiness, or to justify the decision to build the tank in the North End neighborhood.

In addition, Choate had called, and would call, just one eyewitness. Her name was Winnifred McNamara, a widow who lived at 548 Commercial Street, across the street from where the tank had stood. Her demeanor and testimony appeared to do as much to hurt the defense as help it. McNamara said she was hanging laundry on the roof of her home just after 12:30 P.M. on the day the tank collapsed. Just before she saw the roof "push away" from the tank, McNamara testified that she had seen smoke rising from the vicinity of the tank. "I saw smoke rising, and then the whole top slid off ... just as a dish on a table would slide off, and then the molasses walked up, just walked up, and you know the froth and the smoke, like, walked up to the top, but I didn't see the sides going out ... I heard a sound like this: r-r-r-r-r, a kind of heavy sound. In a few minutes I was lifted from the corner over to that corner, and I was hit on the side, and I pitched back on the broad of my back, and after that I couldn't tell no more."

But under cross-examination, McNamara became agitated when Hall pressed her to identify from where the smoke billowed and what type of pipe protruded from the top of the tank. Three times, McNamara threw her hands into the air, left the witness chair and threatened to do "some damage" if she were compelled to testify further. Nonetheless, she complied immediately when Ogden ordered her to sit back down. Hall continued: "Was it a straight pipe or a crooked pipe" he asked. McNamara replied: "No, sir, I couldn't say. I didn't see the pipe, I saw smoke ... I couldn't tell you what was on the top of the tank, sir."

Hall would later ask the court rhetorically—with factories operating on the waterfront, ships moored at the docks, and tugboats chugging through the harbor—"do you think it was possible for anybody to look over the [Charles] river and toward the [Charlestown] Navy Yard at that time of day and *not* see whiffs of smoke and steam?" How, Hall wondered, did such smoke prove the presence of a bomb?

Hall's colleague, Endicott P. Saltonstall, then addressed McNamara about the presence of an anarchist. "Did you notice anything else about the roof at the time you first saw the smoke ... did you see any man, woman, or child on the roof?" he asked. McNamara replied: "No, sir, I did not. No, I did not, sir. I didn't see any man on the roof of the tank at all, sir. No, I did not, sir."

Hall would later say that by selecting McNamara as its only eyewitness, USIA was building its defense around the "testimony of a woman, who, if not insane, certainly showed evidence in the courtroom of being temperamental ... as I have read and considered her testimony, I have been driven to think of that other famous woman in Chicago, whose cow is said to have kicked over the lantern. I think, to use the street slang, that those legends both concern plain bull, and not cow."

The inconsistencies in Wedger's testimony, coupled with McNamara's tentativeness and bizarre courtroom behavior, provided Hall with an opening through which to strike at the heart of the defense. But he still had to battle the tenor of the times and the plausibility of USIA's anarchist argument. To fully discredit the theory of a mysterious bomber, Hall had to show that the tank was unsafe from the beginning, that its collapse of January 15, 1919, and the subsequent destruction that resulted, were inevitable, given the manner in which the receptacle was constructed and the area in which it was located.

He would build his case throughout the late fall of 1920 and the early winter of 1921, first with the testimony of a Boston Building Department employee, then with a steady procession of witnesses who could describe the condition of the tank from the time it was built until the moment it collapsed. Some of them were plaintiffs, like firefighter Bill Connor and stonecutter John Barry, and Hall would also question former USIA employee Isaac Gonzales, in great detail. But most of Hall's witnesses would be clerks and city workers and stevedores, disinterested parties with nothing to gain by testifying against a large national company.

Once these witnesses helped him establish the overall condition of the tank, Hall would train his sights on less cooperative prey. He would seek to cull incriminating testimony from the USIA employee who had the most intimate knowledge of the Commercial Street molasses tank.

His name was Arthur P. Jell.

✤ ✤ ✤

Josephat C. Blain fidgeted on the witness stand, a nervous clerk who worked in the Boston Building Department, and whose boss approved the plans for the foundation of the molasses tank that Hammond Iron Works had submitted in October 1915. Because the tank was considered a "receptacle" and not a "building," Hammond was not required to seek a separate permit nor include the certification of an engineer to build the fifty-foot steel tank itself. However, Blain pointed out, Hammond *did* submit specifications for the tank as part of its foundation permit.

Under Damon Hall's questioning, Blain confirmed that the plans called for specific thickness of each of the seven plates that Hammond used to construct the tank—ring one was to be .687 inches thick, ring two was .625 inches thick, all the way to ring seven at the top of the tank, where the plans stated that the ring measured .312 inches in thickness. It was according to these specifications that the city issued the permit for the foundation and the tank.

Hall then read in open court Hammond's answers to questions regarding the thickness of the walls of the tank. Hammond's sworn statement showed that the thickness of every plate was less than what was called for in the plans. For example, the plans showed ring one— the bottom plate—would be .687 inches thick, but Hammond delivered a plate that was .667 inches thick. Plans called for the top plate, ring seven, to be .312 inches thick; Hammond delivered a steel plate that was .284 inches thick.

Hall said: "In every single one of those rings, this reputable Hammond Iron Works [delivered steel plates] that were less than the specifications called for ... they were like all other steel manufacturers in the country, hurrying to fill war orders, and in every instance, they furnished steel less than the specs called for."

USIA lawyer Charles Choate claimed that the differences were not large enough to be a factor, and that there was a "recognized custom of tolerance" in accordance with guidelines set forth by the American Society for Testing Materials. "No inspector would be warranted in rejecting a plate if it came within the above-mentioned tolerances," Choate argued.

Hall scoffed: "Your Honor, how long would an argument of that kind last before the Massachusetts Supreme Judicial Court? If a street car operator says, 'I ordered axles that were sufficient to carry my car and not break, but there is a rule among car builders that they can furnish something less than I ordered and I accepted the axles under this rule. True, they are not what I ordered, and true, they are too light, but that is a rule that carbuilders follow.' How long would the Supreme Court take to consider a defense of that kind? That is what this whole tolerance question comes down to."

Hall had shown that the walls of the tank were up to 10 percent thinner, and thus, by definition, weaker, and less able to withstand pressure, than Hammond Iron Works had stated in the plans it had filed with the Boston Building Department.

Or put another way, the steel manufacturer had lied to the city.

Charles Choate continued to plead that the difference in thickness was so small that there would be no discernible difference in strength, and perhaps technically, he was correct. But in the battle for credibility, Hall had scored another victory.

Hall then called his "average" witnesses, who testified to the actual condition of the tank, the natural result, as Hall framed his questions, of a giant steel structure that was rushed to completion and built below specifications. The North End waterfront tank was flawed from the beginning, the plaintiffs argued, and remained flawed for the entire time it stood.

First, Frances Brown, a clerk for the Bay State Railway at the time of the flood, whose second-story office window was right across from the tank, said she noticed "several times, that molasses flowed down the sides of the tank ... at the time when the molasses boat would come in, around that time, before or after, I would notice it oozing out," Brown said. "I would notice it and call it to the attention of the girls [in the office]; in fact, we all noticed it. Several times, I saw it on the ground."

William Foster, a marine engineer on fireboat 31, concurred, asserting: "The tank always leaked after it was put up. I noticed some of the vertical seams; the bottom ones leaked pretty badly. From the top, you could also see the molasses dripping out and running down the sides of the tank." And then, Foster's unmistakable implication that USIA had attempted to literally cover up the leaking problem: "The tank kept leaking right up to the time of the collapse, but you could not notice it so much at the last, because they repainted the tank ... it was kind of a dark reddish brown and you couldn't see the molasses as clearly."

Philip Lydon, a stevedore for the Revere Sugar Refinery who worked at the North End Paving Yard from 1916 to 1918, said when molasses ships pulled into port, he and several other men would go to the tank and watch. Before a fence was erected around the tank, prior to America's entrance into the war, Lydon said he leaned against the tank frequently while crews pumped molasses into the steel structure. "We could feel it, the vibration, bulging in and out," Lydon said. "There was always a big leak, too, near the junction of the second and third plates ... molasses ran down the side of the tank, enough for the children in the neighborhood to be there every day to get a dose of it. They would be there from early morning till late at night."

While Charles Choate chided Lydon for "leaning" against the tank during working hours ("I have seen workmen do that when they were working for the city, but I didn't know they had to have a tank to hold them up."), he couldn't shake Lydon's testimony about the leaks. Nor did he endear himself to the witness with the snide comment about slacking: "The only time I used to go there [to the tank] was at meal hours," Lydon shot back.

Hall's next witness, paving yard night watchman Henry Minard, corroborated those who came before him. "I noticed that all summer before the accident, it leaked," Minard said of the tank. "I noticed that boys used to come down there with small cans and hold them under the seams . . . more on a hot day than on a cool day."

On cross-examination, Choate succeeded in getting Minard to acknowledge that, occasionally, "bums looking for a place to sleep" would enter the waterfront area through a small gate "that was never locked, on account of the firehouse being down there . . . but if I saw them, I would throw them out." Minard also admitted that others "who didn't belong" were often in the waterfront area, but Choate's focus on possible "evilly disposed persons" did not disguise the fact that he chose *not* to address the leaking issue in his cross.

Hall's next two witnesses went beyond the leaks in their description of the tank. Charles Caffrey, a stableman at the paving yard when the accident occurred, confirmed that the leaks were constant and that children "used sticks and cans to get molasses." But he also said he "frequently" heard sounds from within the tank, "sounds like thunder, like rumbling . . . I heard it most any time I was near the tank." Unfortunately for Choate and USIA, under cross-examination, Caffrey went further:

Choate: Didn't you think the noise could be the sound of freight cars, or street cars, or the elevated trains?

Caffrey: Well, no, not exactly. It was more of a roll, like thunder.

Choate: When you first heard it, did you think it was a thunderstorm?

Caffrey: I didn't, because I knew what it was.

Choate: What was it?

Caffrey: It was something inside of the molasses tank, bubbling and rolling, something you could hear roll heavily. I think the molasses must have been boiling, or doing something.

Choate: You think it was the boiling of the molasses that made a roar like thunder?

Caffrey: Yes.

Damon Hall, who must have been gleeful about Caffrey uttering the phrase "boiling molasses" during Choate's cross, finished his string of "disinterested" witnesses by calling firefighter Stephen O'Brien to the stand. O'Brien, a twenty-year veteran of the Boston Fire Department, had worked at the Engine 31 fireboat as a marine engineer from 1911 until the day of the disaster, though he was not on duty on January 15, 1919.

But O'Brien *was* at the waterfront many days during Hammond's construction of the tank, and his engineering curiosity drew him frequently to the work site. It was his observations about the nature of the construction that Hall focused on during questioning:

Hall: Tell us, Mr. O'Brien, how you saw them putting in the rivets, and what you saw them do before they put the rivets into the plates.

O'Brien: I saw them drift two holes in, holes that didn't match up.

Hall: What do you mean by "drift"?

O'Brien: Well, the two holes would come about an eighth of an inch from being fair, from matching up. So they put what we call a drift pin in—a steel instrument about ten or fifteen inches long, tapered at the end to the size of the hole—and gave it two or three cracks with a sledge hammer. Then they pull out the drift pin and put the rivets in.

Hall: Well, how many times have you seen this, when one hole didn't match up with the second hole?

O'Brien: I couldn't tell just how many times. They worked day and night.

Charles Choate attempted unsuccessfully to shake Hall's witness, growing frustrated with O'Brien's insistence that he could see the misaligned plate-holes even from a distance. "You have got very good eyesight, haven't you?" Choate asked.

"Well, I never wore glasses," O'Brien said.

"Perhaps you'd better," Choate snapped, and dismissed O'Brien.

✤ ✤ ✤

Damon Hall could not have asked for a better performance from his "no name" witnesses. Each of them had been articulate, unwavering in their testimony, and most importantly, credible.

With the foundation established, Hall called Isaac Gonzales, and the two caulkers, Patrick Kenneally and John Urquhart, to strengthen his case about the tank's substandard construction. Kenneally and Urquhart described how they tried to stem the sheer number of leaks. Gonzales told of the scale-flakes from the tank's inside walls raining down on him, his unsuccessful attempts to convince Jell that the tank was in danger of falling, and his own observations of the leaks. "It leaked enough to make a pool, about a pail of molasses in twenty-four hours," Gonzales testified. "The leaks were principally in the horizontal seams but in the vertical ones, too. I would spread enough sand to keep the molasses from flowing onto the railcar tracks. There was no place that I could say it was not leaking."

After establishing for Ogden the physical condition of the tank, Hall called as witnesses five men who described themselves as explosives experts. They were sailors stationed on ships in Boston Harbor when the tank collapsed. All had served as ordnance machinists and detonation workers during the war; they were men who, like Hugh Ogden, had seen combat in Europe and were all too familiar with the sound of a shell screaming toward the ground and the pounding, deafening blast afterward. They testified that when the tank collapsed they heard rumbling sounds like thunder, or tearing sounds like rending wood, or sounds like a building collapsing.

But each of these dynamite and TNT experts were adamant that the sound they heard was *nothing* like the thunder produced by a high explosive.

None of the experiments USIA conducted to prove that a bomb had destroyed the tank, none of the professors and academicians who testified about the angle of the blast in the replica tank, could match the simple veracity of these combat-tested men who were a few feet from the tank when it collapsed.

USIA's anarchist defense, built on testimony from paid experts— its *theory*, as Hall disdainfully labeled it—thus far had been shredded by solid testimony from average citizens who knew what they saw and described it in no uncertain words. It wasn't over yet, but USIA was reeling; the plaintiffs needed just one knockout punch to end the fight. Damon Hall knew this and so did Charles Choate.

It was why Hall wanted nothing more than to question Arthur P. Jell, and Choate wanted just as badly to keep USIA's assistant treasurer off the stand.

March 4, 1921, Washington, D.C.

When Republican Warren G. Harding rode in a Packard Twin Six from the White House to the Capitol on the morning of March 4, 1921, he became the first president to arrive at his inauguration in an automobile instead of a horse-drawn carriage. This symbolized both the dramatic political change that had taken place in the country with Harding's election, and the beginning of a new era of innovation, commerce, and prosperity in America, led by Big Business.

Proving the pundits correct, Harding and his vice-presidential running mate, Massachusetts Governor Calvin Coolidge, had swept into office in November, burying their Democratic opponent, Ohio Governor James M. Cox. Harding collected 404 electoral votes and won thirty-seven states, compared with Cox's 127 electoral votes and eleven states. The popular vote margin was even more impressive— 61 percent to 35 percent (Socialist Eugene V. Debs garnered 3 percent of the popular vote).

Moreover, Harding's coattails were long and their fabric sturdy. Republican congressmen and senators were elected across the country, and the GOP piled up a 150-vote majority in the House and a twenty-two-vote majority in the Senate. "The Republican wave, still rising, has invaded rock-ribbed Southern and border States ..." the *Boston Globe* reported. "It's an avalanche to Harding." The *Boston Herald* said the election returns "accentuate the stupendous overturn in government." Women, voting nationwide for the first time following the passage of the 19th amendment in August 1920, cast their ballots overwhelmingly for Harding, who was elected on his fifty-fifth birthday.

In Massachusetts, the Harding victory was even more striking, thanks in part to the influence of the popular Coolidge, who won the admiration of voters for his leadership during the Boston police strike. Cox, the Democrat, carried only two small towns in the Bay State. Nearly 90 percent of Massachusetts' voters went to the polls, a full third of them women, and political experts estimated that about three-quarters of women voted for the Republican ticket. More than sixty thousand women cast ballots in the city of Boston alone, and Harding and Coolidge carried the capital city by a plurality of thirty thousand votes, the first time Boston had given a Republican a plurality since William McKinley in 1896.

The stunning GOP victory was seen nationwide as a repudiation of Woodrow Wilson's policies and politics—his dogged attempts to draw the United States into a League of Nations and his unfriendliness toward Big Business. So devastating was Wilson's defeat that fiery Democrat William Jennings Bryan only half-jokingly called for a constitutional maneuver that would allow Wilson to resign in December 1920 and Harding to assume the presidency three months before the scheduled inauguration.

Harding recognized the mandate the country had given him and used words and symbols on inauguration day to usher in the new era. Under a brilliant sky, a Marine Band, "gay in scarlet coats and bright blue trousers," sat in front of the inaugural kiosk, while the steps of the Capitol were guarded with color guards of "regulars and sailors ..." noted the *New York Times*. "Viewed from an upper window of the Capitol ... (were) the reds, greens, and browns of women's hats," women whose participation in the inaugural, for the first time in American history, was more than ceremonial, and whom Harding rewarded for their support by providing hundreds with prime seating locations at the inaugural.

During his thirty-seven-minute inaugural address, Harding, the country's twenty-ninth president, spoke first on the topic closest to the hearts of most Americans: the sovereignty of the United States. He justified the country's decision not to participate in the League of Nations that had become so closely associated with his predecessor, and which finally came into being without U.S. support on January 20, 1920. "We recognize the new order in the world, with the closer contacts which progress has wrought. We crave friendship and harbor no hate," Harding said. "But America, our America . . . can be a party to no permanent military alliance. It can enter into no political commitments, nor assume any economic obligations which will subject our decisions to any other than our own authority."

But it was Harding's secondary inaugural theme that was the subject of greater interest to America's business leaders: the need to fuel the country's economic progress by freeing Big Business from the regulatory shackles that Wilson and Congress had imposed during the war. The message played like sweet music in boardrooms and factories across America—to the emerging automobile, aviation, and rubber magnates; to the burgeoning steel, chemical, and construction industries; to the Wall Street financiers and investment bankers; and indeed, to industrial corporations like United States Industrial Alcohol. Though many of these companies, USIA included, had benefited enormously from war-related contracts, they were now hobbled by excessive regulations in a peacetime economy.

Harding outlined the remedy: "I speak for administrative efficiency, for lightened tax burdens, for sound commercial practices, for adequate credit facilities, for the omission of unnecessary interference of Government with business, for an end to Government's experiment in business, and for more efficient business in Government administration."

Harding had called for freeing America from international entanglements that could weaken her and freeing American business from regulations that he believed could weaken the economy. As if to symbolize this new freedom, his first executive order was to reopen the gates to the White House grounds to the general public for the first time since Wilson had ordered them shut when the United States had entered the war on April 6, 1917. The *New York Times* reported: "Crowds poured through all the entrances like water through a broken dam . . . The crowds streamed across the lawns from all four sides

and some pressed their faces against the White House windows."
Noted the *Boston Herald*: "Immediately after the gates swung open,
the crowd . . . thronged in . . . [then] news of the issuance of the order
spread about the city and inaugural visitors and Washingtonians
added a visit to the White House ground to the list of history-making
events they had witnessed during the day."

✶✶✶

Harding's hope for a richer, stronger America would be dampened
briefly by a severe, though short, depression in the latter part of 1921
and early 1922. But the vision of his inaugural was realized shortly
thereafter when the economy recovered and began an eight-year era
of prosperity that would become known as the Roaring Twenties.
Harding, his administration wracked by scandal, his life cut short
while in office by high blood pressure and heart disease, received
little credit for the boom; much of that went to Calvin Coolidge,
who assumed the presidency in 1923 upon Harding's death, and was
elected in his own right in 1924.

Still, Harding's 1921 inaugural marked the beginning of a new
stage in America's economic growth. Men like Henry Ford and Alfred F. Sloan of General Motors, and Harvey Firestone and Frank
M. Seiberling of Goodyear Rubber, helped the country's auto production jump from 1.5 million cars in 1919 to nearly 5 million in
1929, and spawned the first "auto sections" in American newspapers.
America built roads, schools, and factories. Electrification of those
factories and modern assembly-line methods created a boom in
manufacturing production. Capital became plentiful as banks loos-
ened the reins on credit to keep up with the growth. The stock market shot up.

New money in the marketplace, coupled with a white-hot economy, spurred innovation and consumer spending. Wages of working
Americans grew, and the onset of installment buying allowed them
to purchase more for their families. The 1920s marked a consumer
goods revolution—electric toasters, irons, phonographs, radios,
plumbing fixtures, and automobiles. While immigrants and black
Americans still faced discrimination and tough economic prospects,
most of the country prospered.

In November 1920, KDKA in Pittsburgh would begin service,

marking the birth of regular American radio broadcasting. Two years later, there would be five hundred stations on the air. The movie business also grew during the 1920s, as the American public flocked to theaters to see Mary Pickford, Rudolph Valentino, Douglas Fairbanks, and Charlie Chaplin.

American business was at the pinnacle of its influence. About two hundred corporations controlled more than 20 percent of the nation's wealth. The large corporations thrived, both financially and in the public's eyes; companies like International Harvester, H. J. Heinz, Singer Sewing, Ford, General Motors, U.S. Steel, AT&T, and du Pont saw themselves not only as leaders in their industries, not only as job-creation machines, but as leading institutions in society. As wages grew and labor opportunities abounded in the 1920s, Big Business saw itself as a benefactor that bestowed both financial rewards and a sense of self-worth to those whom it employed. By developing new, often revolutionary products, by moving the country forward, Big Business believed it was doing more than making money; it was doing something *virtuous*. "The man who builds a factory builds a temple—the man who works there worships there," Calvin Coolidge said.

It is hard to overestimate the symbolic impact of Warren Harding's inauguration, the overwhelming sense of excitement and promise it created among America's entrepreneurial and corporate elite. The power and influence of Big Business had been curtailed during Wilson's eight-year tenure, profitable war years notwithstanding; corporate leaders believed that a Republican administration offered virtually limitless prospects, new hope at the start of a new decade.

✼✼✼

USIA and its lead attorney, Charles Choate, must have felt some of that hope. Choate's case had absorbed a series of body blows by Damon Hall's relentless procession of witnesses; perhaps the country's changing mood toward business, exemplified by Harding's resounding victory, would induce Hugh Ogden to look more favorably on USIA's version of events.

Many of Boston's finest private men's clubs, several of which Ogden belonged to, had celebrated the GOP victory in November, most holding receptions for former governor Calvin Coolidge for becoming vice president-elect. Choate believed that Coolidge and Harding, without doubt, were Ogden's kind of men. If the new president, elected by an electoral and popular landslide, was calling for the "omission of unnecessary interference of Government with business," then certainly Ogden would *have* to consider whether a decision against USIA fell into the category of "unnecessary interference." Certainly, he would have to think long and hard about the *ramifications* of such a decision. Would it stifle the expansion of plants and factories if they were required to attain *unattainable* levels of safety? Would it introduce a whole new layer of government regulations and restrictions even while a popular new president had clearly called for the opposite?

For the first time in years, warm winds, favorable to Big Business, were now blowing steadily from Washington. Warren G. Harding's inauguration, and all that it bespoke, must have buoyed Charles Choate's spirits and instilled cautious optimism in the defense. How long that optimism would prevail would depend on how well Arthur P. Jell stood up to questioning three weeks hence in New York City.

✴✴✴

Hugh Ogden's feelings about President Harding's nomination are not part of the historical record, but Ogden's writings and speeches indicate strongly that he would have cast a wary eye toward America's economic prosperity, lest it cloud her vision on bedrock issues of fairness and justice for all citizens.

In a Memorial Day speech in the near future, Ogden would observe: "We have prospered. We have sold goods at high prices. We have accumulated the largest stock of gold any nation ever possessed, but have we done anymore than that? Have we in our blindness gained the whole world and lost our own soul? It was not to ensure material prosperity that our soldiers fought and died ... that the relations of capital and labor might be still further embittered ... We must administer our government upon the broadest and most humanitarian lines so that each citizen shall receive his full inheritance in good roads, good schools, adequate opportunities for higher education, hospital facilities, libraries ... and other institutions that are a public charge for the public good."

Ogden most likely voted for Warren Harding and was no doubt generally inclined to agree with the president's attitudes about government and big business. But the auditor's strength of character, forged on the battlefields of France, and his sense of fair play, made it unlikely that Charles Choate would get his wish, unlikely that Ogden would be influenced by the prevailing economic prosperity or long-term ramifications. Hugh Ogden would consider and decide the molasses case on its merits alone.

Manhattan, Friday, March 25, 1921

The temperature hovered around the mid-80s, the highest ever in Manhattan for the end of March, when Damon Hall, Charles Choate, Henry F. Dolan, and a court stenographer arrived at the elegant Hotel Belmont to question Jell.

Damon Hall was miffed that he had to travel to New York at all. When the plaintiffs had added Jell to the witness list, Choate had tried desperately to prevent the USIA executive from taking the stand by arguing to the Superior Court that Jell's testimony was not directly relevant to the case. The court disagreed and ordered Choate to make Jell available to Hall and the plaintiffs. Choate then pleaded with the court not to compel Jell to testify before Ogden, that traveling from New York to Boston would be an "immense inconvenience" for Jell, and requested instead that Jell be deposed by attorneys from both sides in New York City. The judge agreed, over Hall's vociferous objections; Hall wanted Ogden to be able to look Jell directly in the eye, to watch his comportment under tough questioning.

Hall was not surprised that Choate had chosen the opulent Hotel Belmont as a way to establish Jell's importance and stamp USIA's corporate imprimatur on the proceedings. Far from the neutral surroundings of Hugh Ogden's modest Boston courtroom, the Belmont dripped with haughty pretension. Built at the corner of 42nd Street and Park Avenue in 1906, the twenty-story building, shaped like a tall wedge of cheese, boasted a spacious two-story lobby, grand staircases, floors and walls treated in red marble, mirrored elevator doors, and a dining room and massive sitting room with richly carpeted floors, and great red columns supporting arched ceilings. "New York has added another splendid hostelry to its already rich store," one writer noted when the hotel opened fifteen years earlier. "To this monster hotel, one might aptly apply the expression for large New York enterprises: A city in itself."

Hall believed Choate had chosen the Belmont to gain an edge, perhaps as a means to intimidate, but more likely with the hope that the civility and elegance of the hotel would lessen the tenacity of Hall's questioning. Hall knew the tactic well; it was based on the same theory that said it was perfectly acceptable to criticize a government or corporate leader in private conversation, but impolite to confront him on the same topic face to face. Hall thought Choate was operating on a simple premise: plush surroundings equaled cushy questions.

But for Hall, who was not easily awed amidst resplendence, the trip to New York and the Belmont had just the opposite effect. He was angry at Choate for trying to prevent Jell from testifying in the first place, angrier still that Choate had protested Jell's traveling to Boston to appear before Ogden. To him, that tactic had violated the basic premise of fairness. He viewed Choate as a worthy adversary and, while they were not friends, he had respected the defense counsel for his integrity and love for the law; Choate's successful maneuvering to shelter Jell from Ogden's scrutiny twisted the rules of law in a way Hall found distasteful and disappointing.

Since Ogden would not get to see Jell, it meant Hall's direct examination needed to be more pointed than ever. Jell's answers needed to *jump* from the page when Ogden read the deposition transcript.

The Belmont's cut-glass chandeliers and frescoed walls notwithstanding, Damon Hall planned to tear into Arthur P. Jell like he was in a street fight.

✦✦✦

Hall wasted little time with preliminaries. He quickly established that the forty-two-year-old Jell had spent his entire professional career as a financial administrator, that he had no technical or engineering training, and that he could not read building plans or specifications.

Jell then acknowledged that he had ordered Hammond Iron Works to construct the steel plates for the tank's walls with a "factor of safety" of 3, which led Hall to this line of questioning:

Hall: Was the factor of safety of 3 that you determined the result of any investigation or advice from technically trained engineers, builders, or architects?

Jell: No.

Hall: No?

Jell: No.

Hall: Did you, prior to making that recommendation of a factor of safety of 3, make any investigation whatever as to the factor of safety which the ordinary engineering practice called for?

Jell: No.

Hall: Did you consult *anyone* before making that suggestion as to a factor of safety of 3.

Jell: I don't remember having done so.

Hall: Is it fair to say, then, that you arrived at that in your own mind?

Jell: Not entirely. I had been told in the past by tank manufacturers that they built tanks with a factor of safety of 2. So I figured 3 would be sufficient.

Hall: Do you know what manufacturers told you that?

Jell: I do not.

Hall: Or the size of the tanks to which they referred?

Jell: I do not.

For Hall, it was not enough to show that Jell's "factor of safety" specification was based on no credible knowledge or advice. It was also important that he get Jell to admit what had happened when Hammond Iron Works delivered plans and drawings based on those specifications:

Hall: When Mr. Shellhammer [of Hammond Iron Works] showed you the plans in January of 1915, did you have any talk with him about the factor of safety in the specifications?

Jell: I cannot remember.

Hall: Do you remember that you did?

Jell: No, I do not.

Hall: With such experience as you had, were you able, by looking at the plans and specifications, to determine from them what factor of safety had been provided in them?

Jell: No.

Hall: Did you submit the plans or specifications to any architect or engineer?

Jell: No.

Hall: Did you submit them to the New York office of U.S. Industrial Alcohol? Did you show them to any officer of USIA?

Jell: No.

Hall: Did anyone ask to see them, to inspect them?

Jell: No.

Hall: I want to ask one more time, before I go on with the next line of inquiry, whether . . . the factor of safety as determined upon was the result of any investigation or advice from technically trained engineers, builders, or architects?

Jell: No.

Hall: Your answer is "no"?

Jell: No.

And then, once Hammond had finished the steel plates and delivered them:

Hall: Upon the delivery of the metal for this tank in Boston, did you have any engineer or builder examine the material [to ensure it conformed to] specifications?

Jell: No.

Hall: Or any metallurgist?

Jell: No.

Hall: Did you seek the advice or consult with *any* person outside of the employees of Hammond Iron Works, as to the quality and fitness of the steel which was delivered, or the method of construction?

Jell: No.

Hall: Did you at any time have or ask for *any* test to be made of the steel being fabricated on your behalf?

Jell: No.

Jell then acknowledged that he had been frustrated by delays as he attempted to secure the waterfront site for the tank from Boston Elevated, and that the delay was "causing us embarrassment . . . without a tank of our own, we were compelled to purchase from a dealer in molasses, who charged us a higher price than we could have it delivered at our own tank." Later, after the steel arrived and the sale of the property had been completed, Jell testified that he ordered Hammond to hire additional crews to finish the work before the *Miliero* arrived on December 31, 1915. Work continued right up until the day the molasses ship steamed into Boston Harbor.

Hall: Did you at any time after the tank was erected, and before the steamer arrived, have any investigation made of the tank by any architect, engineer, or man who was familiar with steel construction, as to the sufficiency of the tank as erected?

Jell: No.

Hall: Referring to the contract for the erection of the tank, do you recall that it provided for a water test after the tank was created? That the tank be filled with water to test for leaks?

Jell: Yes.

Hall: Was any water test made of the tank—except by putting in six inches of water, as you have already testified—before it was put into service?

Jell: No.

Hall: Why not?

Jell: Well, for one reason, there was not time ... It would have been impossible to empty the water again before the arrival of the steamer. It would have been impossible to fill the tank. There was not a supply of water at that point sufficient to fill the tank within a reasonable time. We had only a very small water connection and it would have taken many days, possibly have run into weeks, to have filled the tank with water.

Hall: Do you mean by that, or do you not, that if you had made that water test, it would have delayed the unloading of the steamer?

Jell: Yes.

Hall: That is what you mean?

Jell: Yes, sir.

Hall: Did you investigate to see whether there were water mains on Commercial Street which would have afforded ample quantities of water to fill it in much less than weeks?

Jell: I did not.

Relentless, Hall concluded this line of testimony, no doubt secretly cheering Jell's response:

Hall: Any other reasons why the water test was not made?

Jell: It was considered an unnecessary expense.

Hall: By whom was it considered an unnecessary expense?

Jell: By me.

Hall then introduced into evidence Jell's letter to Hammond thanking them for "rushing" the tank's construction, and induced Jell to admit that Gonzales had reported leaks in the tank, though Jell thought his employee was exaggerating or "misinformed." But later, Jell appeared to contradict himself when he said he *had* ordered the tank caulked twice and repainted in response to Gonzales's concerns.

The plaintiffs' counsel then finished his direct questioning of the USIA assistant treasurer:

Hall: Well, now, Mr. Jell, at any time before December 31, 1915 [when the tank was completed], and the date when this catastrophe occurred, did you have any architect or engineer, or any person familiar with steel construction, inspect this tank?

Jell: No.

Hall: Do you know of any such inspection having been made by any such persons?

Jell: I do not.

Hall: Do you know of any engineer employed by the company, or any architect, or expert in steel construction employed by USIA, of your own knowledge, who ever visited the tank prior to the disaster?

Jell: Not to my knowledge.

After a short break in the sweltering meeting room, Charles Choate tried to salvage something for the defense in his cross-examination. Under his friendly questioning, Jell pointed out that USIA had larger molasses tanks in Baltimore that had never had problems (one holding 3 million gallons), and that he trusted Hammond Iron Works because they were a reputable steel manufacturer. When Hammond did not object to Jell's "factor of safety" specification, Jell assumed that his number was sufficient and that Hammond would deliver steel plates with the proper factor of safety. As for testing the tank, Jell said it was for "leaks only" and, in response to Choate's question added, "it hasn't anything to do with the strength of the tank."

Choate focused more on the anarchist activity in the area, the police presence during the war, and the report from Gonzales that a caller had threatened to destroy the tank.

Choate: You did regard his report and this threat as sufficient importance to ask for special protection [guards]?

Jell: Yes.

Choate: And you got it?

Jell: Yes.

On redirect, however, Hall questioned how Jell could "disbelieve" Gonzales's numerous reports about the tank's leaks, but conclude that his comments about the telephone threat were credible enough to ask for extra police protection on the waterfront. "You said you paid no attention to what Gonzales said to you, except in the instance of the police report [due to the phone threat], because you didn't consider him a responsible person," Hall said. "Do you remember saying that?" Jell replied: "Yes."

And then, Hall revisited Jell's claim that the water test on the tank would be for leaks only, not to determine the tank's strength to withstand weight or pressure:

Hall: Did it occur to you, did you have any idea, that the (water test) might give some idea as to the strength of the tank, as well as the leaks?

Jell: No. None whatever.

Hall: That didn't occur to you?

Jell: No, sir.

Hall: One final time, Mr. Jell. Did you ever ascertain, prior to the erection of the Commercial Street tank, by submitting those Hammond plans to *anybody on the face of the Earth,* whether they called for a safety factor of 3?

Jell: I did not.

Finally, Hall addressed Jell's assertion that he relied on Hammond Iron Works' experience and expertise to produce steel plates sufficient to hold 2.3 million gallons of molasses in a tank that stood fifty feet high and ninety feet in diameter.

Hall: Did you have any training or experience that enabled you to determine whether they [Hammond] were skillful and competent people or not?

Jell: I did not.

Hall: And … did you have any knowledge or experience whatever that enabled you to tell whether the construction work was done satisfactorily, or whether the tank was strong?

Jell: I considered the tank satisfactory for our purpose.

Hall: If you will just answer the question … no technical experience of any kind?

Jell: No. None.

Sitting in the Hotel Belmont in New York City, on March 25, 1921, seven months into the molasses hearings, USIA attorney Charles Choate had no way of knowing that there would be two and a half years and thousands of pages of testimony ahead in this monstrous case. He was not clairvoyant, after all.

But he was intelligent and perceptive, and he knew that it would be nearly impossible for the defense to recover from Jell's stunningly damaging deposition—his blatant admissions that no qualified person oversaw the development of the tank's plans or its construction, and worse, that safety had been compromised so egregiously for the sake of time and money.

✧✦✧

With his New York drubbing of Arthur P. Jell, Damon Hall had succeeded in getting two critical pieces of testimony on the record. Earlier, he had shown that Hammond Iron Works had delivered steel plates that were 10 percent thinner than its own plans had stated. Now, Jell had acknowledged that he had relied on Hammond's *reputation only* to assume that the tank would be safe. By definition, when Hammond had lied to USIA and the City of Boston and delivered substandard steel, its reputation had been sullied.

Hall had also gotten Jell to admit that he had not tested the tank before it was filled with molasses, not for any sound scientific or engineering reason, but simply to avoid expense and save time.

Now he needed to lock one more piece into place. The fact that the plates were too thin, and that Jell had not ordered the water test, provided enough circumstantial evidence for Ogden to conclude that the tank was structurally unsound from the beginning; but these facts, *in and of themselves*, were not hard evidence. Hall needed to introduce rock-solid evidence that the tank was poorly constructed, that it was lucky to have stood at all.

For that, he needed the report prepared two years earlier by MIT Professor C.M. Spofford on behalf of the Boston Elevated Company.

✦✦✦

Professor Spofford's report, the result of tests he conducted on pieces of the tank just a few weeks after the collapse at MIT laboratories, received little public attention until Damon Hall introduced it into evidence. Hall believed that the entire Spofford report would carry far more weight than the testimony of other expert witnesses, since one of Spofford's important observations in 1919 had later been corroborated by independent court testimony: The MIT expert had stated in writing shortly after the accident that the tank's steel plates were thinner than the plans had called for, "and were overstrained by the static pressure of the molasses."

This fact alone enhanced the credibility of the entire Spofford report. If he was correct about the thickness of the plates, why would there be any reason to doubt his other conclusions?

In addition to his observations about the plates, Spofford found that the tank had been secured with an "insufficient number" of rivets. As a result, the steel shell was unable to withstand a capacity load of molasses, and the joints simply gave way.

"The tension in these plates should not have exceeded 16,000 pounds per square inch," Spofford wrote, "and a stress as great as 18,000 pounds per square inch is as high as should have been permitted under *any* circumstances." On the day the tank ruptured, the 2.3 million gallons of molasses, 44 percent heavier than water, weighed 26 million pounds and exerted pressure on the tank's walls of *31,000 pounds per square inch*, "a figure nearly double that which should have been allowed," Spofford concluded. Therefore, "the *factor of safety is but 1.8*, while ordinary practice would have called for from 3 to 4."

Damon Hall now had entered into the record a credible expert's opinion that the tank's factor of safety came nowhere near the "3" level Arthur Jell said he had ordered from Hammond Iron Works. Jell said he declined to ask any engineer to inspect the steel plates upon their arrival, and ordered no calculations as to the weight of the molasses and the pressure it exerted on the tank's walls. By definition, this meant that USIA erected the fifty-foot tank on the outskirts of Boston's most congested neighborhood with *absolutely no knowledge whatsoever* of its strength or its capability to withstand pressure from the molasses within.

"In my judgment, the tank was improperly designed, and its failure was due entirely to structural weakness," Spofford concluded. "The formation of gases in the molasses might have increased the head of the molasses somewhat ... [but] the stresses due to the static pressure of the molasses alone were so great that the whole structure was in a dangerous condition ..."

With Spofford's credibility and his explicit conclusions, Hall believed that the plaintiffs had offered irrefutable proof of USIA's negligence.

Thursday, July 14, 1921

Just before 8 P.M., the twelve members of the jury sitting in Dedham, Massachusetts, indicated to Judge Webster Thayer that they were ready to deliver their verdict in the case of the two anarchists charged with murder, Sacco and Vanzetti.

In the six weeks that they had heard evidence in the case of the South Braintree killings, they had developed a sense of camaraderie that would bind them together for the rest of their lives. Today, they would deliver a verdict that would resound across the world.

"Guilty of murder in the first degree," croaked the jury foreman when Thayer asked him for the verdict on, first, Sacco, and then, Vanzetti.

When he heard the words, Sacco shouted out: *Sono innocente! Sono innocente!* They kill innocent men! Don't forget. Two innocent men they kill!" Vanzetti said nothing as he was led away by police officers.

The conviction of the two Italian immigrant anarchists, which could carry a death sentence, would spark a six-year global cause celebre that would include mass demonstrations, letter-writing campaigns, political pleas, and legal appeals that would fill law libraries. Were Sacco and Vanzetti the deceitful, stone-cold killers the prosecution described, who were willing to resort to any crime to advance their anarchist cause? Or were they two innocent men whose immigrant status and anarchist activities made them easy targets for authorities looking to sate the passions of an inflamed public? Or was one guilty and the other innocent?

Scholars and ordinary researchers alike would study and debate the case for years. It would be the subject of legal and academic symposia, debates between conservatives and liberals, book fodder for scores of prominent authors.

Today, however, Charles Choate saw the Sacco and Vanzetti convictions as further confirmation that the public still feared anarchists and believed them capable of deadly violence. That was a glimmer of good news for USIA, which Damon Hall had been pummeling for months.

Choate must have believed that the impact of the jury's decision in Dedham could give him a fighting chance, that it breathed a renewed sliver of plausibility into USIA's case, which now hung by the slimmest of threads in Hugh W. Ogden's courtroom.

July, 1921–July, 1923

As the liability portion of the molasses hearings drew to a conclusion, Hugh Ogden gathered the attorneys from both sides together to announce that he would hear the individual cases on damages forthwith, prior to issuing any decision on liability. Charles Choate argued that the damage testimony *itself* could further prejudice Ogden against USIA, thereby affecting his liability decision. Why not reach a verdict on liability before deciding on damages? If USIA were absolved from culpability, would not the damages portion of the hearings be rendered unnecessary?

Ogden held firm, saying he would render no decision until he had heard all the evidence in the case, including the damage arguments. While he never stated it, Ogden's decision to move forward on damages had to be a signal to both sides that he believed USIA bore at least partial responsibility for the molasses disaster.

For the next two years, Damon Hall called on wives who had lost their husbands and mothers who had seen their sons die in the most horrific way possible, their broken bodies wracked with pain at the Haymarket Relief Station. He called on men and boys whose bones had been crushed and skulls fractured, and on breadwinners who had been unable to work since the accident.

He called on stonecutter John Barry, whose hair had turned white while he was trapped under the firehouse, and whose injuries had forced him to support ten children while performing light duty. "The pain in my back hurts all the time," Barry said. "It's as though my spine is breaking. I can't straighten up; I feel like I am going to fall almost all the time. The doctor says there is no cure."

He called on firefighter Bill Connor, who had been trapped near Barry, who had implored a fellow firefighter to kick debris away from a hole so the molasses could flow out, who heard George Layhe's anguished cries as he succumbed to crushing injuries and smothered in the molasses. Connor tore his shoulder muscles and was placed on injured leave after rescuers pulled him out from under the collapsed firehouse.

Hall called on Martin Clougherty, former owner of the Pen and Pencil Club, whose mother died when her wooden frame house splintered into pieces after smashing into the overhead trestle, and whose brother died slowly in the insane hospital; Clougherty, who had clung to his bed-frame "raft" to stay atop the molasses. He had terrible nightmares after the accident and was bedridden for three months. "My ribs and my chest still hurt," he told the court. "I can't lay on my left side. All across my chest, where the big planks fell on me, anytime I get a touch of cold it just chokes me right up. Even without cold, when I lay on my back in bed at night, I feel like my wind is shutting off." In addition, Clougherty's dreams continued, "bad dreams, with buildings falling over me ... and if I go into a subway, or if I go into a crowd, I feel like I'm being crowded and I need to fight my way out. I have a general feeling of depression all of the time while I'm awake."

The testimony continued with the families of the dead—the Iantoscas, the Distasios, the Layhes, the Callahans, the Breens, and the Martins—each describing how they learned of their loved one's death. Some watched it firsthand, like Giuseppe Iantosca, who witnessed Pasquale being swallowed by the molasses wave.

Charles Choate and the defense did their best to minimize the stories and the suffering, eliciting testimony from doctors who suggested that those who died from molasses asphyxiation did not "suffer" because they were killed so quickly. Defense attorneys even argued that the dead children, Maria Distasio and Pasquale Iantosca, who were collecting firewood near the tank, were "trespassers" and therefore, their families were entitled to no damage awards at all. "A company is under no obligation to make its premises safe for trespassers," one defense attorney sniffed.

During the two years of testimony, the world carried on. Congress officially ended World War I with a joint resolution in July, and in October agreed to separate treaties with Germany, Austria, and Hungary—its final acts in the utter rejection of Woodrow Wilson's League of Nations. Both the American economy and the national standard of living continued to grow. President Harding's Interior Secretary Albert Fall was accused of selling for personal gain the nation's oil reserves at Wyoming's Teapot Dome; the resulting scandal would paralyze Harding's administration and render the president all but impotent until his death in office on August 2, 1923, at the Palace Hotel in San Francisco.

Among the players in the molasses case, plaintiffs' attorney Endicott P. Saltonstall died in December 1922, shortly after the governor had appointed him district attorney for Middlesex County. "He spent his life largely in trying the general litigation which comes before the Superior Court," said one eulogizer, "but he also knew ... the duty of an advocate to come to the relief of those in difficulty and distress."

In May 1922, Hugh Ogden, always the soldier, delivered the Memorial Day keynote speech to the residents of Meredith, New Hampshire, posing the question: "What lesson is there for us in the impressive ceremonies of this day?" It was here that he talked about the need for the government to help each citizen "receive his full inheritance."

In July 1923, Ogden begged the indulgence of lawyers from both sides, informing them that he would be taking a week off to attend a reunion of the 42nd Rainbow Division in Indianapolis. "If you will make some arrangement that will let me go the week of July 12, I would like it very much," he said humbly.

⁂

Finally, in mid-July 1923, three years after it had begun, the testimony ended. For Hugh Ogden, what had begun as a "six week" commitment had lasted longer than his service in the Great War; indeed, longer than America's involvement in the European struggle.

In three years, Ogden twice had inspected the waterfront premises where the tank stood, had listened to 920 witnesses whose testimony covered more than twenty thousand pages, and had examined 1,584 exhibits.

It wasn't over yet. For the next eleven weeks, Ogden would hear closing arguments, both on the liability and damages portions of the cases. The lawyers would be as garrulous as ever; their closing statements would cover another 4,600 pages of court transcripts.

After that, the talking would cease and Hugh Ogden could finally render his decision.

August 17, 1923

Two weeks after closing arguments began in the molasses trial, Vice President and former Massachusetts Governor Calvin Coolidge was formally administered the oath of office by Chief Justice William Howard Taft, himself a former president. Coolidge, born on the most American of holidays, July 4, was fifty-one-years-old. He initially had been sworn in as the nation's thirtieth president by his father, a notary public, on the night Warren Harding died.

Coolidge was governor of Massachusetts in 1919 when the molasses tank collapsed.

Now he was the third president to serve during the extraordinary court case that had followed.

≁ TWELVE ≈

"A SORDID STORY"

Thursday, September 20, 1923

If Charles Choate could have chosen the time to deliver a closing argument in defense of the virtues of a large American industrial corporation, he would have been hard-pressed to select a more opportune month than September 1923. The economy was expanding, production had reached new heights, Americans had money to spend, and Big Business, unencumbered by the government interference of the war years, was the roaring engine that was powering the prosperity.

September in Boston exemplified the economic optimism and confidence that was sweeping the country. More than a million people had traveled through the city over the Labor Day holiday, breaking all records. The travelers were lured by promising weather and improved business conditions, according to the *Boston Herald*. Railroads and steamships, their terminals jammed, "reached the limits of their resources and have thrown up their hands while hoping for the best" in their efforts to accommodate the vacationing public. Highways to the north, west, and south of Boston were filled, "miles distant ... with a boiling current of motor cars ... for 20 miles or more on most of the trunk roads, the greatest possible speed was a sluggish five miles an hour."

Labor Day travel had been September's first positive economic signpost in Massachusetts. Many others followed.

Textile mill owners predicted that their factories would be operating at full capacity for the fall months, which would mean full employment as well.

More than ten thousand people witnessed the opening of a new commercial airport in East Boston on September 8 that would transform Boston into an international aviation and economic center (and would one day be named for another prominent Boston judge-soldier, Lt. Gen. Edward Lawrence Logan).

Employees of the Boston Edison Electric Illuminating Company celebrated the company's generation of a connected load of five hundred thousand kilowatts, enough power to light one hundred thousand homes or a continuous line of lamps set eighteen inches apart on both sides of a roadway from Boston to San Francisco.

And on September 18, just two days before Choate delivered his closing statement, the National Motor and Accessory Manufacturers Association Convention opened in Boston, with organizers predicting that nearly 4 million cars and trucks would be produced and sold in 1923, making it the "greatest year in the automotive industry's history." One Studebaker executive crowed: "The automobile is so interwoven into our national life that the production and sale of motor cars is a fixed and stable business that nothing can undermine."

Textile companies. Electric companies. Aviation companies. Automotive companies. Charles Choate knew that these were reputable, established, rock-solid organizations that were responsible for America's economic expansion and higher standard of living.

United States Industrial Alcohol was in the same class—a major employer, a leader in its industry, a national company with many smaller suppliers who depended on its success. To single USIA out, to find it liable for the molasses disaster and force it to pay exorbitant damages in this lawsuit, would be a step backward, a return to excessive government regulations and restrictions that contributed to the economic stagnation immediately following the war.

Again, Choate hoped Auditor Hugh Ogden would see it the same way.

✦ ✦ ✦

"What is more plausible?" boomed Choate as he rose to begin his closing remarks. "Did this tank collapse because of structural weakness, or did it collapse because of an agency set in motion by some unknown third person who had access to it? This is where we come to; that is where we are at grips." Choate suggested to Hugh Ogden that the choice was obvious, so long as Ogden could overcome his "reluctance to find that a thing was destroyed by dynamite in a civilized place like the City of Boston."

Choate briefly countered the plaintiffs' claim that the tank was improperly designed and constructed to withstand the weight and pressure of 2.3 million gallons of molasses. "The tank was built by experienced tank builders," he said. "They had built thousands of them ... the tank size presented no unusual problems to the Hammond Iron Works ... it was designed by them with an experience of years and successful construction and maintenance behind them. There was no use of defective or improper material. There was no employment of unskilled or inexperienced men in the construction of this tank. It was a good workmanlike job, done by experienced, workmanlike people, out of first-class material."

Beyond that, Choate argued, January 15, 1919, was "an ordinary winter day, without extreme wind or other extremes for our climate that all buildings did not withstand without the slightest consequence." In addition, he pointed out that the tank had been "filled to capacity about a dozen times" before the accident happened [actually, seven times]. "If it did not have sufficient structural strength to withstand a load of molasses which was in it at the time of the disaster, it would have failed the first time that it was filled with a similar load."

No, Choate said, a review of the evidence, circumstantial as it was, could lead only to the conclusion that dynamite destroyed the tank. Nor should the fact that the evidence was only circumstantial weaken the defendant's case. "You haven't got any evidence to the effect that a man went there and placed dynamite there," Choate conceded, "but there are as many human eyes that saw a man place dynamite there, as human eyes saw the metal stretch and these pieces gradually give way."

What was important for Ogden to consider, Choate argued, was the radical climate in Boston and the country at the time, the analysis USIA's expert witnesses provided, the results of their experiments with the replica tank, and the testimony of Winnifred McNamara, the "closest eyewitness to the tank," who saw a puff of white smoke near the manhole on the tank's roof just before it collapsed.

"This tank was in a section of the city which the authorities had recognized required special guard during the existence of war time conditions," Choate pointed out, in "danger of destruction from persons with perverted minds ..."

Choate recounted the anarchist activity in Boston and emphasized that USIA's role in the manufacture of munitions would have fueled the ire of violent anarchists operating in the North End. He reminded Ogden of the North End Police Station bombing. He stressed that a bomb had been discovered and disarmed at USIA's Brooklyn plant *before* the Boston disaster, and that an "incendiary fire" had destroyed the Brooklyn facility not long afterward. He said that the company had lost two steamships at sea, "with no explanation . . . all we know is that one apparently broke in two and went to the bottom. The other one disappeared; nobody ever knew what became of it, and nobody ever heard of a living soul upon it.

"Then there is the evidence of the man who was there [Isaac Gonzales], of the telephone threat, where he was called up on the telephone and told that somebody was going to destroy the plant," Choate said. "Evidently, somebody in the community, for some reason, wanted to destroy property used in this way . . . The threats against this property, the printed threats posted, threatening all property in that section of the city, present a most unusual background when you come to study the occurrence of a catastrophe like this."

Again, Choate urged Ogden to suspend any disbelief he might have that anarchists could act so brazenly. "It is a surprising thing to find, and a man living in an orderly community can't reconcile himself very quickly to the fact that there are people who think that way and are disposed to act that way, unless he is confronted by the fact that these things do happen. They happen in just this peaceable community in which we live . . ."

The results of the Baltimore experiments and the McNamara testimony offered additional powerful circumstantial evidence that an explosion was *exactly* what had happened on Commercial Street, Choate said. "In Baltimore, our experts built a tank and filled it with molasses," Choate recounted. "They placed the dynamite carefully in the vicinity of the manhole. They lighted the fuse. White smoke came up—exactly the way Mrs. McNamara saw it in Boston in 1919. Then the charge was detonated and the tank split at the manhole, and a piece that weighed forty or fifty pounds was blown out forty or fifty feet by that explosion. You cannot get two accidents exactly alike, but it is illuminating . . . the effect of intentionally placing a charge of dynamite in relatively the same position as we believe it was placed in this [Boston] tank."

Choate claimed that the Baltimore experiment lent credence to McNamara's description of the scene she witnessed from the rooftop while hanging her laundry. "She was a perfectly respectable, worthy Irish woman, a little temperamental and a little restive under the cross-examination of the plaintiffs' lawyers, but unquestionably honest and meaning to tell exactly the truth as she knew it . . . it is inconceivable that she could have imagined that particular phenomenon of the smoke coming out of the top of that molasses tank, unless it was there . . ."

Choate said Ogden's responsibility, absent strong physical evidence on either side, "traces of which have all disappeared," was to consider which scenario was most *plausible* in determining the cause of the Commercial Street disaster.

"One theory, so far as direct evidence is concerned, is just as good as the other," Choate concluded. "[But] the experience of mankind in this region where this tank stood, is that there is a very *great* possibility of a destruction by explosion, just as we claim . . . the experience of mankind, so far as we have been able to get from the evidence in this case, is that there is a very *remote* possibility of a tank of this kind falling by its own structural weakness. Tanks vastly less strong have stood vastly more serious experiences and have not failed. Everybody agrees that this tank, in view of present knowledge, could have been built better than it was, but that doesn't prove that it collapsed because it wasn't strong enough to stand the stress. And that is the real bite of the case—whether, built as it was, it was stout enough to stand that stress, *even if you could have built a better one.*"

Choate rested his case, concluding his eloquent close just before 4 P.M. One of the plaintiffs' attorneys, George L. Mayberry of the Boston Elevated Company, asked to express, "on the record . . . that we feel we have been favored by listening to an extremely able argument."

The lead plaintiffs' attorney, Damon Hall, said nothing for the record. But it was not lost on him, nor, he hoped, on Hugh Ogden, that Charles Choate had delivered his entire closing argument without addressing the deposition testimony of USIA assistant treasurer Arthur P. Jell.

In the nearly two hundred pages of trial transcript that recorded his close, Choate hadn't even mentioned Jell's name.

Monday, September 24, 1923

At precisely 10 A.M., Damon Everett Hall adjusted his spectacles, stood, and faced Auditor Hugh Ogden's bench to deliver the most important closing argument of his professional career. Light rain, Boston's first in more than three weeks, tapped against the window, the only sound in the otherwise hushed courtroom. Hall, the son of a Methodist clergyman, was approaching his forty-eighth birthday and had been practicing corporate and trial law in Boston since 1899. But never had the fate of so many depended on the strength of the case he would summarize today.

"There never was, and there *never could be*, any legitimate defense to this catastrophe," he opened dramatically, "which in January of 1919, caused property damage to the extent of more than a million dollars, which brought pain and suffering to scores of people, and which blotted out the lives of more than a score of people, bringing death to them in one of its most horrid forms."

Ridiculing the essence of USIA's defense, Hall continued: "This alleged crime of a mythical anarchist, climbing at high noon up the side of a fifty-foot tank, in the heart of a busy city, with hundreds of people about, emerging to its roof, dropping in the manhole a mythical bomb after lighting the fuse, and then disappearing down the side of the tank in perfect peace and safety, through the railroad yard, and out into the city and then disappearing into thin air, is, I submit, nothing but the sheerest romance. Such crimes are generally committed in the dark by mortal men, not at high noon by ghosts. According to all of the experience of mankind, of course, when such crimes are contemplated or committed, they do not do it at open noon-day, with hundreds of people about, but they seek the darkness of night in which to do it."

Hall called USIA's claims a "ghostly defense," citing the erratic testimony of Winnifred McNamara, the imprecise conclusions of the Baltimore experiments with the replica tank, and the contradictory testimony offered by state police chemist Walter Wedger. Hall said: "To the grand jury in 1919, Wedger had testified, 'I am very much of the opinion that if the tank had had the proper factor of safety ... there would not be any chance for the thing to give way.' What was the court to make of this contradiction? I can't attempt to account for what Wedger said on the witness stand here, that this tank was blown up by dynamite. It is inexplicable upon any theory of sanity or honesty—and no one questions Wedger's sanity."

Hall chided USIA for basing its entire defense upon a theory, without a shred of evidence that any "evilly disposed person" had been in the vicinity of the tank. "Defenses which are founded upon pure theory have done more to give a black eye to the administration of justice in our courts than all other kinds of defenses put together ... the public is sick to death of theories, of the kind of insanity that comes at the moment of the crime and disappears the moment after the crime."

The plaintiffs' attorney handled the "anarchist defense" with sarcasm, claiming the anarchist was "an intelligent ghost, I have to admit, because he knew that the January bargain sales were on and, that for the first time in all of history, Mr. White, the [tank's] caretaker, was to leave at twelve o'clock that day and go up town to meet his wife on a shopping tour, leaving the tank unattended." Further, Hall said, the lack of broken glass outside of the windows that were smashed by the molasses wave also meant that, "these ghostly anarchists with their ghostly bombs produced ghostly dynamite explosions that we mortals have never heard of—and that is, the concussionless explosion."

Hall said the defense's claim, argued so ably by Charles Choate, "was a strain upon any man's credulity." The real cause of the molasses disaster was the negligence of the company, "inconceivable only in its sordidness and carelessness of human life, but in no other respect —it doesn't require you to stretch your imagination and to go into the nether world ... it is a claim based on common sense principles."

The key plaintiffs' contention, Hall said to Ogden, was that "from its inception in the mind of Arthur Jell, to its end, this tank, this structure, in the heart of a great city, planned and designed to hold 26 million pounds of liquid above the surface of the ground, was *erected, operated, and maintained without a word of advice from any competent authority whatever,* either as to its sufficiency for the purpose intended, or as to its condition during its life."

The defense, Hall argued, tried to hide this fact from the outset of the hearings. "They didn't tell you the facts about this tank. They left its birth and earlier years shrouded in complete mystery, and they did this deliberately and purposely because they were afraid to have the facts known ... that this tank was constructed before we entered the war, when corporations were reaping the first rich profits of the war by the sale of goods to foreign governments ... they wanted to keep that background from you. They rested their case without calling a living soul who was responsible for the erection of their tank ... They hoped to slide through without this utterly sordid tale being revealed to you."

USIA also fought the plaintiffs' motion to compel Jell to testify, Hall pointed out, and then refused to let Ogden see "the man charged with the duty and responsibility of erecting this tank, and who lived with it until it fell ... now I don't blame them for that attitude, because the story that you get from Jell was, as I have said and repeated, one of the most sordid stories that it is possible to imagine, where everything was sacrificed for money. I don't blame them for not wanting you to see him or hear him."

Hall reviewed Jell's testimony, first his inability to read plans and blueprints because he had "been a bookkeeper and accountant all of his life," and then his decision not to consult anyone about the factor of safety. "Think of it!" Hall shouted. "Taking a shot in the air that way [on the factor of safety of 3], this man about to erect a tank to hold 26 million pounds, above the surface of the Earth, in a crowded section of the city! A clerk, a bookkeeper ordered to construct such an engine of destruction as this tank, given blanket authority to do it, but not knowing enough about plans or specifications to read them, and not even submitting these plans to a competent engineer. It is almost inconceivable, but those are facts. They had to erect that tank in a rush, because they were losing money by storing molasses elsewhere. We are not asking you to wander off into the realm of ghosts and hobgoblins."

Jell and USIA compounded their negligence, Hall said, by failing to properly test the tank once Hammond Iron Works had completed the job. "So of course, this structure, planned and executed and thrown together as it was, leaked from the very start," Hall said.

Jell's ignorance of blueprints and construction practices also meant that he lacked the knowledge to recognize that the steel plates

Hammond delivered did not conform to plans, Hall said (a fact that, by definition, also refuted Choate's claim of Hammond's integrity). Jell's stubbornness and desire to keep USIA's business running at "top speed" caused him to generally ignore the warnings of Isaac Gonzales and others that the tank "leaked each and every day." And even though Jell ordered the tank caulked twice, Hall said his disregard for the soundness of the structure and the safety of the neighborhood was epitomized by his decision to paint the tank and "disguise" the flow of molasses down its sides.

"When you take this background into consideration, wouldn't you expect this tank to leak?" Hall asked Ogden. "Actually, after you have heard this story, you are more likely to ask, 'Great heavens! Did the tank stand at all?' That is the first question you would ask."

Not only was USIA guilty of negligence for the manner in which the tank was constructed, Hall argued that the company made matters worse by deciding to locate the fifty-foot-tall steel structure in the heart of a busy neighborhood. "You can't collect and imprison such an enormous liquid volume above the surface of the ground, without realizing that if it gets loose, widespread devastation is going to follow," Hall said. "If the thing is erected far from human habitation, you get property damage. If it is erected in the midst of the city, you get property damage and loss of life. If it is erected near a playground furnished by the city for children to play in, the effects of the thing getting loose are about as horrible to contemplate as a thing possibly could be."

It was USIA's desire for profits that led Jell, the company's employee, to cut corners on safety, Hall argued, the ultimate cause of the Commercial Street tragedy.

"You have the company saying, 'To hell with the public, give us the tank,' and the attempt to save a few dollars comes into play," Hall said. "So you have this man [Jell], trying to save a few dollars by not having an architect examine the plans. You have him trying to save a few dollars on the storage charges of molasses, and therefore having this tank put up as a rush job. And you have him disregarding the provision—the eminently wise provision—of a test of the tank, because the water would have cost them a few dollars ... It shows absolute incompetence and an absolute and utter disregard of the rights of the public, of the people on the streets, of the people in the houses and buildings adjacent to where this structure was erected."

Several hours after he had begun his closing argument, Hall summed up simply: "When I said that this was a sordid story, I submit that I was entirely right."

Saturday, September 29, 1923

Damon Hall started and finished his close on Monday, September 24. After a few additional closing arguments during the week from lawyers for Boston Elevated and the City of Boston, Auditor Hugh Ogden declared the molasses flood hearings over on Saturday, September 29, 1923. It was the 341st day of testimony, concluding three years and one month after it had begun, and more than four and a half years after the disastrous flood. The trial was the longest and most expensive civil suit in Massachusetts history.

Nothing in the record indicates why Ogden held the final session on a Saturday, something he refrained from doing throughout the trial. Perhaps he did not want the marathon hearings to continue into a thirty-ninth month; perhaps he simply wanted to get it over with.

Whatever the reason, Ogden had heard from the last of the lawyers and the experts, the last of the eyewitnesses and the victims, the last of the doctors and the grieving relatives. Now he could review the exhibits and the twenty-five-thousand-page transcript at his own pace, in the quiet of his office, without interference, and write his final report for the court.

Technically, his opinion would be advisory in nature, but he knew he held the future of the case in his hands; his report would carry crucial weight in any litigation. If he found in favor of the plaintiffs, and awarded damages, USIA would almost certainly settle the case based on Ogden's recommended amounts, rather than risk a jury using the auditor's decision as ammunition to increase the damage awards significantly. As the *Boston Globe* noted calmly: "They [USIA and its insurance underwriters] do not believe that the aggregate claims would be very great, as the persons affected were, for the most part, of the wage-earning class." If the auditor found in favor of USIA, the plaintiffs would face the daunting task of convincing a jury that he had ruled unjustly, an unlikely probability that would give even the feisty Damon Hall pause.

For all practical purposes, Hugh Ogden alone would decide the monstrous molasses flood case.

August 17, 1924, Paris, France

The invitation from the military governor of Paris had arrived at a good time.

For ten months, Hugh Ogden had pored over the transcripts from the molasses hearings, reviewing exhibits and underlining important portions of testimony. At the same time, he had resumed a near normal workload in his own law practice. A trip to France, with his wife, Lisbeth, and several members of the family, was a welcome break.

But this had been more than a pleasure trip. In recognition of his notable service during the World War, the French Republic had decorated Odgen with the Cross of Officer in the Legion of Honor, the highest decoration France could bestow for military service. The simple but impressive ceremony, followed by a state luncheon, had been held five days earlier at the Hotel des Invalides. In Boston, later in August, the French Consul General would present Ogden with the official certificate that accompanied the decoration.

Now, sitting in his own room at the Hotel Brighton after several days in Paris, Ogden penned a short note describing the honor to Horace Lippincott in the University of Pennsylvania alumni office: "My friends among the alumni will be interested in learning of a very inspiring occasion," he wrote. Ogden had good reason to be proud; he was one of the few men who had received both France's Legion of Honor decoration and America's Distinguished Service Medal.

Once again, Hugh Ogden, the soldier, had been honored for his meritorious service.

Hugh Ogden, the auditor, would return home within days to begin writing his decision in the molasses flood case.

November 4, 1924

Calvin Coolidge was elected president in his own right, trouncing Democrat John W. Davis of West Virginia and Progressive Robert

LaFollette of Wisconsin. With the country prosperous and at peace, with the integrity of the executive branch restored after the Harding scandals, the Republican slogan, "Keep Cool and Keep Coolidge" resonated with voters. Coolidge won 54 percent of the popular vote and 382 electoral votes, to 29 percent and 136 electoral votes for Davis, his closest opponent.

In his inaugural address on March 4, 1925, Coolidge trumpeted the country's economic vitality: "We have sufficiently rearranged our domestic affairs so that confidence has returned, business has revived, and we appear to be entering an era of prosperity which is gradually reaching into every part of the Nation . . ."

Coolidge said that Democratic proposals for imposing excessive taxes upon business and the wealthy, while tempting, were counterproductive to the overall economy, detrimental to the poor, and contrary to the American way of life. "The method of raising revenue ought not to *impede* the transaction of business—it ought to *encourage* it," he said. "We can not finance the country, we can not improve social conditions, through *any* system of injustice, even if we attempt to inflict it upon the rich. Those who suffer the most harm will be the poor. This country believes in prosperity. It is absurd to suppose that it is envious of those who are already prosperous . . . The wise and correct course to follow in taxation, and all other economic legislation, is not to destroy those who have already secured success, but to create conditions under which everyone will have a better chance to be successful."

Alluding to his overwhelming victory at the polls, Coolidge added: "The verdict of the country has been given on this question. That verdict stands. We shall do well to heed it."

April 28, 1925

Eight weeks after the inaugural, Auditor Hugh W. Ogden issued his own verdict.

In the wake of the president's call for a vigorous pro-business climate in America, Ogden held that United States Industrial Alcohol, one of the nation's largest industrial corporations, was liable for the collapse of the molasses tank on Boston's waterfront.

Ogden's fifty-one-page special report on liability, submitted to the

Superior Court of Massachusetts, had the organization and detail one might expect from an author with a military background, and the fluid, often dramatic writing style that a lawyer would employ to argue his case.

Ogden rejected outright USIA's claims of sabotage, citing the company's failure to produce any evidence to support its claim. "No bomb or high explosive and no traces of a bomb or high explosives were discovered at or near the scene of the accident," he wrote. "No anarchist or other evilly disposed person was seen at or near the tank upon the day of the accident. No evidence was offered to connect the [defendant's] statements of fact [about anarchist activity in the area] ... with this accident, its cause or effect ..." Pointing out that the tank's concrete foundation was not damaged at all, Ogden dismissed USIA's claim that a ten-pound dynamite bomb could have been detonated inside the tank without making any impression in the foundation. And Ogden agreed with the plaintiffs' contention that no "concussive force" accompanied the tank's collapse, more evidence that no bomb had exploded: "Photographs taken upon the day of the accident, and within a few days thereafter, do not disclose any amount of broken glass in windows above the level of the first story (where the molasses wave reached)."

Absent evidence of an explosion, or any deliberate act to destroy the tank, Ogden said he was left to conclude that the tank collapsed due to structural weakness. While the auditor considered the testimony of the expert witnesses on each side, he did not attach great weight to their words, noting that their conclusions often canceled each other out. "Amid this swirl of polemical scientific waters, it is not strange that the auditor has at times felt that the only rock to which he could safely cling was the obvious fact that at least half the scientists must be wrong."

Still, Ogden pointed out that the one area in which *all* the experts agreed was that the tank should have been built with a greater factor of safety. "From the outset, I am faced with the defense experts saying that, while in their opinion the tank was safe as built, they would not build it the same way if they were called on today to design a tank to hold the same load ... I cannot help feeling that in their position the defendant's experts do not quite have the courage of their convictions as stated ... what justification can they have for [favoring] increasing the size of the plates, raising the factor of safety, and thus strengthening the tank if the tank was properly designed and 'safe' for every purpose for which it was designed?"

If the defendants' experts admitted that they would have built a stronger tank, then USIA's decision to use steel plates that were *thinner* than the plans called for appeared even more egregious in hindsight, Ogden said. Further, "no inspection was made of the tank by any architect, engineer, or any other person familiar with steel construction between the time it was completed, December 31, 1915, and the date of its collapse." Refuting USIA's claim that the tank was safe since it had been filled to capacity several times before its collapse, Ogden said: "Every time the tank was filled with molasses and emptied there was a bending back and forth of the lap joints which in time was bound to weaken the joints beyond the position of safety."

Ogden reserved his harshest criticism for Arthur P. Jell and the USIA management that allowed him to oversee the project.

"He at no time visited any other plant which was in operation, he had no technical or mechanical training, could not read a plan or tell from an inspection of specifications what factor of safety was provided for in them, could not read a blueprint for the erection of a tank, consulted no engineer, builder, or architect as to what was a proper factor of safety, and made no investigation regarding what factor of safety ordinary engineering practice called for," Ogden stated. "He made no personal investigation as to factors of safety, and did not talk with any representative of the Hammond Iron Works about factors of safety. He had blanket authority to enter into any necessary contract for the construction of the tank and the equipment to be used with it, given to him by the president of the defendant company."

Jell and USIA compounded their negligence in late 1915 when "work was rushed (on the tank) so that it might be completed before the arrival of the steamer that was due on December 31. The only test which the tank received prior to the ship's arrival was by running six inches of water into it. This was in part because there was no time, in part because in the opinion of Mr. Jell it would be too expensive, and in part because he did not think it was necessary."

Perhaps most damaging to Jell and USIA, according to Ogden, was that once Isaac Gonzales and other "third parties" reported that molasses leaked from the tank's seams, little was done to shore up the structure. In the section of his report entitled "Leaking at the Joints," Ogden's objective tone clearly becomes more accusatory, his anger toward USIA more evident.

"It does not seem conceivable that a responsible official of the defendant could have been definitely advised of danger from leaks of a tank of this description and failed to take any action whatever to guard against collapse ... We have the testimony of a number of witnesses, most of whom were not plaintiffs or related to the plaintiffs, and all of whom testified to substantial leaks in the seams ..." The fact that USIA ordered the tank caulked twice was insufficient action to prevent collapse, but "material evidence that the condition of the joints was being affected to their detriment by high stresses. I think if leaking in the joints was plain to third parties, it should have been plain to the defendant. It certainly existed long enough and was marked enough to have been brought to their attention."

In his strongest and most emotional language in the report, Ogden said USIA should have recognized that "there was sufficient evidence of trouble available to a reasonably competent management to cause it to investigate and see whether something ought to be done in the interest of common safety. As a matter of fact, the repetition of these 'weepings' suggested nothing to [USIA] administration in Boston, and accordingly, nothing was done by the administration in New York. I cannot help feeling that a proper regard for the appalling possibility of damage to persons and property contained in the tank in case of accident demanded a higher standard of care in inspection from those in authority."

Finally, Ogden declared, in many ways the design and construction of the tank was doomed from the beginning by historical circumstances. But far from absolving the company for this, Ogden strongly suggested that USIA used extraordinary world conditions to provide cover for its own negligence:

"The general impression of the erection and maintenance of the tank is that of an urgent job, the product of the world conditions in force at the time," Ogden said. "In 1915 both steel and powder were high and going higher. There was an acute demand for both from the armies of Europe. The pressure upon our manufacturing concerns was enormous to turn out a maximum amount of steel and of explosives, and new plants and enlargements of old plants were in order from day to day. I believe that this plant was the product of the conditions of the time, and that to those who lived through those years, and kept their eyes and ears open to their lessons, this appears in the speed of its erection, the size of the plates, the nature of the joints, the omission of a strength test, the small factor of safety, and the absence of every kind of skilled technical supervision and inspection by the defendant—from the date the plates landed in Boston up to the time of the disaster."

The auditor summed up his conclusion simply: "I believe and find that the high primary stresses, the low factor of safety, and the secondary stresses, in combination, were responsible for the failure of this tank."

✻ ✻ ✻

It is not entirely clear whether Charles Choate formulated his "anarchist defense" out of desperation—convinced that he had no other choice based on the evidence—or whether he felt that such a strategy would appeal to Hugh Ogden's set of beliefs and, ultimately, influence the auditor's decision in USIA's favor. If Choate's defense was based on the latter assumption, he had badly misjudged Hugh Ogden.

On the surface, Choate's approach would appear logical. The auditor was educated, civic-minded, and well-to-do, and certainly would not have identified with the plaintiffs, a group of working-class Italian immigrants and Irish city workers. There is also no doubt that Ogden, as a soldier and a patriot, would have despised both the motives and methods of the anarchists. And, as a conservative businessman, he more than likely shared USIA's concern about excessive government regulations and interference. Had he been a lesser man, the type of man Choate had counted on, one who let his personal feelings—and perhaps prejudices—guide his legal judgment, a ruling in favor of USIA would have been simple and generated little controversy.

But Ogden had a deeper set of beliefs, and they were grounded in a sense of fairness and justice. They had been formed early in his life, through the influence of his minister father and Ogden's own interest in religion, and then strengthened by his years of military service and his love for the law. His religious training taught him to treat men with decency and dignity, regardless of their backgrounds or social standing. His years as an Army judge advocate, and a civilian attorney, taught him that adherence to the evidence was the only fair way to review and decide a case.

In the molasses case, the evidence was clear, and Ogden ruled the only way he could have. Though he never publicly stated his personal opinion on USIA's defense strategy, he almost certainly would have been insulted that it was built entirely on speculation and innuendo, and perhaps worse, that it attempted to appeal to his perceived cultural and personal biases. Hugh Ogden was a bigger man than that. He had entered private law practice after his service in the World War determined to contribute to society, to make a difference, to help people. By basing his decision in the molasses case on the evidence alone, by refusing to be cowed or swayed by Charles Choate's specious defense, by seeking and finding the truth, he had succeeded.

�֍ �֍ ✖

After finding against USIA on liability, Ogden turned to the damages portion of the case—the amount each victim or family of the deceased would receive. Again, these were advisory in nature and would set the stage for a jury trial, unless the two sides agreed to settle once they heard Ogden's recommendations.

Ogden recommended an estimated $300,000 in total damages, equivalent to about $30 million today, still a relatively small sum considering the harshness of his report on USIA's negligence. The small amount was most likely based on the low-income wage-earning status of most of the victims. The figure included an average of $6,000 to the estates of those who were killed, more than $25,000 to the City of Boston for the buildings in the North End Paving Yard, and another $42,000 to the Boston Elevated Railway Company, mainly for the damage caused to its overhead trestle and track bed.

There was an emotional aspect to Ogden's damage awards; the auditor was put in a position of determining who "suffered" more in the disaster. Because their loved ones were killed instantly, for example, the families of Maria Distasio, Pasquale Iantosca, and Bridget Clougherty received $6,000 in damages (the Distasios received another $2,500 for the fractured skull suffered by Maria's brother, Antonio, who survived). Firefighter George Layhe's beneficiaries received $7,000, with the extra $1,000 for the pain and suffering he endured during his hours trapped under the firehouse, before he smothered when he was no longer able to hold his head up above the molasses.

The family of James McMullen, the Bay State Railway foreman who was scolding Maria Distasio the moment before the tank's collapse, received $7,500, including $1,500 for pain and suffering. "He suffered with infection and delirium until the Sunday [after the flood]," Ogden noted. Relatives of Flaminio Gallerani, whose body was found under the pier eleven days after the accident, were awarded $6,300. "[His] fright and terror and mental revulsion against impending death, I find to be very great," Ogden said.

For those who survived, Ogden also had to determine "degrees of suffering," from property damage and minor injuries to permanent afflictions and conditions. To the family of a four-year-old girl who had been knocked down by the wave in her home and cracked her two front teeth, Ogden awarded $400, noting they were the girl's "first teeth."

Others received more. Martin and Teresa Clougherty were awarded $2,500 each for the injuries they received when their house was smashed (and another $1,800 for the destroyed house), with Ogden noting that Teresa "has been virtually housebound except to attend her mother's funeral." In her interrogatory, Teresa stated: "I have suffered since and am still suffering from the effects of my injuries, and I am informed that my sufferings are due to the shock. I have more or less constant handshaking, loss of sleep, loss of appetite, apprehension and nervous exhaustion." Ogden awarded no money to Stephen Clougherty, who died in the insane asylum eleven months after the flood, concluding that the accident had "nothing to do with his death."

Walter Merrithew, who was rescued by the deaf mute in the freight house, received $500 for an injured leg.

Ogden awarded firefighter Bill Connor $4,468, "including doctor bills," for his injuries and pain and suffering. Connor, who was out of work for four months, eventually returned to light duty and was later assigned to the Fire Prevention Bureau.

Stonecutter John Barry, who had morphine injected into his spine three times as rescuers clawed to dig him out from under the firehouse, was awarded $4,000 by Ogden, who noted: "He will never be materially better. His back and knee will give him more or less pain as long as he lives."

✤✤✤

Damon Hall was ecstatic about the victory, but dissatisfied with Ogden's damage awards. He promptly insisted on a jury trial to determine damages.

Charles Choate and the other USIA attorneys immediately offered to negotiate, and the two sides reached a "private" agreement within hours. "It was estimated that if the company had not settled, but permitted the case to go to trial and eventually lost, it would have lost hundreds of thousands of dollars in costs of court," the *Boston Globe* reported. "It is estimated that a jury case would have taken six more months."

The private agreement reached between USIA and the plaintiffs was made public when USIA reported its 1925 financial results. The company took a charge against profits of $628,000 "due to the Boston tank accident," ultimately agreeing to damage awards more than double those that Hugh Ogden had recommended.

Damon Hall, the tough street-fighting lawyer who had agreed to represent a collection of poor immigrants and city workers against a large industrial corporation at the zenith of Big Business popularity in America, had demanded true financial justice from USIA—and got it without a jury trial.

In the process, Hall's clients, the 119 plaintiffs, had received a double victory: Hugh Ogden's verdict, and USIA's speedy agreement to more than double the damage awards, itself a tacit admission of the company's guilt.

More than ten years after Arthur P. Jell had secured the property on which to build the monstrous tank, more than six years after the tank had collapsed, spewing forth a crashing deluge of 2.3 million gallons of thick, viscous liquid across the Commercial Street waterfront, the Boston molasses flood trial had come to an end.

August 22-28, 1927

At 11:15 P.M. on August 22, Boston's Charlestown prison, surrounded by eight hundred police, its walls and catwalks lined with machine guns and searchlights, was eerily silent. The streets around the prison had been roped off for a half mile, and those who lived within the area were ordered to stay indoors.

Across the Charles River, crowds gathered on the Boston Common in front of the State House, their eyes focused on the lights burning in the governor's office.

Inside the prison, the warden walked into the death house, where Nicola Sacco was writing a letter and Bartolomeo Vanzetti was pacing in his cell. "I am sorry," the warden said. "but it is my painful duty to inform you that you have to die tonight." Vanzetti whispered in reply: "We must bow to the inevitable."

A seven-year legal battle to stop Sacco and Vanzetti's executions had failed. In May 1926, the Supreme Judicial Court of Massachusetts upheld their convictions and denied their motions for a new trial. Just two weeks ago, on August 10, 1927, Supreme Court Justice Oliver Wendell Holmes denied a request that he stay the executions, ruling that the case was a state, not a federal, matter. The Supreme Court denied a final petition on August 20.

Earlier this day, demonstrations protesting the executions had taken place across the country and in cities around the world. More than a hundred armed police officers surrounded the U.S. Capitol building in Washington, D.C., guarding against violence, and sixty miles away from Boston in Worcester, Massachusetts, a courthouse in which trial judge Webster Thayer was presiding over a criminal case was patrolled by armed troopers. In Paris, a general strike had halted traffic, and the American embassy was ringed with tanks to protect it from rioters. Large protests had also taken place in England, Switzerland, Germany, Italy, Portugal, Australia, Argentina, and South Africa, all to no avail.

Massachusetts governor Alvan T. Fuller left the State House shortly after midnight, unswayed by a bombardment of last-minute pleas to intervene and spare the two condemned men, including a long, tearful visit by Sacco's wife and Vanzetti's sister. "Good night, gentlemen," he said as he passed through the group of waiting newspapermen gathered outside the State House.

At half past midnight, the morning of August 23, 1927, Sacco was strapped into the electric chair in the Charlestown prison, shouted "long live anarchy!" and then said quietly, "farewell my wife and child and all my friends." The warden nodded and electricity surged through Sacco's body.

Moments later, Vanzetti was led into the death chamber. He said softly: "I wish to say that I am innocent. I have never done a crime, some sins, but never any crime. I am an innocent man." With that he shook hands with the warden and the guards and took his place in the chair. "I now wish to forgive some people for what they are doing to me," Vanzetti said. He was dead minutes later.

The next afternoon, Dr. George Burgess Magrath, the medical examiner who had plodded through the molasses flood wreckage in his rubber hip-boots and later viewed the broken bodies of the flood victims in his morgue, performed the legally required autopsies on Sacco and Vanzetti. For several days, the bodies of the two anarchists lay in state at the Langone Funeral Home in Boston's North End, where thousands of people visited to offer their respects.

On Sunday, August 28, thousands more congregated in the North End Playground, adjacent to where the molasses tank once stood, to take part in an eight-mile funeral procession across the city to Forest Hills Cemetery. More than two hundred thousand people thronged the route to pay tribute to the two Italian anarchists, "one of the most tremendous funerals of modern times—a gigantic cortege that marched over streets strewn with flowers ..." reported the *Boston Globe*. "Never in this history of Boston has there been a demonstration quite like it."

Sacco and Vanzetti were cremated shortly afterward.

With a few isolated exceptions, the anarchist movement, which provided U.S. Industrial Alcohol with the centerpiece of its unsuccessful defense in the molasses case, died with them.

Epilogue

-+->-<-+-

T he ten-year timeline of the molasses flood story, which began in 1915 when USIA built the tank and ended with Hugh Ogden's decision in 1925, offers more than a dramatic prism through which to view a tumultuous decade in Boston and America. The flood saga ex- emplified and directly influenced events that changed the region and the nation in the short term, and shaped them for years to come.

First, the flood essentially ended three hundred years' worth of high-volume molasses trade in Boston and New England. While some molasses distilling took place in the city up until World War II, the in- dustry never resumed its level of importance. Sugar prices dropped markedly after the First World War, and sugar replaced molasses as a sweetener. New technologies in the production of high explosives and smokeless powder soon eliminated the need for munitions com- panies to rely on industrial alcohol distilled from molasses. Molasses, which had played such a key role in the American Revolution, the slave trade, the rum business, and in munitions production, slowly disappeared as a staple product in America and as a critical part of the New England economy.

The disaster's effects also had a long-term impact on construction safety standards in Boston and across the country. Shortly after the flood, the Boston Building Department began requiring that all cal- culations of engineers and architects be filed with their plans and that stamped drawings be signed, a practice that became standard across the country. The molasses case influenced the adoption of en- gineering certification laws in all states, as well as the requirement that all plans for major structures be sealed by a registered profes- sional engineer before a municipality or state would issue a building permit. Interestingly, the Boston molasses flood did for building con- struction regulations nationwide what a subsequent Boston disaster, the great Coconut Grove nightclub fire, did for fire code laws.

The flood also taught Italian immigrants in Boston and elsewhere the importance of becoming involved in the political process to pro- tect their rights and their interests. Because most Italian immigrants shunned politics and eschewed citizenship prior to World War I, USIA was able to erect its huge storage tank with barely a whimper of protest from the North End neighborhood. Following the molasses hearings, during the late 1920s and early 1930s, the citizenship rate among Italians increased sharply. There were many reasons for this, to be sure, but one of those was a growing realization among Italians that citizenship and the right to vote was the only way to control their neighborhood and their destiny. Not surprisingly, as citizenship and assimilation among Italians increased, anti-immigrant sentiments began to wane.

Finally, and most importantly, the molasses flood and the court decision that followed marked a symbolic turning point in the country's attitudes toward Big Business, which for most of the first quarter of the twentieth century had been subjected to few regulations to safeguard the public (government mandates during the First World War dealt more with taxation and production quotas than worker or public safety issues). Damon Hall noted in his closing argument: "When this tank was built, the first rush of the war was on, the opportunity was open to American contractors to make big money, and so they [USIA] said, 'to hell with the public, give us the tank.' "

After the molasses hearings, despite continued economic prosperity and a strong pro-business attitude in Washington, the public began to fight back. Hugh Ogden's strong language and clear verdict against USIA in 1925 showed that the country had come a long way in ten years; a corporation *could* be made to pay for wanton negligence of the sort that led to the construction, with virtually no oversight or testing, of a monstrous tank capable of holding 26 million pounds of molasses in a congested neighborhood.

The feeling that Big Business could not be trusted to police itself grew stronger in the late 1920s and early 1930s. Citizens demanded, and got, broader regulations and government oversight in the marketplace, especially after prosperity ended with the stock market crash of 1929 and the onset of the Great Depression. It was the people's skeptical attitudes toward business that helped elect Franklin Delano Roosevelt president in 1932, fueling the popularity of the New Deal and a new era in America. "The money changers have fled from their high seats in the temple of our civilization," Roosevelt said during his inauguration speech. "We may now restore that temple to the ancient truths. The measure of restoration lies in the extent to which we apply social values more noble than mere monetary profit ... I pledge you, I pledge myself, to a new deal for the American people. Give me your help, not to win votes alone, but to win in this crusade to restore America to its own people."

�ֹ ✵ ✵

As the flood itself has receded in Boston's collective memory, so, too, have the players in this tragedy. Most have faded quietly into history, and some disappear entirely (Isaac Gonzales, Giuseppe Iantosca, and John Barry, to name a few). Still others, most notably the legal luminaries, continued their prestigious work and earned public recognition until they died, but since then, their names have been relegated to history's footnotes.

For the most part, these were ordinary people caught up in a tragic event, one that ushered in a year of turmoil in the United States, and later, served as a catalyst for government to impose new safety regulations on industry to protect the public.

Here is what we know about some of the people who were part of this story:

LUIGI GALLEANI, the deported leader of the Italian anarchist movement in America, was eventually arrested by Mussolini's Fascists in Italy. He spent three years in prison, and was then exiled to an island off the Sicilian coast. In February 1930, in failing health, he was allowed to return to the mainland, where he retired to the mountain village of Caprigloia. He died of a heart attack on November 4, 1931 at age seventy, shortly after returning home from his morning walk.

WILLIAM CONNOR, the Boston firefighter who was trapped under the firehouse and heard George Layhe's cries for help, died on February 6, 1951 at age seventy. He remained a Boston firefighter until 1940, but his injuries hindered his career. He was reduced in rank to a "hoseman" in April 1920 because he could not handle full duties. He retired with a disability pension of $1,400 per year.

NATHANIEL "NAT" BOWERING, Connor's buddy who kicked debris away from the hole to allow molasses to flow out, died in 1975 at age eighty-six. He remained a firefighter until 1956, but recurring back and spine injuries, traced to the time he spent trapped under the firehouse, nagged him through his career. He retired with a disability pension of $3,240 per year.

MARTIN CLOUGHERTY, who clung to his bedframe "raft" and rescued his sister, Teresa, from the flood, remained a proprietor of a Revere, Massachusetts, hotel during the 1920s, after the Pen and Pencil Club closed on January 17, 1920, when Prohibition went into effect. We know nothing more about him.

ANTONIO DISTASIO, Maria's brother, who suffered a fractured skull in the flood, went on to become a boxer and fought two hundred bouts under the name "Kayo." He died at age eighty-six after caring for his wife, who was hospitalized with Alzheimer's disease. "She's the most beautiful girl in the world," he told a *Boston Globe* reporter who visited his apartment in 1990. "I got two bedrooms here and I'm waiting for her to come home, but it looks bad. Every time I talk about it, I start crying."

ARTHUR P. JELL, assistant treasurer of USIA, worked at the company's New York City headquarters throughout the hearing and while Ogden was writing his verdict. Little is known of Jell; records are inconclusive, but they indicate that he lived in New Jersey, later moved to Maryland, and died in 1963 at age eighty-five.

CHARLES F. CHOATE, JR., lead lawyer for USIA, who argued passionately in favor of the "anarchist" theory, collapsed from an apparent heart attack in U.S. District Court on November 30, 1927, two years after Ogden's decision, and three months after Sacco and Vanzetti were executed. Choate was taken to nearby Massachusetts General Hospital (where he was a vice president of the board), where he had a second heart attack and died, ending a distinguished legal career.

The law firm Choate started in 1898 with John Hall, later joined in partnership by Ralph A. Stewart, became Choate, Hall & Stewart, today one of Boston's most prestigious law firms.

DAMON HALL, lead attorney for the plaintiffs, who won the case (and not the "Hall" in Choate, Hall & Stewart), died in his hometown of Belmont, Massachusetts, a week before Christmas in 1953, just two weeks after his seventy-eighth birthday.

After the molasses trial, he went on to serve as special assistant attorney general of Massachusetts in a legislative investigation of the

Boston Police Department in 1930, and was named a member of the Salvation Army advisory board in Boston. He was active in Belmont town politics for many years.

His description of the flood rings as true as any words about the disaster: "It was a tremendous calamity which would appeal to everything that is human in mankind, yet was treated with the utmost indifference by the defendant."

HUGH W. OGDEN, auditor and soldier, died on September 3, 1938, at age sixty-six, while he and his wife, Lisbeth, were on holiday in Bath, England. Ogden, who had been born in Bath, Maine, made the trip to his "sister city" annually. "He was one of Boston's most prominent attorneys and a soldier with a distinguished record," the *New York Times* reported in its obituary.

Closer to home, the *Boston Herald* editorialized: "With hardly an exception, his clients became his friends. They trusted him. Nobody will ever know how many cases he took for which he received only a nominal fee or none at all, simply because he saw a duty which somebody ought to perform."

It is likely, though, that Hugh Ogden the soldier would have been most pleased and honored by the ceremony at the American Legion Post in his hometown of Brookline. The post commander presented Lisbeth with a framed copy of the official resolution memorializing Ogden's career, and offered these words:

"Colonel Ogden was a distinguished soldier, a conscientious and upright citizen, an eminent and brilliant lawyer, and a true and devoted Legionnaire ... We will miss his friendly greeting, his kindly smile, and his unselfish service ... He was a modest man, a tolerant man, a brave man, a sincere man, and—above all—an honorable man."

The plaintiffs in the Boston Molasses Flood case would no doubt agree.

Boston Molasses Flood — List of Deceased

→>-<←

	Name	Age(1)	Occupation
1.	Patrick Breen	44	Laborer (North End Paving Yard)
2.	William Brogan	61	Teamster (2)
3.	Bridget Clougherty	65	Homemaker
4.	Stephen Clougherty (3)	34	Unemployed
5.	John Callahan	43	Paver (North End Paving Yard)
6.	Maria Distasio	10	Child
7.	William Duffy	58	Laborer (North End Paving Yard)
8.	Peter Francis	64	Blacksmith (North End Paving Yard)
9.	Flaminio Gallerani	37	Driver
10.	Pasquale Iantosca	10	Child
11.	James H. Kinneally	Unknown (4)	Laborer (North End Paving Yard)
12.	Eric Laird	17	Teamster
13.	George Layhe	38	Firefighter (Engine 31)
14.	James Lennon	64	Teamster
15.	Ralph Martin	21	Driver
16.	James McMullen	46	Foreman, Bay State Express
17.	Cesar Nicolo	32	Expressman
18.	Thomas Noonan	43	Longshoreman
19.	Peter Shaughnessy	18	Teamster
20.	John Sieberlich	69	Blacksmith (North End Paving Yard)
21.	Michael Sinnott	76	Messenger

(1) Ages listed are according to death certificates; these were sometimes incorrect, especially for immigrants, for whom the actual date of birth was not always known.

(2) In the language of the day, a "teamster" was, literally, a man who drove a team of horses, usually transporting a wagon full of goods.

(3) Though Damon Hall and Martin Clougherty argued strenuously that Stephen Clougherty's death in the insane asylum was caused by the trauma he suffered in the molasses flood, Hugh Ogden disagreed and awarded no damages for Stephen's death.

(4) No death certificate exists for James Kinneally. We do know, from testimony of his wife, Mary, that the couple had been married for thirty years at the time of his death. Together, they had nine children—only five of whom were still alive when Mary testified in Hugh Ogden's courtroom.

Bibliographic Essay
✦➤◄✦

Along with the allure of telling the molasses flood story for the first time came a flutter of uncertainty about my chances of uncovering sufficient documentation to breathe life into a little-known subject—with secondary sources scarce, primary source material would be essential to *Dark Tide's* foundation.

With help (see the acknowledgments), I struck gold. Most of the narrative and characters relating to the molasses flood in *Dark Tide* are based on three rich primary sources:

✦ *Dorr v. U.S. Industrial Alcohol*, the forty-volume, twenty-five-thousand-page transcript of the three years of molasses flood hearings, housed in the Social Law Library in Boston, Massachusetts.

✦ *Reports on Damages*, four boxes of Hugh Ogden's individual awards to the victims of the flood and their families, housed in the Massachusetts Superior Court archives (Suffolk County): Box 1, Docket numbers 110980-114349; Box 2, Docket numbers 114350-115592; Box 3, Docket numbers 116777-118392; Box 4, Docket numbers 121269-126172 (April 1925).

✦ Hugh Ogden's final *Auditor's Report* to the Superior Court that he issued in April 1925 (copies of which are included as part of the transcripts and contained in each damage award case).

These sources, especially the transcripts, provide stunning, often riveting, firsthand accounts from eyewitnesses, victims, family members of the deceased, and expert witnesses. One can hardly imagine a richer trove of primary source material than testimony from people who are under oath, especially when attorneys from each side asked many of the same questions I would have if I could speak to these people today. In addition, because the attorneys needed to establish the backgrounds of all the witnesses, the transcripts offer rich biographical and background information, as well as insight into the characters of all of the participants. Finally, but no less importantly, the transcripts contain important vital records, including the death certificates of those who perished in the flood, and other documents critical to the case—for example, the full exchange of letters between Arthur P. Jell and the Hammond Iron Works (including the incriminating correspondence in which Jell commends and thanks Hammond for "rushing the tank" to completion).

Ogden's damage reports contain his summary and assessment of every individual's suffering or financial loss, and his rationale for awarding the amounts he did; the latter, especially, provides a revealing look into the auditor's character and thought process. Ogden's final fifty-plus page report offers rich background on the disaster, and tells us as much about Ogden as it does about how he weighed the testimony and evidence. Ogden is a careful writer, setting the scene remarkably well in the report, and tackling each of the major issues with literary verve and methodical analysis.

In addition to the report itself, Ogden attached exhibits to his final document that included the lease agreement between USIA and Boston Elevated for the waterfront property on which the tank was built; the set of specifications for the tank and the steel plates that Hammond Iron Works prepared for USIA; and USIA's permit request to the Boston Building Commissioner.

This book is the first published account to draw on most of these sources. To my knowledge, neither the twenty-five-thousand-page transcript nor Ogden's damage awards have ever been cited before.

Many lines in the original double-spaced transcript pages are underlined in heavy black pencil, which I believe Ogden made as he reviewed the case in preparation for his report. When Hugh Ogden turned over the forty volumes to the Social Law Library in April 1928, he said in his cover letter: "I decided the evidence on damage in a separate report in each case. Of these latter, I have no copies available. They are on file, however, and if anyone is interested to see the way in which the matter of damages was handled, the evidence is available in the files of the Superior Court." Evidently, there was little or no interest up to the time I tapped these records to research this book. I broke the seal on many of the individual damage awards—they had lain apparently untouched in the archives for eighty years—my white gloves sooty with fine, black dust.

It should be noted that excerpts from Ogden's final report have been included in a handful of magazine articles written about the flood.

Other primary source material includes:

✣   *The Hugh W. Ogden Collection* from the University of Pennsylvania. It includes correspondence from Ogden to Horace Lippincott, some of Ogden's Army correspondence, many of his writings and speeches, and newspaper articles about him.

✣   *Numerous Boston Fire Department records*, including call reports, incident reports, property loss reports, and personnel cards of the key men from the Engine 31 firehouse.

✣   MIT Professor Spofford's *Special Examination of Commercial Street Premises of Molasses Tank*, which he conducted at the direction of the Boston Building Department.

❖ Commonwealth of Massachusetts Supreme Judicial Court, *In the Matter of Purity Distilling Company*, Frederick M. Harrison, Petitioner, "Petition for Dissolution" (November 30, 1917, No. 28316 Eq.). The petition was granted, and all Purity assets, including the molasses tank on Commercial Street, subsequently became assets of U.S. Industrial Alcohol, Purity's parent company.

❖ Boston Municipal Court, *Inquest Docket Sheets* (pertaining to victims of the molasses flood), prepared and filed by Judge Wilfred Bolster (March 1, 1919).

❖ *Proceedings in the Supreme Judicial Court for Suffolk County Upon the Presentation of a Memorial of Endicott Peabody Saltonstall* (May 26, 1923), and *Proceedings in the Supreme Judicial Court at Boston in Memory of Charles Francis Choate, Jr.* (May 25, 1929).

❖ *Harvard Law School Secretary's Report, No. 1, Class of 1897* (May 1899) and *Harvard Law School Secretary's Report No. 1, Class of 1902* (April 1904).

I used the primary sources, mainly the trial transcript, to form the heart of the book's narrative, weaving in my knowledge of the event or the time period gleaned from other sources. For example, the prologue's description of Isaac Gonzales's late-night runs through the North End are drawn directly from his testimony; the intense heat that is described is taken from news accounts and weather reports of the time.

In some cases, I have built the dramatic narrative and drawn conclusions based on a combination of primary and secondary sources, and my knowledge of a character's background and beliefs. For example, Hugh Ogden's letter to Lippincott from the Cosmos Club in Washington, D.C., is real; Ogden's concerns about the manner in which the country has been thrown into turmoil is my interpretation based upon what I know of Ogden's patriotism and his soldier's attention to order.

Secondary Sources

Throughout the book, on virtually every subject, I consulted hundreds of pages of newspapers, primarily in the *Boston Globe*, the *Boston Herald*, the *Boston Post*, the *Boston American*, and the *New York Times*. Most of these are referenced directly in the text. Other secondary sources that I consulted as background, or from which I quoted, are most helpfully cited and grouped according to the following categories.

The Flood Itself

Since there have been no previous books written about the molasses flood, my secondary sources were limited to the newspaper accounts and a smattering of magazine articles and retrospectives through the years.

Among the most helpful were Burtis S. Brown's "Details of the Failure of a 90-foot Molasses Tank" in the *Engineering News-Record* (May 15, 1919); Richard WeinGardt's "Molasses Spill, Boston, Massachusetts (1919)" in Neil Schlager, ed., *When Technology Fails: Significant Technological Disasters, Accidents, and Failures of the Twentieth Century* (Gail Research Inc., 1994); Dr. V.C. Marshall's "The Boston, Mass., Incident of January 15, 1919" in the *Loss Prevention Bulletin* (Number 082); and my own "Death by Molasses" in *American History* (February 2001).

Other articles I looked at included: Robert Bluhardt's "Wave of Death" in *Firehouse* magazine (June 1983); Aldon H. Blackington's "Molasses Disaster" in *Yankee Yarns* (New York, Dodd Mead, 1954); Michele Foster's "Triangle Trade's Revenge on the North End" in *Northeastern University Department of History Newsletter* (Winter 1994); Ralph Frye's "The Great Molasses Flood" in *Reader's Digest* (August 1955); Priscilla Harding's "The Great Boston Molasses Disaster of 1919" in *The American Legion Magazine* (December 1968); and John Mason's "The Molasses Flood of January 15, 1919" in *Yankee Magazine* (January 1965).

Anarchists, 1919, Sacco and Vanzetti

Many trees have been felled to record virtually every aspect of the Sacco and Vanzetti case, but the story of the anarchist movement in America has received comparatively little attention. For that reason, I am most grateful to Paul Avrich for his fine book, *Sacco and Vanzetti: The Anarchist Background* (Princeton, New Jersey, Princeton University Press, 1991), by far the most comprehensive work on both the anarchist underpinnings of the Sacco and Vanzetti case, and the anarchist movement in Boston and the United States. Avrich's work provides much of the source material for the anarchist discussion in this book, and is well worth reading.

Other works that cover both the anarchist issue and the turmoil that rocked America in 1919 included Louis Adamic's *Dynamite: The Story of Class Violence in America* (New York, Chelsea House, 1983); Emma Goldman's *Living My Life* (New York, Knopf, 1931); Zachary Moses Schrag's *1919: The Boston Police Strike in the Context of American Labor* (Cambridge, Mass., Harvard College, 1992, honors thesis for bachelor's degree); Francis Russell's *A City in Terror: 1919, The Boston Police Strike* (New York, The Viking Press, 1975); Rudolph J. Vecoli, ed., *Italian American Radicalism: Old World Origins and New World Developments* (Staten Island, N.Y., American Italian Historical Association, 1973); and Colston E. Warne's *The Steel Strike of 1919* (Boston, D.C. Heath and Company,

1963). For a later perspective on the 1920 midday bombing of Wall Street, I also referred to Nathan Ward's "The Fire Last Time: When Terrorists First Struck New York's Financial District" in *American Heritage* magazine (November/December 2001).

The source material available on the Sacco and Vanzetti case is too lengthy to list in its entirety here, but I found the following most helpful: *The Sacco-Vanzetti Case: Transcript of the Records of the Trial of Nicola Sacco and Bartolomeo Vanzetti in the Courts of Massachusetts and Subsequent Proceedings, 6 vols., 1920–7* (New York, Henry Holt & Company, 1928–29); Herbert B. Ehrmann's *The Case That Will Not Die: Commonwealth vs. Sacco and Vanzetti* (Boston, Little, Brown, 1969); Felix Frankfurter's *The Case of Sacco and Vanzetti: A Critical Analysis for Lawyers and Laymen* (Boston, Little, Brown, 1927); Robert H. Montgomery's *Sacco-Vanzetti: The Murder and the Myth* (New York, The Devin-Adair Company, 1960); and Francis Russell's *Tragedy in Dedham: The Story of the Sacco-Vanzetti Case* (New York, McGraw-Hill, 1962).

Italian Immigrant Experience in Boston and America; Immigration in General

The historiography of the Italian immigrant experience in America is lengthy, if largely unknown. Two works that I relied on heavily for this book are William DeMarco's fine study *Ethnics and Enclaves: Boston's Italian North End* (UMI Research Press, Ann Arbor, 1981, a revision of his Boston College thesis); and my own history master's thesis, *From Italy to Boston's North End: Italian Immigration and Settlement, 1890–1910* (Boston, University of Massachusetts-Boston, 1994). Both of these works have complete bibliographies for interested readers, but I also examined specific references for this book which are worth noting.

For good general studies on Italian immigration and Italians settling in the United States, see Erik Amfitheatrof's *The Children of Columbus: An Informal History of Italians in the New World* (Boston, Little, Brown, 1973); James A. Crispino's, The *Assimilation of Ethnic Groups: The Italian Case* (New York, Center for Migration Studies, 1980); Robert F. Foerster's *The Italian Emigration of Our Times* (Cambridge, Mass., Harvard University Press, 1919); Patrick J. Gallo's *Old Bread, New Wine: A Portrait of Italian Americans* (Chicago, Nelson-Hall, 1981); Luciano Iorizzo's and Salvatore Mondello's *The Italian Americans* (Boston, Twayne Publishers, 1980); Jerry Mangione's and Ben Morreale's *La Storia: Five Centuries of the Italian American Experience* (New York, Harper Collins, 1992); Humbert Nelli's *From Immigrants to Ethnics: The Italian Americans* (Oxford and New York, Oxford University Press, 1970); and Lydio F. Tomasi, ed., *The Italians in America: The Progressive View, 1891–1914*.

For a greater understanding of a more pertinent theme discussed in this book, the discrimination and assimilation difficulties Italians suffered as they struggled to become Americans, see Betty Boyd Caroli's *Italian Repatriation from the United States, 1900–1914* (New York, Center for Migration Studies, 1973); Alexander DeConde's *Half Bitter, Half Sweet: An Excursion into Italian-American History* (New York, Charles Scribner, 1971); Iorizzo's and Mondello's *The Italian Americans*; two fine books by Richard Gambino—*Blood of My Blood: The Dilemma of Italian Americans* (Garden City, New York, Doubleday and Company, 1974); and *Vendetta: The True Story of the Worst Lynching in America: The Mass Murder of Italian-Americans in 1891, the Vicious Motivations Behind it, and the Tragic Repercussions that Linger to This Day* (New York, Doubleday, 1977), which focuses on the New Orleans lynching case referred to in this book; and Michael J. Piore's *Birds of Passage: Migrant Labor and Industrial Societies* (New York, Cambridge University Press, 1979).

For general studies of immigration and immigrants in Boston, see Roger Daniels's *Coming to America: A History of Immigration and Ethnicity in American Life* (New York, Harper Collins Publishers, 1990); Herbert J. Gans's *The Urban Villagers* (New York, The Free Press, 1962); Oscar Handlin's *Boston Immigrants: A Study in Acculturation* (Cambridge, Mass., Harvard University Press, 1941); John Higham's *Strangers in the Land: Patterns of American Nativism, 1860–1925* (New Brunswick, Rutgers University Press, 1988); and Stephen Thernstrom's *The Other Bostonians: Poverty and Progress in the American Metropolis 1880–1970* (Cambridge, Mass., Harvard University Press, 1973).

Woodrow Wilson, World War I, and Munitions

Historians and authors have long struggled to interpret and make sense of the ghastly and destructive war that pulled a reluctant United States from the insulation and isolation of the "long nineteenth century," and thrust it onto the world stage and into the uncertain future of the twentieth century. Similarly, the struggle continues to this day to capture the often tortured complexity of Woodrow Wilson, the man and the president.

In my view, some of the people who have succeeded admirably at these challenges are: John Milton Cooper, Jr. in *The Warrior and the Priest: Woodrow Wilson and Theodore Roosevelt* (Cambridge, Mass., Harvard University Press, 1983); Marc Ferro in *The Great War: 1914–1918* (London, Ark Publishing, 1973 in English; published first in French, 1969); Oron J. Hale in *The Great Illusion: 1900–1914, The Rise of Modern Europe* (New York, Harper & Row, 1971); Meirion and Susie Harries in *The Last Days of Innocence: America at War, 1917–1918* (New York, Vintage Books, 1997); Richard Hofstadter's "Woodrow Wilson: The Conservative as Liberal" in *The America Political Tradition and the Men Who Made It* (New York, Alfred Knopf, 1948, 1973); Paul Kennedy in *The Rise and Fall of the Great Powers* (Lexington, Mass., D.C. Heath & Company, 1987); and Charles Callan Tansill in *America Goes to War* (Gloucester, Mass., Peter Smith Publishers, 1938; reprinted by special arrangement by Little Brown, 1963).

While all of these works touched on the production of arms and munitions, the most helpful summary and analysis of this specific topic was Colonel Leonard P. Ayres' *The War With Germany: A Statistical Summary* (Washington, Government Printing Office, 1919). Prepared for the War Department, this work provides a comprehensive and impressive numerical summation, complete with charts and graphs, of the massive effort a country must undertake to feed, clothe, supply, train, transport, and arm more than 4 million men fighting a war half a world away.

For complete texts and analyses of the inaugural addresses of Wilson, Harding, and Coolidge, I also referred to Davis Newton Lott's *The Presidents Speak: The Inaugural Addresses of the American Presidents, From Washington to Clinton* (New York, Henry Holt, 1994).

Molasses Industry and Slave Trade

Volumes have been published on American slavery in the South, but certainly the subject of the molasses industry and the slave trade benefiting the *northern* colonies needs to be examined more thoroughly. Nonetheless, there are several fine works that deal with this topic.

By far, the most thorough and beneficial analysis I found on the economic benefits of rum and molasses to the American colonies was John J. McCusker's *Rum and the American Revolution: The Rum Trade and the Balance of Payments of the Thirteen Continental Colonies* (New York & London, Garland Publishing, 1989). Within this remarkably rich and well-documented work is a chapter most valuable to my research entitled: "Molasses in the Continental Colonies: Its Importation, Consumption, Distillation, and Re-exportation."

As for the slave trade itself, I also drew from and found most helpful Phyllis Raybin Emert, ed., *Colonial Triangular Trade: An Economy Based on Human Misery* (Carlisle, Mass., Discovery Enterprises, 1995); James Pope-Hennessy's *Sins of the Fathers: A Study of the Atlantic Slave Traders, 1441–1807* (New York, Alfred A. Knopf, 1968); Peter Kolchin's *American Slavery, 1619–1877* (New York, Hill and Wang, 1993); Daniel P. Mannix's *Black Cargoes: A History of the Atlantic Slave Trade, 1518–1865* (New York, The Viking Press, 1962); and Isidor Paiewonsky's *Eyewitness Accounts of Slavery in the Danish West Indies and Graphic Tales of Other Slave Happenings on Ships and Plantations* (New York, Fordham University Press, 1989).

There are many books about tension in the American colonies leading up to the American Revolution, much of it spawned by the Sugar (or Molasses) Act, and fueled by the Stamp and Tea Acts. Two of the best are I.R. Christie's *Crisis of Empire: Great Britain and the American Colonies, 1754–1783* (New York, Norton & Company, 1966); and Pauline Maier's *From Resistance to Revolution: Colonial Radicals and the Development of American Opposition to Britain, 1765–1776* (New York, Random House, 1972).

Other Boston History, History of Time Period

For a broad overview of Boston history, including its rough-and-tumble politics during this time period, see Jack Beatty's *The Rascal King: The Life and Times of James Michael Curley, 1874–1958* (Reading, Mass., Addison-Wesley, 1992); Richard D. Brown's and Jack Tager's *Massachusetts: A Concise History* (Amherst, Mass., University of Massachusetts Press, 2000); and university historian at Boston College and preeminent Boston historian Thomas H. O'Connor's *The Boston Irish: A Political History* (Boston, Northeastern University Press, 1995) and *The Hub: Boston Past and Present* (Boston, Northeastern University Press, 2001).

Finally, I found the following works helpful for background on topics specific to this book and for general historical background. Articles and listings included: H.W. Frohne's "The Hotel Belmont," in the *Architectural Record* (July 1906); J. B. Martindale, founder, *Martindale's American Law Directory* (New York, G.B. Martindale, January 1919, January 1924, January 1930), and *The Martindale-Hubbell Law Directory* (New York, Martindale-Hubbell, Inc., 1940); *Moody's Analyses of Investments* and *Moody's Manual of Investments: American and Foreign* (New York, Moody's Investors Service, various issues 1914–1936); Distinguished Biographers Selected from Each State, eds., *The National Cyclopedia of American Biography* (New York, James T. White & Company, various years).

Books included: Edward Behr's *Prohibition: Thirteen Years That Changed America* (New York, Arcade Publishing, 1996); Pete Davies's *American Road: The Story of an Epic Transcontinental Journey at the Dawn of the Motor Age* (New York, Henry Holt, 2002); Gina Kolata's *Flu: The Story of the Great Influenza Pandemic of 1918 and the Search for the Virus That Caused It* (New York, Simon & Schuster, 1999); and Arthur M. Schlesinger, Jr.'s *The Crisis of the Old Order: The Age of Roosevelt* (Boston, Houghton Mifflin, 1957).

Acknowledgments

-+->-<+-

Writing may be a solitary act, but I can verify that writing a *book* is far from a solo effort. I'm deeply thankful to the many friends, family members, colleagues, and well-wishers who have helped me along the way with encouraging words and kind deeds.

Some have selflessly shared their time and talents to lend a hand with the technical aspects of the book, such as helping with research or reading the manuscript. Others have provided me with emotional strength by expressing enthusiastic interest in my progress, or displaying an unconditional willingness to listen to my (endless) chatter about the story. A few have done both. I can be a bit of a "molasses geek" once I really get rolling on this topic—I'm grateful that no one ever made me feel that way.

The strength of any nonfiction book starts with good research, so I'll start there as well. My profound thanks go to Elizabeth Bouvier, head of archives, Massachusetts Supreme Judicial Court, who tracked down Hugh Ogden's damage awards and his final report, and later, discovered the forty-volume transcript of the molasses flood hearings. Neither of us was sure the latter *actually* existed, which was why one of the highlights of my research was Elizabeth's call to me on an August morning to say that, after much dogged searching, she had located the transcripts (I was at the Social Law Library in Boston that afternoon to begin reading the first volume). Elizabeth also found Judge Bolster's inquest notes.

I'm indebted to Brian Harkins, head of reference, June Strojny, director of library operations, and the entire staff at the Social Law Library in Boston, who were helpful, courteous, and efficient during the course of my research. That includes the copy center team, one of the most responsive groups I've seen. The time I spent at SLL at a small desk in a quiet upstairs nook, perusing thousands of pages of transcripts, was among my most enjoyable on this project.

Other repositories that have my thanks are the UMass-Boston Healy Library, where I spent hours in the microfilm room, the University of Pennsylvania archives, Harvard Law School archives, MIT Special Collections Library, and the library at Boston University.

Bill Noonan, Boston Fire Department archivist, provided me with most of the photos in this book, and dug up general BFD records and information on individual firefighters (George Layhe, Bill Connor, Nat Bowering, and others). The BFD has a storied history and a proud tradition, and Bill is an outstanding chronicler and custodian of each. I'm appreciative of his enthusiastic support from the very beginning.

For encouraging this book in its early stages and his kind comments thereafter, author Thomas O'Connor, university historian at Boston College, has my gratitude, as does my friend, BC professor of history Jim O'Toole, for his strong support and the regular conversations we share on writing, history, and politics.

I offer my sincere thanks to Cecile Wright, Peter Stavropulos, and Jonathan Burbank, my colleagues and friends at Bull Information Systems, for giving me the chance to pursue my dream of writing this book. *Dark Tide* certainly would not be in your hands today—and may never have been finished at all—without their flexibility and willingness to try something different. I hope I have lived up to the confidence they have shown in me. I will never forget it.

My longtime and dear friend Ellen Keefe provided invaluable assistance and encouragement throughout this project. She spent tireless hours helping me with the research, reading the manuscript, and lending her legal expertise. She has also served as a "molasses ambassador" of sorts, spreading word of my progress and building anticipation for this book with her family, friends, and professional colleagues. I cannot thank her enough for everything she has done. *Dark Tide* is a richer work for her involvement; I am richer for her friendship.

My agent, Joy Tutela, at the David Black Literary Agency, has believed passionately in this book from the start. She has been an advisor, a confidante, an editor, and a friend, and has fulfilled those roles with grace, enthusiasm, honesty, humor, savvy, and class. She has helped temper my expectations when necessary and celebrate my achievements when appropriate. Her first name is also an apt description of what it's like to work with her. There would be no book without her. Thanks for everything, Joy.

Amy Caldwell, my editor at Beacon Press, had the "big picture" vision to recognize that *Dark Tide* was more than a disaster story, and edited the manuscript thoughtfully, shrewdly, and with great care. I was also inspired by the enthusiasm Amy and the rest of the Beacon team showed for the book.

I'm immensely grateful to my parents, Rose and Tony Puleo, for their interest, their pride, and their love. They have always encouraged me, and have been in my corner each and every day, throughout this project and always. I'm honored and humbled by all they have done for me.

My final and deepest debt of gratitude is to my "First Lady," my wife and best friend, Kate. There are no words that can convey either the full measure of her contributions or the miracle of our love. She is my music and my inspiration, a great source of my creative strength. Throughout the research and writing, she has stood where she always stands—at my side—supporting and encouraging me, fulfilling the role of counselor and confidante, offering gentle criticism and unabashed enthusiasm, listening to my daily updates as though nothing could be more important. If that weren't enough, she is one of the best copy editors and proofreaders I know. To say that I could not have completed this book without Kate seems like the most inadequate of tributes—I can't imagine making it through the day without her. For all of these reasons, and because she is the greatest blessing of my life, *Dark Tide* is dedicated to her.

Each of these people has contributed immeasurably to this book, and their efforts have only enhanced its quality. Any shortcomings, mistakes, errors of omission, or faulty analysis are my responsibility alone.

Index

→>◄←

Page numbers in italic refer to illustrations.

Adams, John, 50
Aetna Chemical Company, 58
Africa, 47–48
alcohol. *See* grain alcohol; industrial alcohol
"American Anarchists, The," 176
American Federation of Labor, 77, 156
American Legion Post, 238
American Revolution, 47, 49, 50, 234
American Society for Testing Materials, 187
American Woolen Company, 146
"Anarchist Fighters, The," 150, 176
anarchists: activity after declaration of war, 58–59, 61–63; arrest of Graudat, 151; arrest of Spanish, 145; collapse of molasses tank and, 112; crackdown on, 146; deportation of, 79, 151, 159–160; economic conditions and, 144; on end of, 233; fire at USIA Brooklyn plant and, 158; "GO-HEAD" notices, 79, 150; Hayden (Albert F.) and, 150–151; Immigration Act and, 79; as issue in civil trial hearings/report, 166–167, 171, 172–174, 175–178, 185–186, 192, 209, 215–216, 218–219, 225, 228; Italian, 19, 35–36, 42, 63, 79, 95, 145–146, 148, 233; IWW (Wobblies) and, 42; Jell and, 75; May Day and, 146–148; missing steamers and, 154; molasses tank as target for, 19; North Square riot and, 43; shooting of Clemenceau and, 145; Slater and Morrill Shoe Company employees and, 166; U.S. government response to, 61–63, 66–67. *See also* Berkman, Alexander; bombs/bombings; Galleani, Luigi; Goldman, Emma;

Sacco, Nicola; Valdinoci, Carlo; Vanzetti, Bartolomeo
Anti-Saloon League, 74
assimilation, 32, 36, 235
Associated Press, 175
auto production, 195
automotive industry, 214
Avrich, Paul, 35, 62, 147, 150, 151, 177

Barnard, John F., 133
Barry, John: after flood, 135–136; civil trial damage awards and, 230–231; civil trial hearings damages testimony and, 210; day of collapse of molasses tank and, 103–105, *106*, 116–119, *117*, 124–125, 126; discrimination and, 28; just before collapse of molasses tank, 94; testimony in civil hearing, 186; today, 236; on work of, 29
Barry, Mary, 124
Barry, Veronica, 124–125
Bay State office building, 108
Bay State Railway/Railroad, 2, 108, 188, 230
Berkman, Alexander, 62, 159–160
Bessie J., 92, 98
Bethlehem Steel Works (Pennsylvania), 18, 156
Big Business, 192, 193, 194, 196, 197, 198, 231, 235
Blain, Josephat C., 186–187
Bolsheviks/Bolshevism, 144, 146, 152, 160
Bolster, Wilfred, 134–135, 141–142, 180
bombs/bombings: Brooklyn plant, 39–40, 216; of Eddystone Ammunition Corporation, 58–59; Gonzales's report to Boston police about threat